The Space Industry of the Future

The Space Industry of the Future consists of the first instance of guidance for the space industry on how value creation in space can occur for the greater benefit of humanity using principles of capitalism and sustainability. The timing of this book is ideal given (1) sustainability challenges facing humanity and (2) that the growth of the commercial space economy is now occurring at a rate never seen before. This book presents an opportune guide written for technical, business, and policy practitioners alike that frames how this industry growth should occur from an integrated values and commercial perspective. This perspective is presented in the context of the modern technical capabilities of space systems relative to the world's greatest problems.

The guidance contained in this book for the growing commercial space industry includes considerations beyond profit seeking alone. This guidance is founded on a bespoke value creation criteria to apply in the context of for-profit outer space activities that, if used, will result in the maximum value creation that a company is capable of. The criteria are developed and presented through a rigorous discussion on capitalism, economics, value theory, the circular economy, stakeholder management, and ethics. The value creation criteria are then discussed at length in relation to the space industry.

The primary audience for this book is practitioners within the space industry; this includes investors, business managers, policy makers, engineers, and scientists. The secondary audience includes students and researchers, as well as a growing range of parties interested in space policy and entrepreneurship.

Mark W. McElroy Jr works as a technical manager in commercial satellite propulsion projects. Previously, he worked as an engineer at NASA for nine years. In his initial years at NASA, Dr. McElroy obtained a PhD in Aerospace Engineering and performed research on aerospace composite structures. Later, he became involved in technical management within the Artemis campaign to send humans to the Moon and Mars. Dr. McElroy's roles in the Artemis campaign included system management in the Orion exploration vehicle program, technical consulting in the next generation space suit program, and serving as the Assistant Chief Engineer in the Gateway lunar space station program. Through Dr. McElroy's tenure at NASA, he has gained a broad exposure to the space industry in both the United States and Europe offering a thorough vantage point on how a diverse set of modern space companies operate, manage projects, innovate, and create value. Prior to his time working in the space industry, Dr. McElroy was a structural engineer in the naval shipbuilding and gas turbine industries.

The Space Industry of the Future

Capitalism and Sustainability in Outer Space

Mark W. McElroy Jr

Routledge
Taylor & Francis Group

LONDON AND NEW YORK

Cover image: Getty Images

First published 2023
by Routledge
4 Park Square, Milton Park, Abingdon, Oxon OX14 4RN

and by Routledge
605 Third Avenue, New York, NY 10158

Routledge is an imprint of the Taylor & Francis Group, an informa business

© 2023 Mark W. McElroy Jr

British Library Cataloguing-in-Publication Data
A catalogue record for this book is available from the British Library

Library of Congress Cataloging-in-Publication Data
Names: McElroy, Mark W., author.
Title: The space industry of the future : capitalism and sustainability
in outer space / Mark W. McElroy.
Description: Milton Park, Abingdon, Oxon ; New York, NY :
Routledge, 2023. | Includes bibliographical references and index. |
Identifiers: LCCN 2022013738 | ISBN 9781032341446 (hardback) |
ISBN 9781032215082 (paperback) | ISBN 9781003268734 (ebook)
Subjects: LCSH: Space industrialization. | Aeronautics, Commercial.
Classification: LCC HD9711.75.A2 M34 2023 |
DDC 338.00919—dc23/eng/20220322
LC record available at https://lccn.loc.gov/2022013738

ISBN: 9781032341446 (hbk)
ISBN: 9781032215082 (pbk)
ISBN: 9781003268734 (ebk)

DOI: 10.4324/9781003268734

Typeset in Times New Roman
by codeMantra

To Hieu

Contents

Preface

Preface

Novelist Toni Morrison once said, "If there's a book that you want to read, but it hasn't been written yet, then you must write it." Morrison's quote captures precisely how this book on the space industry of the future came to be. The process of writing this book for me started in 2019. Around this time is when I began to become aware of the prolific growth of the commercial space industry. My awareness came about as a result of a growing leadership role at NASA in human spaceflight programs that offered me a high-level perspective on the space industry. This perspective is one I found through things like conference and workshop participation, work in projects like the Orion crew capsule and Gateway lunar space station, hallway chats, and a heightened attention to industry news. It became apparent to me that while humans have been active in space for decades, never before has there been such an opportunity for commercial activity to drive significant expansion of the industry. Furthermore, I began hearing estimates that this trend would only continue and that the space industry would grow several times over by the 2030s into the range of trillions of dollars. Like a lot of people, this seemed quite exciting to me and I began to wonder about the possibilities. Both financial and technical.

On the surface, prospective space industry growth appears to be a tremendous opportunity to make money. A new frontier of economic possibility analogous to the origins of many other now-established industries. The early participants in the commercial space industry stand to financially benefit the most in the coming years. Below the surface, beyond simply the prospect to profit, some intriguing questions emerge. If it is a given that there is money to be made, are there certain profitable activities in space that are more important than others? What is the best way to make money in space that has the maximum positive impact on humanity? What are the specific technical challenges and specific business opportunities associated with space industry growth? What is the relationship between societal and financial goals in an entrepreneurial effort in space? What does value creation mean precisely in space and how best can preferable outcomes of the space industry be deliberately pursued? In short, what *should* be done in space? These were the questions that came to my mind back in 2019 as I was considering the implications of growth in the commercial space industry. And so, I sought out looking in literature for some answers.

There are many books and articles out there on the commercial space industry. I'd like to think I've read them all at this point, though more are coming out all the time now. In my search for answers to the questions listed above, I came across quite a lot of information related to opportunities and challenges in the space industry of the future. I found work across many authors covering business models, technology frontiers, exploration goals, policy, finance, and history. In all of this, I found relatively consistent themes of both enthusiasm for progress and embracing an increasingly commercial approach, a hand-off of sorts from a historically government-led industry. I failed, however, to find any work that satisfactorily answered my questions posed above. I found nothing that offered a critical and thorough assessment of what *should* be done in space, given the opportunities and technical capabilities that now exist. A lot *can* be done in space now, but what *should* be done is a different question. Eventually, I realized also that it is a loaded question with no straightforward answer. Unsatisfied in my initial literature search, but no less intrigued, I began a deeper look into the topic. I did not know at the outset, but my investigation would take me beyond simply assessment of the space industry into realms of philosophy, economics, ethics, capitalism, and sustainability.

So what exactly does a book about the space industry of the future have to do with philosophy, economics, ethics, capitalism, and sustainability? Everything, at least that is what I found. Initially, I intended to avoid a foray into philosophy and ethics as I considered these subjects off-topic. I soon found these disciplines though to offer a useful perspective in understanding what is most important for businesses to do. Financial considerations aside, most people can grasp the concept that companies are capable of doing good for humanity. And if this is accepted, it also becomes evident then that some companies may do more good than others based on the nature of their products, services, operations, etc. It is natural to prefer (given a choice) the maximum benefit to society that a company can offer. Therefore, understanding how to proactively reach this goal is desirable. Philosophy, economics, ethics, capitalism, and sustainability are all instrumental to this end. I set about figuring out how to apply these disciplines directly to economic growth in the space industry.

Part of this effort involved an early conclusion on my part that maximizing benefit to society using space systems can be best achieved using commercial methods. Government has been doing good in space for decades, so why such an emphasis now on a commercial approach? Why turn to capitalism in space for the future? The simple answer is that the most good possible, that is, the greatest possible benefit to humanity, cannot be achieved by noncommercial means alone. Governments will continue to create value in space for years to come and this is a good thing, but humanity stands to realize orders of magnitude more value from space systems if capitalism is used. Generically, this is not a new concept, but due to reducing orbital launch costs and other technological advancements, it is one whose time has come for implementation in the space industry. After examining closely the history and functionality of capitalism, its strength and potential in space became even more compelling to me than I realized going in.

With this perspective, one thing that I've tried to do in this book is make the case for use of capitalism in space. A big part of this argument though is that use of capitalism today does not entail the same things that it has in the past. It happens that the rapid growth of the commercial space industry is occurring in parallel with a global economic transition toward a new sustainable version of capitalism. In 2022, it has become gravely obvious that any large-scale application of capitalism that is not sustainable is dubious as to its actual value to humanity. Given that global negative repercussions of an unsustainable implementation of capitalism are now beginning to materialize, demand for corrective action is spreading. Application of capitalism in the space industry must be sustainable for it to be compatible with human prosperity.

Despite the high relevance of sustainability challenges in today's world, I found a particular lack of literature concerning sustainability in the space industry. To begin to address this apparent gap, I've included it as a major theme throughout the book. I approach this topic by including a generic summary of sustainability challenges and ongoing efforts around the world to address them through an evolution of how capitalism is implemented. I eventually draw conclusions that concerning the space industry, sustainability is achieved both through adhering to specific "do no harm" responsibilities aligned with global sustainability trends and by contributing to specific proactive commercial solutions in this area. Details on both of these perspectives are included.

And so eventually in my investigation, answers to my initial questions related to "what *should* be done in space?" had crystalized. I found that the answers require understanding of philosophical and ethical considerations in order to maximize the good that can be achieved by a company in space. I found that achieving as much good as possible is best realized using capitalism. And I found that supporting sustainability is a prerequisite of sorts in this effort. At a certain point, in my mind all of this began to appear in the form of a finite statement about the future space industry that could be expressed in a book. And the fact that I found no such book to exist previously motivated me further to publish my findings. I will note here that I have written and published this book in my personal capacity outside of my official duties as a NASA employee. All information and insights in the book are obtained entirely from publicly available sources.

In formulating my conclusions into writing, I eventually converged on expressing the concept that the overarching goal for the space industry of the future is to *maximize value creation*, and this necessarily involves considerations of goodness, economics, and sustainability. And while what is described here so far sounds fairly academic, I wanted the ultimate presentation to be something actionable and pragmatic. Theoretic background is described in the book; however, this background is leveraged to ultimately form a succinct value creation criterion to be used by for-profit organizations. The criterion is labeled *stakeholder intrinsic value* and it is intended to be used by space industry professionals to assess products, services, activities, decisions, and more to help them configure their organizations to maximize value creation. After formulation of the concept, stakeholder intrinsic value is discussed at length in the context of specific opportunities in the space industry.

The proposition is made throughout this book that the stakeholder intrinsic value criteria should be applied to maximize value creation in the space industry. There are several notable limitations in this proposition though that I would like to acknowledge up front and suggest as areas for future work. First is a lack of application. This book serves to formulate and introduce the concept of stakeholder intrinsic value in the space industry. Applied demonstrations are a logical next step that has not yet occurred. Second, there is no precise scoring system presented for stakeholder intrinsic value assessments. This will be an important feature to be able to compare results of different assessments. A scoring system likely is best developed in the context of applications. Third, there is the matter of allowable impacts. This book suggests that decisions on what is an allowable impact on the environment or on society by a company is left to collective decision by a company and its stakeholders. While this decision can come about in ways that are thorough and informed, there is nothing to say that one given stakeholder group, even one with all perspectives represented, can be the final arbiter as to the allowable impacts from a given company. This is an ongoing challenge stretching beyond the space industry that this book does not attempt to solve.

Who are the intended readers for this book? One way to view the entire book is from the perspective of a prospective space entrepreneur. Of all the means by which to make money in the growing space industry in the coming years, which should one pursue? Which are most important to humanity and how can they be assessed at the same time for commercial potential? Investors have an equally critical role as company founders in the future space industry and may have a similar interest in this book as entrepreneurs. Space company managers may also be interested in reading this book. Given that there is a logical preference for space systems to benefit humanity as much as possible, how can organizations be configured and run to best realize this goal? And knowing that this must occur by definition in ways that achieve profit complicates the question further. Managers will find insight in this area throughout the book. Finally, the book may also be of interest from the perspective of technical innovators in the space industry. Just like entrepreneurs, investors, and managers, innovators have a key role in realizing both profit and benefit to humanity. Discussion on value creation herein can help guide research and development activities as much as it can business decisions.

This book offers guidance to entrepreneurs, investors, managers, and innovators in the space industry that are interested in maximizing value creation in their organizations. It is written though to be accessible by anyone interested in the commercial space industry. Overall, my hope is that this book can serve as one small contribution toward realizing a space industry of the future that is as successful and beneficial to humanity as possible.

1 Introduction

One trillion dollars. This is the size that the global space economy is expected to reach in the 2030s [1, 2]. The space industry has been growing steadily in recent years toward this milestone at a rate never seen before. For context, the global space economy is approximately $450 billion in size as of 2020 [3], which is up 55% from a decade prior. The consistent year-after-year growth that has been happening involves areas across the industry, including launch vehicles, small satellites, navigation services, telecommunications, tourism, remote sensing, research, and much more. And while government space budgets have been trending upwards globally, the main engine behind space industry growth is commercial activity. In 2020, commercial activity represented approximately 80% of the industry [3]. Private investments such as corporate, angel, venture capital, and stock sales reached historic peaks of $8.9 billion in 2020 [4] and upwards of $10 billion in 2021 [5]. Up until as recently as 2014, this number was consistently less than $1 billion annually. The result of this growth is simply more value created from space for more people than ever before, and there can be no mistake that this is due to the growing commercial nature of the industry. After all, finite government space budgets can only go so far. As the relative proportion of value created by governments in the space economy shrinks, commercial entities assume a newfound responsibility.

While governments will always have a regulatory role, it falls now upon entrepreneurs, managers, investors, and innovators to develop new commercial space systems that are devised to benefit humanity today and in the future to the greatest extent possible. This responsibility can be characterized generically as maximizing value creation. A business opportunity or strategy must involve a substantive assessment of what form of value creation is the most important to undertake and how it can occur in a way that results in a true net benefit for society. Three concepts are involved in an assessment of a given value creation scheme: importance, sustainability, and profitability. These concepts are not in competition with one another; rather, they are complementary and are all necessary for maximizing the net benefit to society that an organization can offer.

DOI: 10.4324/9781003268734-1

Benefiting society through solving problems and meeting demands is precisely why companies exist in the first place. It should be uncontroversial that this is the preferable outcome of the space industry of the future. To achieve this outcome, those leading the way must have a clear grasp of value theory and commercialization in the context of space systems. This book formulates these concepts into a bespoke unified value theory called *stakeholder intrinsic value*. The case is made that a commercial approach based on maximizing stakeholder intrinsic value criteria is the best means to expand the space industry in lasting ways that support human prosperity. This necessarily involves considerations of sustainability, commercial potential, and discerning which opportunities exist that stand to benefit humanity the most. Each of these topics is examined in detail in the following chapters.

This book serves primarily as guidance for space industry entrepreneurs, managers, investors, and innovators whose goal is to maximize value creation in their organizations. After completing the book, readers should come away with a better understanding of the following topics, specifically in the context of the space industry:

- How to discern relative importance among numerous value creation schemes
- Commercialization criteria
- Responsibilities and commercial opportunities relative to support of sustainability goals
- An actionable methodology for designing a company purpose and/or strategy that maximizes value creation

Unique Value from Space Systems

The space industry stands to create value for humanity that is not possible by any other means. Just what is the nature of this unique value proposition? This question is addressed throughout the book; however, conclusions from the most recent decadal study on Earth observation, performed jointly by numerous science and space-affiliated organizations, offer some introduction to the topic [6]. One of the findings from the report is quoted below.

Finding 1.1: Space-based Earth observations provide a global perspective of Earth that has:

- Over the last 60 years, transformed our "scientific understanding" of the planet, revealing it to be an integrated system of dynamic interactions between the atmosphere, ocean, land, ice, and human society across a range of spatial and temporal scales, irrespective of geographic, political, or disciplinary boundaries.
- In the past decade in particular, enabled "societal applications" that provide tremendous value to individuals, businesses, the nation, and the world. Such applications are growing in breadth and depth, becoming

an essential information infrastructure element for society as they are integrated into people's daily lives.

The decadal study quote elicits two questions already alluded to that this book is framed around:

1   What can space bring to the table in terms of human benefit that is truly unique?
2   How can these capabilities be applied in the most productive but sustainable manner possible to create value for humanity?

On the first question, consider Earth observation satellites. Think of remote sensing satellites in low Earth orbit as allowing humanity to watch a movie of itself. The setting is the thin biosphere shell surrounding Earth in between the planet's crust and the upper atmosphere. The plot follows system changes over time related to human interaction with environmental elements like fresh water, breathable air, fertile soil, geology, vegetation health, and weather. The plot also covers features of human society like poverty, food production, pollution, the spread of disease, industrialization, and economic growth. It is only space systems that can offer this godlike vantage point and allow one to watch the evolving story of humanity and planet Earth. This capability has become key in maintaining the technical and social systems that sustain the world population.

Remote sensing is not the only specialized benefit that space can offer. Global navigation and telecommunications networks are also enabled by space systems in ways that are not possible with ground infrastructure. The functionality of the modern world depends on these kinds of resources in space. Insight into some of the greatest questions of the universe and nature are also enabled by space systems focused on scientific discovery. Even indirect benefits like global inspiration, national unity, and spin-off economic activity that come from watching and participating in space endeavors are significant forms of value that the space industry is especially suited to provide.

The second question elicited by the decadal study quote is related to how to best leverage space system capabilities to humanity's benefit. Capitalism has been used for centuries to do exactly this in other industries. Throughout history, there has been no more successful socioeconomic system than capitalism in terms of the sheer scale of human lives it has uplifted and saved. Specifically, this system involves seeking voluntary win-win transactions that address mass societal needs through the most efficient provision mechanisms possible. This is what capitalism has done for humanity in the past and it can be used in the space industry to do good in the world going forward.

The second question also invokes the concept of sustainability. Sustainability, by definition, means that something can continue indefinitely without interruption or failure. This would be a good thing for civilization and the human species, and so, a broad generic answer to the second question is to "use capitalism in ways that are sustainable." This concept is discussed extensively throughout the book. Capitalism in the space industry is not a new concept, however, so why has it not occurred already to a greater extent if it has so much potential? The following section provides an introduction to answering this question, though additional commentary on this topic also exists in later chapters.

Space Industry Commercialization: A Brief Introduction

The space industry started in the 1950s and 1960s. In this era, activities in space were 100% government-funded and conducted only by the United States and the Soviet Union. Achievements by these two nations in space were considerable and included advances in rocketry, robotic spacecraft, satellites, and human spaceflight. The pinnacle of these achievements no doubt came in 1969 with NASA landing humans on the Moon in the Apollo program. This was an achievement so far ahead of its time, only 50 years later in the 2020s is humanity on the cusp of repeating this feat in NASA's Artemis program (aptly named after the sister of the ancient Greek god Apollo). Echoed by science fiction author Arthur C. Clark in a 2007 interview [7], "a technological mutation that should not have occurred until the 21st century" is how William Sims Bainbridge described spaceflight in his 1976 book, *The Spaceflight Revolution: A Sociological Study* [8]. Really any of the space achievements in the 1950s and 1960s may be seen as "technical mutations," in that they were compelled to occur by the will of wealthy governments rather than as organic responses to demands from society. Generally, until such a demand exists and the means to meet it exist, commercialization does not come into the picture.

In the decades following the birth of the space industry, technology has improved, capital has become more and more available, and safety lessons have been learned. Additionally, what is viewed as possible from space systems has expanded as well. This evolution was largely driven by continued government-financed initiatives; however, as the industry continued to mature, commercial opportunities began to emerge. Commercialization in space started with telecommunications in the 1990s and now is spreading to other areas like remote sensing and tourism. This progress is due largely to improvements in launch services. Up until the 2000s, reliability, performance, and relative safety of rockets came at an extraordinary cost on the order of hundreds of millions of dollars per launch. Hardly something that most start-up companies or investors would be interested in or able to accommodate for a new business idea. Today, all of these factors have changed. Cost, technology, and safety are all finally at levels conducive to widespread entrepreneurialism and commercial value creation. This is a relatively recent development and so the commercialization of the space industry is now just beginning.

The Space Industry Today

Today, the global space industry has in place a highly capable industrial base. The industry infrastructure and expertise are finally mature enough to be used as an entrepreneurial foundation for new companies and new ideas. The potential exists to establish self-sustaining value creation for society from space via commercial activity. One of the exciting implications of this development is that creating value in space is now possible for many organizations ranging far beyond just wealthy governments. The creativity, innovation, and efficiency that come with the use of free-market capitalism have been unleashed. This is how humanity will continue to derive more and more value from space going forward.

To continue with Bainbridge's analogy, space activity in the 1960s may have been a "technical mutation"; however, this mutation has caught on and proven itself a positive factor in the evolution of human civilization. Largely, what has allowed this mutation to begin to proliferate is the introduction of competition and reusability in the orbital launch industry. Launch providers that embrace reusable rocket designs, manufacturing innovations, and management efficiency can launch payloads at a cost that can be an order of magnitude less than legacy rockets. These innovations are now the backdrop of a newfound market where new launch companies and legacy launch companies are in fierce competition to create the most reliable and cost-effective rockets ever produced. This is a prime example of capitalism working to increase efficiency, open access to more people, and ultimately realize more value creation overall.

Increased access to the space economy for entrepreneurs is not just thanks to cheaper launch services. Advances in technology, computational tools, artificial intelligence, data mining, and machine learning are enabling many new players to create "value-added" capabilities using data collected by legacy government space organizations. Beyond government systems, new technologies like satellite constellations and small satellites are also opening up the prospect of data collection itself to commercial entities. Additionally, project management innovation is having an effect. Public-private partnerships, fixed-price contracts, increased international collaboration, and launch rideshare opportunities are making space activities cheaper and more accessible. All of these factors combined with reduced launch costs are enabling the emergence of the commercial space industry.

Amazon founder and CEO, Jeff Bezos, has explained partially the motivation for his own space company, Blue Origin, in this same context. As Bezos says, the advent of reusable rockets and cheap launch costs is akin to the advent of the internet. There were no entrepreneurs plotting and planning the next great online business before the internet existed. As soon as it did exist, it acted as a common infrastructure for entrepreneurs to use and innovate around. Space entrepreneurialism was limited in the past because there was no common infrastructure in place to facilitate entrepreneurial activity. Now with affordable launch services, the possibilities open up. The vast majority of benefit and economic activity to follow will be dreamed up and executed not today by the launch providers themselves but in the future by other entrepreneurs that take advantage of their products and services.

The growth of the commercial space industry is no coincidence. It is the result of a transfer of certain roles in space from the government to industry. In some cases, this is intentional and proactive on the part of governments to facilitate formation of a commercial space economy. Intentional because this is the only means to continue the growth of value creation in space in a way that is proportional to the needs of society and does not involve ballooning government budgets. As this growth and transfer of roles occur, governments can shift their focus and limited resources toward new initiatives that are not yet ready for commercialization.

Prominent examples of this hand off in the space industry are evident in NASA's Commercial Resupply Service (CRS) program and the Commercial Crew Program (CCP). After decades of launching cargo and crew to low Earth orbit, the US government decided in the 2008–2009 time frame that this service should be provided commercially for the International Space Station (ISS) going forward. This view was founded on mature capabilities in industry and is documented in a 2009 NASA report titled *Review of United States Human Space Flight Plans*. In addition to a desire to capture more efficiency and innovation from industry, this would allow NASA to focus more of its resources on the next frontier, deep space exploration. This hand off was implemented via public-private partnerships and increasing use of fixed-price contracts where the cost of hardware development was shared by the government and industry. Also, the government played the role of guaranteed customer by agreeing to purchase six to seven crew and cargo flights to the ISS each year [9].

In addition to flight contracts, the industry partners involved in CRS and CCP benefit by getting support from NASA to develop a new product/service to offer broadly in a commercial market to other customers. The government benefits by development cost-sharing and ultimately getting a way to low Earth orbit that is cheaper than it could have achieved on its own. The cost reduction is due to the inherent efficiency resulting from competition and profit-seeking in markets. In this case, NASA leveraged modern industry potential to create the market for low Earth orbit access.

As hoped, creation of the low Earth orbit launch market turned out to be a win-win for government and industry. The cost to launch cargo to the ISS used to be as high as \$93,000/kg using the space shuttle [10]. Today, the cost is approximately \$23,000/kg using a commercial SpaceX Falcon 9 rocket.[1] The CCP has had a similar outcome regarding cost savings; however, exact prices are not disclosed publicly. Estimates place the cost per seat for sending crew to the ISS on a SpaceX Dragon spacecraft at \$55 million [11]. The cost per seat for the Russian Soyuz spacecraft is approximately \$90 million [12] and, looking back further, the cost per seat on the spaces shuttle was \$137 million[2] in 2021 dollars. Commercial provision of cargo and crew to the ISS offer examples of the win-win benefits that commercialization can bring.

NASA's commercial cargo and crew programs are high-profile examples of successful commercialization efforts in the space industry. This is just scratching the surface, however, and this book covers the full breadth of possibilities for commercialization in space. There's a lot that can be done in space and a lot that will be accomplished in the coming years in terms of increasing commercial activity. This makes it all the more important for industry leaders to be cognizant of not just the commercial potential but also which activities in space stand to benefit society the most.

What Should Be Done in Space?

A major theme in this book is reflecting on what should be done in space. What can be done in space is a different matter and is receiving no shortage of attention and energy from inside and outside the industry. This enthusiasm is fortunate and exciting to be sure, but it makes it all the more critical for participants to have awareness and understanding of the impacts that, good or bad, space systems have on society. And once one takes this perspective, certain activities emerge as more useful and more important. Certain activities create more value. One of the core purposes of this book is to shed light on how to undertake a critical analysis from this perspective.

Philosophy professor James Schwartz, a self-declared space enthusiast, reflects on this same topic asking, "…what the fundamental purpose of spaceflight is or should be…" [13]. A strong advocate for the value of science from space, Schwartz begins by suggesting that a basic answer is simply to "…provide new markets for economic activity." Are "new markets for economic activity" not enough to justify anything really? Anything as long as it creates value and is not harmful to something else? After all, where economic activity exists, human achievement, sustenance, and prosperity exist also. If a new space economy is nothing more than an expanded sphere of existence for people to live, work, play, etc. in a manner that is compatible with the sustainability of humanity and the planet, this would appear to be a valid end to pursue in itself.

Expanding humanity's economic sphere of existence into space could involve value creation in many forms. Establishing human colonies off-world to ensure the long-term survival of humanity. Advancing frontiers of science and knowledge. Adventure, recreation, exploration. Earth observation, telecommunications, weather prediction, global internet, navigation services. Space resources harvesting. National prestige, political influence, security. Technology innovation spin-offs. Educational inspiration and stimulation of the economy. Pursuit of wealth. All of the means for value creation listed here are examined in this book, so that the reader may become more adept at grading relative importance and discerning which *should* be pursued commercially as priorities. In other words, which opportunities stand to create the most value for humanity. Capitalism is an inextricable element of this discussion.

Capitalism Today

The use of free-market capitalism is already resulting in more value creation in space for more people than ever before. This is a good thing and it is the best approach to continue to derive more and more benefit for humanity from the space industry. It so happens that the growth of the commercial space industry coincides with rising momentum around the world to redefine how capitalism functions overall. This is motivated by planetary sustainability problems that threaten the prosperity of humanity. The manner in which capitalism and industrialization have functioned historically is partially to blame. As capitalism evolves in the near term to address these challenges, the space industry must form and grow also according to the new sustainability-conscious economic paradigm. If this occurs, the size of the space industry and the amount of value that it can offer humanity are effectively limitless, given the vast expanse of space.

The cost of using capitalism in its traditional form is increasingly untenable environmental degradation. Increasingly untenable because it now threatens not just the long-term but also the short-term prosperity of civilization. This predicament is the cumulative result of a macro-scale pattern seen repeated historically in nations adopting capitalism. The first step is industrialization, whereby production increases resulting in many new jobs and overall economic growth. This is not to be understated as it entails uplifting out of poverty potentially millions or even billions of people over time into a "middle class" where basic needs are met and luxuries like recreation and comfort become possible. As industrialization occurs, there is a dramatic rise in energy consumption, natural resource use, and greenhouse gases emitted into the atmosphere. The rise of the middle class and rise in pollution do not continue forever though, and eventually both plateau. The final stages of economic advancement involve the transition of the now wealthy nation to one with even more wealth and one consisting of more and more advanced, high tech, service-based, and other "clean" industry activities.

While the economic process described is transformational in terms of increasing prosperity and eliminating poverty, hunger, disease, lack of education, and more, there are some notable problems. A nation in the final stages of transitioning to a "clean" industry is deceiving in terms of any actual reduction of pollution. As author Kate Raworth puts it in *Doughnut Economics*:

> ...cleaning up a nation's air and water by shifting from manufacturing to service industries doesn't eliminate those pollutants: it sends them overseas, letting someone else, somewhere else, feel the burn while those

back at home import the neatly packaged finished product. That means it's a strategy for environmental clean-up that cannot be followed by all countries because eventually there will be nowhere left to outsource the pollution.

[14]

Until waste associated with production and consumption is reduced significantly, all of the value obtained from an advanced industrialized economy appears to come at terrible costs overall.

If the developing world were to realize the economic transformation associated with industrialization in the same way that countries in North America, Europe, and parts of Asia so effectively did, global environmental problems like climate change and resource depletion would become far worse than they already are. For example, every person on Earth uses an average of 16 kg of resources each day, including minerals, fossil fuels, and biomass. The western world uses 57 kg/day [15]. If developing countries were to follow suit and mimic the same evolution from a dirty to a "clean" economy and adopt the same levels of consumption seen in western nations, material demand would necessitate more minerals that exist on Earth [16]. Not to mention that the pollution and waste produced with this level of resource use would overwhelm the planet. If everyone on Earth is to have a decent life meeting some universally acceptable level of health and prosperity, something has to change.

Unfortunately, the planet is already being overwhelmed by existing levels of human-caused greenhouse gas emissions in the atmosphere [17]. As a result, humanity is beginning to experience the negative effects of a changing climate. In the summers of 2020 and 2021, a scourge of wildfires like the modern world has never seen consumed millions of acres of forest in the western United States. Similarly unprecedented wildfires devastated Australian forests in 2019 and 2020. In 2020, there was one point when six simultaneous tropical storms or hurricane systems existed in the Atlantic Ocean and Gulf of Mexico. A 2021 study published in *Nature* uses archived satellite data going back 20 years to reveal that glacier melt is now occurring at double the rate seen in 2000, thereby accelerating sea level rise [18]. Broadly speaking, other effects of climate change that can now be observed include fresh water shortages, food shortages, exhaustion of agriculture productivity, poor health of the oceans, and increasingly severe natural disasters.

Strain on the economy is another perspective on how climate change negatively affects humanity. Since 1980, weather-related insurance losses have risen fivefold and uninsured claims have doubled [19]. Weather conditions alone can impact a US state's Gross Domestic Product (GDP) by up to 13% and the national US GDP by 3.4% [20]. Similarly, heat-induced labor productivity loss is estimated to be around $2.5 trillion by 2030 and up to 4% of GDP by 2100 [21]. In a best-case scenario where all existing national emissions reduction commitments are met (which is not on track currently), average global temperatures can be expected to rise to at least 2.2°C above preindustrial levels [22]. This level is well beyond the threshold of 1.5°C that scientists have identified as the maximum for which the worst impacts of climate change could be avoided. A full account of depressing statistics chronicling all of the negative impacts of climate change could go on.

These impacts are more than just an inconvenience; they have real quantifiable influence on the economy and peoples' livelihoods. The source of these problems is related to unsustainable resource use and waste production at rates that degrade the ability of the planetary system to sustain life. Growing at a rate of 3% per year, the global economy doubles every 25 years. Historically, every 1% increase in GDP is accompanied by a 0.4% increase in resource usage [23]. As GDP growth continues using the current system, resource usage increases, and more and more waste is deposited into the environment degrading the very ecological conditions that make the economy (and life) possible in the first place.

This unfortunate trend is occurring as predicted by Donella Meadows et al. in the 1972 report, *The Limits to Growth* [24]. *The Limits to Growth* predicts that humanity will eventually exceed Earth's carrying capacity. That is, humanity would exceed the capacity of the planetary life support system. Estimates place humanity already at 140% of the planet's carrying capacity as of 2010 [25] and predict that 200% will be reached by the 2030s without corrective action [26]. The repercussions of exceeding the carrying capacity of the Earth are nothing less than a reduction in quality of life, a reduction in security, increased inequality, food insecurity, political instability, and an ultimately reduced global population. There really is no other option but to change how modern capitalist economies function if humanity is to prosper in the long term.

In summary, capitalism is not just dollars and cents on paper, it is a real interacting element of the planetary system now that influences the health of the environment and civilization. Enjoying nature firsthand and appreciating the outdoors in a visceral sense is not required anymore for motivating environmental conservation. The stakes are much higher today and they transcend ideologies about anything other than a desire for long-term human prosperity. Sustainability is now a prerequisite for a strong economy.

Capitalism + Space: Next Steps

What is the future of capitalism given the gravity of some of its problems? Is it possible to continue to enjoy the uplifting benefits of capitalism and industrialization but do so in a way that eliminates negative costs to the planet and society? The short answer is yes, but this involves the need for an evolution of how companies operate. A company is nothing more than a contrived organization of people, resources, and contracts that are configured to meet a demand. Companies are literally the value creation tools of society. If a company does not create value, if it does not benefit society, then there is no reason for it to exist. Humanity today is demanding more and more that companies be responsible and create value in ways that are sustainable. This is because it has become obvious that, despite appearances, companies that are not sustainable actually do not create value in the long term! The key for capitalism going forward is to continue to utilize humanity's best value creation tools, companies, but change how they operate so their products and services are not provided at the expense of critical environmental and social systems.

A shift in the economy along these lines has already begun. This modified implementation of capitalism is garnering grassroots support around the world as people grow more aware of the problems *and* the solutions related to sustainability that are associated with how companies operate [23]. The way that businesses function is changing to become more purpose-driven and considerate of stakeholders beyond owners and shareholders. While the rate of change needs to be faster, companies in industries across the world are reducing waste, utilizing renewable energy, increasing supply chain accountability, adopting service business models, and focusing more on community and employee well-being. These practices put together define what is emerging as a new sustainable implementation of capitalism.

The emergence of the commercial space industry and the emergence of a global sustainable economy are occurring simultaneously. The commercial space industry must form in ways that are both profitable and in line with sustainable economy principles if maximization of benefit to humanity is the goal. And this is not impossible. This book describes thoroughly how commercial value creation in space can occur in this manner.

Look Ahead

In Chapter 2, there is a deep dive into capitalism. What it is? How did it form? Why did it form? Why is it so important relative to the space industry? Discussion is also included on efforts underway to evolve capitalism in order to eliminate its flaws while maintaining its advantageous features. This portion of the discussion includes examination of concepts like the Triple Bottom Line, the circular economy, and stakeholder management. In Chapters 3 and 4, these principles are applied in devising a bespoke value theory, *stakeholder intrinsic value*, for application in the space industry. Stakeholder intrinsic value is a combination of concepts drawing from ethics, philosophy, profit-seeking, sustainability, intrinsic value, stakeholder management, and capitalism. The result is a succinct set of guidelines for use in the space industry. The proposition is made that to maximize value creation, companies in the space industry should pursue activities/decisions that are most compliant with the stakeholder intrinsic value criteria.

In Chapter 5, the discussion turns more closely to the space industry itself and how stakeholder intrinsic value creation can be realized in this context. This starts with assessing principles of economics to indicate what kinds of activities are conducive to commercialization. This includes a generic review of common activities in space as well as an examination of numerous historical examples. Next, in Chapter 6, this insight is combined with the stakeholder intrinsic value concept to study further which specific activities in space can both occur commercially and address the most pressing needs of humanity. Much of this discussion is framed around addressing the UN Sustainable Development Goals. In Chapter 7, there are several additional topics addressed related to the space industry and commercialization focused on human spaceflight and deep space exploration. Finally, in Chapter 8, all of the stakeholder intrinsic value creation opportunities in the space industry that the book discusses are tabulated and a cursory assessment is made as to which are most important.

Some readers may wish to go directly to Chapter 5 and skip over the immediately following chapters on capitalism and value theory. This may be reasonable for those already well versed in these fields; however, all of the discussion specifically on value creation in the space industry in later chapters is heavily framed around the concept of stakeholder intrinsic value. Therefore, it is recommended that those inclined to skip Chapters 2–4 should at least read the section titled "Stakeholder Intrinsic Value: Defined" located toward the end of Chapter 4. For readers interested in the background and complete formulation of the concept of stakeholder intrinsic value creation in the space industry, read on.

Notes

1 Because of mission complexity, the cost to deliver cargo to the ISS is higher than delivering a payload (i.e., satellite) elsewhere in low Earth orbit. The cost to deliver a payload to orbit currently is $2,600/kg using a SpaceX Falcon 9 rocket and $1,500/kg using a SpaceX Falcon Heavy [185]. The previous cost for the space shuttle to deliver a payload to orbit was $65,400/kg in 2021 dollars [185].
2 An average space shuttle flight near the end of the program was $450 million [271]. Adjusting for inflation and assuming a flight delivers four crew to the ISS (same as SpaceX Dragon), this comes out to $137 million per seat. The cost is less if more crewmembers are assumed for a given shuttle flight.

2 Capitalism

Capitalism is the socioeconomic system that has guided civilization to unprecedented levels of prosperity over the last several hundred years. Those that participate the most tend to enjoy the most wealth where in this context wealth has a broad definition beyond money. Wealth to be had from capitalism includes things like food to eat, security, housing, education opportunities, healthcare, recreation, time for hobbies, a meaningful job, a prospect for retirement, and the means to enjoy all of these things with one's family and friends. While capitalism in its current form has brought more people more of the items in this list than any other socioeconomic system in human history, it does have its share of problems. There are corruptive elements in capitalism, there are many who are excluded unfairly, and there are negative costs to the planet and society that have now risen to an untenable level.

While unignorable challenges do exist, the benefits of capitalism are easily compelling enough to motivate continuing with the system overall but working to address its problems. This is the challenge of today that must be overcome in order to continue to maintain and expand human prosperity. The space industry has a role in this story, but before examining the possibilities of this role, a better understanding of capitalism itself is useful. This understanding helps justify the proposition in this book to use capitalism for value creation in space by illuminating how it came to be and ultimately how its principles apply in this context. This chapter covers the past, present, and future of capitalism.

Capitalism: The Basics

Capitalism is a system where capital is invested to generate a profit for the investors. Typically, capital refers to money and the investment is used by a business to create value via provision of a product or service. The free market is a central feature of modern-day capitalism and is where supply of and demand for products and services are linked. Participants enter the market either as sellers or buyers seeking voluntary win-win transactions. Ideally, buyers walk away with their wants satisfied and sellers walk away

DOI: 10.4324/9781003268734-2

with a profit. Win-win. The market reacts in real time to resource shortages, regulation changes, and consumer demand. It reflects and accommodates also the personal ethics and morals of participants through their purchase choices. Competition among sellers in markets drives an endless pursuit of greater and greater efficiency in value production. Entrepreneurialism, innovation, and technological advances are key features of this process that are rewarded if executed well. The result overall of free markets is something decidedly democratic, in that anyone can participate and winners and losers are decided by merit, not politics, ideology, or some other corruptive influence. In short, markets exist to link supply and demand and they do so through an endless series of win-win voluntary transactions in the most efficient manner possible.

By using capital investments to create a value production apparatus (i.e., a company) and a marketplace to link it to demand and distribution, large swaths of the population are engaged economically. Those engaged wake up every day with an organized structure and purpose in life. Go to work, get paid, take care of your family, help a few people out that need it, and have some fun in your spare time. For those that can participate in this system, food, healthcare, and security are all available. Poverty is reduced, crime is reduced, and war becomes more trouble than it is worth. The insatiable forces in human nature to innovate, and to struggle, and to compete, and to learn, and to explore, and to grow are given a productive outlet. Participants are not locked into a daily desperate fight to survive.

While production of goods and services occurs via markets in capitalism, this approach is made possible by certain government functions. Left completely unfettered, free markets will tend toward consolidation, monopolies, cost externalization, political influence, and exclusive policies that increasingly benefit those with capital over the general population. The most fundamental roles of the government to support market functionality and avoid these pitfalls are to guarantee access to markets, enforce the right to own private property, and enforce the rule of law in an unbiased manner. Market transactions occur in part only because participants have confidence that the terms of the transactions will be enforced legally if necessary. Also, the notion that anyone can "own" private property, such as land or a business, and benefit economically from it is established and enforced by the state. Market transactions don't work without this concept. In addition to providing a regulatory framework, the state can also promote market access and functionality by providing basic public services for all to use such as public education, industry infrastructure, fundamental R&D, and acting as a guaranteed customer for burgeoning industries.

If the business-government partnership is optimized, the outcome is win-win all around. Most obviously, a well-functioning market benefits the companies and customers that are directly involved. Less obvious are other indirect benefits. Governments are financed by the taxation of people and companies so any government services like police, firefighters, socialized healthcare, parks, etc. are funded indirectly through free-market capitalism. Charities, nonprofits, and nongovernment organizations (NGO) also offer crucial value to humanity in ways that companies and governments may not. These types of organizations typically obtain funding through donated capital that originated in profit-seeking market activity as well.

The resonance between capitalism and human nature can explain why it is so effective. All participants in modern free-market capitalism have the same goal on the surface and this is to pursue profits. Love it or hate it, this motivation works because it taps into a part of human nature that everyone has and that is the gratification of their own selfish goals. After all, if profits are realized, they can be applied to satisfy almost any material want one should have for themselves or for others they care about. Additionally, the potential means to pursue profit are highly diverse and can cater to almost anyone's particular interests and skills. The clever bit though is that capitalism positions these selfish acts such that they benefit others involved at the same time. To quote economist Adam Smith:

> It is not from the benevolence of the butcher, the brewer, or the baker, that we expect our dinner, but from their regard to their own interest. We address ourselves, not to their humanity but to their self-love, and never talk to them of our own necessities but of their advantages.
>
> [27]

The profit-seeking motive has proven capable of driving formation of complex organizations of people and limited resources to innovate, collaborate, and consistently produce value demanded by society. Profit-seeking companies are by far the most efficient and equitable means humans have ever devised for meeting society's needs. More often than not, the value produced as a result of profit-seeking would not exist otherwise. The power that humanity has to achieve great things using the profit-seeking motivation is not to be ignored or cast aside.

The profit-seeking motive is so compelling and so successful that maximization of financial capital historically has come at the expense of other forms of capital, such as environmental and social. This is the primary flaw in modern capitalism. Maximizing profits at the expense of social and environmental systems that are critical for humanity cannot continue indefinitely without major disruptions to prosperity and the global economy. That said, profit-seeking is too powerful of a tool to abandon. Collectively, humanity stands to continue to gain from its use as long as it can be brought more into balance with other critical needs. Upcoming sections describe efforts underway to this end. Overall, the importance (and rarity, historically speaking) of a system that offers the societal benefits that capitalism does cannot be overstated. The next section provides a historical perspective in order to help strengthen further the argument made throughout this book for application of capitalism in space.

History of Capitalism

A company is merely a system of contracts and collaborations among people to maximize efficiency in production and use of information. These organizations have evolved within capitalism as increasingly effective tools of society for creating value. The upcoming discussion traces the formation of companies as value creation tools for humanity through six milestones across history: (1) merchant trade caravans, (2) multigenerational trade firms, (3) publicly traded companies, (4) labor markets and private property, (5) industrialization, and (6) shareholder primacy. A summary is provided at the end of this section highlighting why exactly these historical milestones help justify the use of capitalism today for value creation in the space industry.

Merchant Trade Caravans

The earliest form of capitalism, merchant capitalism, evolved first between Arabia and China around the 8th century as long-distance trade. At this time, Europe was not yet involved as the European economy had collapsed in the 5th century when the Western Roman Empire fell. However, by the 12th–15th centuries, long-distance trade across sea routes among Europe, Arabia, and China had increased dramatically. Global trade gradually became centered in northern Italy in cities like Venice, Genoa, and Florence and increasingly less so in Arabia and China. To reduce risk, merchants would travel in caravans over land or in fleets of ships. These "companies" of merchants based out of northern Italy are the origins of modern-day business organizations.

A necessity arose to be able to conduct long-distance business without transportation of gold and currency. Merchant companies increasingly used cashless transaction techniques such as bills of exchange and credit through the 14th and 15th centuries. Some of these merchant companies formed into multigenerational family firms. Eventually, these institutions moved beyond the scope of family-inherited wealth to business enterprises, still multigenerational, but with changing owners and with a distinct legal identity. Advancements in legal frameworks for company shareholding, business contracts, and partnerships had not occurred in China or Arabia, and therefore constitute a distinctly European contribution toward the ability of companies to create value. As financial success increased in northern Italy, the competitiveness of this region decreased and there was a gravitational economic pull across Europe to the relatively open societies at the time in Antwerp and Amsterdam.

By the 16th century, the capitalist center of Europe was based primarily in Antwerp and Amsterdam. The first stock exchanges were established in Antwerp in 1531 and the Dutch East India Company (DEIC) became the first publicly traded company in 1602. The DEIC was modeled very much after the previous merchant enterprises formed in northern Italy; however, it was more sophisticated in legal and ownership structure. The company's capital was permanent and owned by the enterprise itself, not by individuals. It was financed by many investors, that is, shareholders, but these investors were not owners of company capital and were not involved directly in management of the company. Also, the shareholders were limited to wealthy members of the aristocracy. While enormously profitable for these investors, there was no semblance of features seen later in capitalism such as a free market, division of labor, or industrialization.

Companies, shareholding, bills of exchange, credit, contracts, multigenerational firm management all are concepts that were first conceived of as ways to expand value creation capabilities of society. This is precisely why these concepts survive to this day. Still, despite these advances happening with capitalism in Europe and global trade leading up to the 17th century, capitalism was still a relatively minor element of most people's lives. It was far from the society-shaping force that it is today. It would not be until industrialization when the masses became directly engaged in value creation that the benefits became more widespread and the near-universal veil of poverty would begin to be lifted.

Industrialization

Up until the 18th century, the vast majority of the European population was still poor and primarily engaged in activities focused on subsistence or serving a lord or dictator. This system, feudalism, consisted of an aristocracy that compelled the general population into service and production (i.e., value creation) through the threat of physical violence. This system began to change first in Holland and England, which also not coincidentally is where the highest degree of political freedom existed compared to other locations in Europe. It happened that, compared to other nations, feudalism in England was centralized in power such that stability and labor were more enforced by the central government than by landowners themselves. These conditions permitted labor markets to form where landowners would award production work to the lowest bidder. It also went the other way, in that workers would seek out the highest wage possible. A result of these evolving relationships was the organization of land into defined parcels often marked physically by fences or walls to be rented and used for production. One approach for catalyzing capitalism somewhere it has not yet taken hold is to do exactly this, grant ownership of parcels of land, thereby creating capital with a stroke of a pen to be used for investment into production.

At the time, changes in manufacturing industries were occurring as well. Previously, manufacturing industries were structured around guilds that provided stability, organization, an apprenticeship format, and guaranteed employment in many cases. At the same time, guilds tended to impede innovation. Mining and textiles are examples of industries that did not have guilds. Powered by long-distance trade and demand, it was these industries specifically that first began to see their production apparatus organized according to principles of modern capitalism. Put simply, capitalism demanded profit, greater profit came from greater output, and greater output came from innovations in the way production occurred. This motivation to improve production methods was the catalyst of the industrial revolution.

The industrial revolution occurred in England in the 18th century, and combined with England's military strength, it resulted in centralization of the European economy in London. The industrial revolution consisted of a process where large cotton mills would hire specialized workers in order to support expanding and increasingly mechanized production lines. As this approach to cotton production spread, intense competition among many mills grew. This, in turn, motivated continuous innovation and efficiency on the part of producers. Large-scale benefits of capitalism for society started to emerge related to productivity, organization of social structures, stability, reduction of conflict and war, increased education, and the existence of disposable income. Economist Adam Smith captured in 1776 a functional description of the capitalist system in his highly influential publication, *The Wealth of Nations* [27]. Smith included comments on individual liberty, capital investment, division of labor, supply and demand, free markets, and trade all as important features of capitalism. Quite the contrast from prominent apparent alternatives at the time like feudalism and slavery. While merchant capitalism was the dominant form of capitalism still in the 18th century, Smith portrayed a shift further into a version of capitalism based more on consumerism and individuals participating directly in the markets rather than just aristocrats and trading companies.

This shift toward Smith's vision in England represents the inflection point where the capitalist system became defined by perpetual expansion, growth, and innovation. This was caused by industrialization and the increasingly direct and voluntary participation of the general population in the economic system through markets and organized labor. Industrialization changed capitalism profoundly in terms of technological advances, an increase in energy consumption, and in terms of extending the benefits to masses of people rather than the few that own capital.

Shareholder Primacy

Company management structures and bureaucracy continued to grow in complexity leading to what many consider the prominent form of capitalism in the 20th century, managerial capitalism. Managerial capitalism was characterized by organizations where business decisions were made by paid managers rather than owners. In this era, the geographic center of capitalism was also shifting once again, this time from London to the United States. Following managerial capitalism, the modern American implementation of capitalism emerged in the 1970s. This change in perspective was led by the Chicago school of economics as shareholder primacy.

The shareholder primacy ideology was popularized by the University of Chicago professor Milton Friedman in his famous article, *The Social Responsibility of Business Is to Increase Its Profits* [28]. This ideology argues that if shareholder profits are prioritized above all else by business managers, the outcome will be the greatest production of value to society that a company is capable of. The other part of shareholder primacy according to Friedman, after maximizing shareholder profits, is that the rule of law must be obeyed. This is important because here there is an implicit assumption that large-scale societal and environmental problems will be managed and mitigated by the government.

An area of criticism of shareholder primacy is that it drives managers to seek profits anywhere that it is possible no matter the social and/or environmental costs. In cases where laws are insufficient to mitigate large-scale problems, a shareholder primacy approach can do real harm to humanity by prioritizing profit at the expense of critical environmental and social systems. As the value creation tools of society, it is questionable if companies engaged in unsustainable practices like these are serving their core function. It would appear that a company is not creating value if its actions result in reduced human prosperity. Shareholder primacy can also motivate profit-seeking in the short term at the expense of even the business itself and its productivity in the longer term. Managers and investors alike in this scenario may not suffer the long-term consequences necessarily, because after the short-term gains have been realized, they can move on and repeat the pattern somewhere else. Overall, it is not clear that shareholder primacy results in maximum value creation as intended.

Shareholder primacy has come to be adopted thoroughly in the mainstream since the 1970s, but is this ideology actually a matter of law? The de facto answer might as well be yes, given the degree to which shareholder primacy has been embraced; however, the legal community is not unanimous on this matter. Within state case law, the legality of shareholder primacy is contested, as numerous judicial rulings can be cited to support a legal argument for both shareholder primacy and opposed ideologies [29, 30]. Internal law, defined by a corporation's charter or articles of incorporation when it is founded, is somewhat less contested in this area. The articles of incorporation are an important place to define guidelines for sustainable management approaches, a statement of purpose, and an outline of any details that may be perceived as running counter to shareholder primacy. This is perhaps the most effective opportunity to attract like-minded investors, board members, and employees that share in the company's vision and management approach.[1] Beyond internal law, the law doctrine known as the business judgment rule says that managers may use profits as they see fit as long as they adhere to the company's charter, the use is to the benefit of the company, and their decisions are not tainted by fraud or a conflict of interest.

As with case law, the interpretation of the business judgment rule relative to legal adherence to shareholder primacy is contested [29, 30].

In addition to defining terms in the charter, choice of legal structure is another way to support company activities that may be perceived as contrary to shareholder primacy. Use of shareholder primacy is associated generally with the most common legal structure for a company, a C corporation. There are several other for-profit legal alternatives to C corporations for businesses that offer more flexibility and legal backing for prioritizing goals in addition to profit maximization. Community Interest Company (CIC), Low-Profit Limited Liability (L3C), and Benefit Corporation are all in this category. Benefit corporations, in particular, have been authorized in 35 US states and are becoming more and more common, including now instances of publicly traded benefit corporations (PBC) [31].

History of Capitalism: Reflecting on the Space Industry

The preceding sections have traced the evolution of capitalism over six historical milestones: (1) merchant trade caravans, (2) multigenerational trade firms, (3) publicly traded companies, (4) labor markets and private property, (5) industrialization, and (6) shareholder primacy. Each of these milestones sheds light on why features of capitalism formed in the first place and why these features are desirable to help value creation in the space industry. The truth is, the lasting features of capitalism exist today only because they were found to result in enhanced value creation. The following list highlights observations from the history of capitalism and provides an implicit argument that the features described are means by which to maximize value creation in space:

- The origins of companies are groups of profit-seeking individuals (trade merchants) collaborating in order to collectively reduce risk. More value creation is possible by an organized profit-seeking group than by an individual.
- Company structures grew in sophistication in order to increase value creation capabilities. Enhanced value creation came about through cashless transaction methods, financial tools, public stock offerings, multigenerational firms, and advanced managerial structures.
- Investors of capital into a value creation scheme are motivated by the prospect of personal gain; however, this only occurs if the investment results also in creating value for others. Profit-seeking was found to be a highly effective driver of value creation.
- Industrialization and the use of markets increased value creation through directly engaging large swaths of people in both the supply and demand sides of the economy. Private property rights and labor markets were enablers for industrialization.

- Value creation using capitalism was most successful in nations with more political freedom.
- Shareholder primacy revealed to an extent not seen before the effectiveness of the profit-seeking motive in enabling production. In doing so, however, an imbalance formed between the performance of social, environmental, and economic systems. This suggests a proactive means to ensure sustainability is necessary to balance profit-seeking with other critical needs.

Externalization

The biggest flaw in how free-market capitalism is implemented today is that markets are prone to externalizing certain critical costs from transactions. A key element necessary for a market to function is that the participants in a given transaction have all of the information that they need to make an informed decision. This is necessary to properly assign value based on utility, scarcity, and costs associated with a transaction. It is not logical to make a business transaction where one incurs a net loss on themselves, but that is exactly what is happening potentially if all relevant information is not available to help guide a decision. Bigger picture, it's not logical to utilize a system of value creation for society that is permissive of value losses in transactions that accumulate and negatively affect everyone.

Another way to view externalized costs is the notion of a hidden subsidy. Market transactions that impose costs on the environment and society occur as if remediation of the associated negative impacts is subsidized. If there was no such subsidy and all information was factored into a transaction, those remediation costs would have to be borne by the parties directly involved. For example, unmitigated greenhouse gas emissions have occurred because there has always been an implicit assumption on the part of consumers and producers of fossil fuels that the atmosphere could absorb any waste emitted. Until recent decades, the cost of emitting greenhouse gas has effectively been subsidized by a biosphere capable of absorbing the amounts emitted. Today, this natural subsidy is not enough and the bill is coming due in the form of environmental impacts, including, among other things, sea level rise, strain on agricultural productivity, municipal flood management, higher rates of disease and insect infestation, mass migration away from at-risk coastal communities, more frequent and more severe natural disasters, and loss of economic productivity due to extremes in heat. These costs are part of the original transactions where they were externalized whether the direct participants included them or not.

In economic terms, externalities may be seen as inefficiencies in value creation. If externalities are found to exist and they are then subsequently accounted for in transactions, the cost of production as a whole appears to shift upwards. In this instance, the optimized production level where value to consumers is maximized overall results in a lower production rate at a higher cost to consumers compared to if externalities are ignored. In this case, the cost to consumers is best characterized not as *higher but rather more accurate*, as it reflects both financial costs of production and broader costs to society. Conversely, not accounting for externalities in transactions results in production levels that are higher than socially desirable overall [32]. In other words, production levels that do more harm than good.

The reality today is that modern capitalism suffers from pervasive cost externalization. While this is not a new thing, the scale of the global economy has reached a level where externalized costs are overwhelming critical social and environmental systems. Because these systems are so foundational, an accelerating erosion of human prosperity is occurring now as a result. Clearly this trend is undesirable and therefore there is a strong motivation to rectify this flaw in modern capitalism so that humanity can continue indefinitely to enjoy the benefits stemming from free markets and profit-seeking. The next section describes efforts underway and practical methods to achieve this goal.

The Future of Capitalism

When it comes to survival, humans are historically adept at adaptation and innovation. It's a defining feature of the species. The solution to sustainability problems associated with modern capitalism is to adapt the system to today's challenges and the challenges of the future. Modify the way food, energy, and all products are produced. Modify the way people move around, consume natural resources, and dispose of waste. In short, modify the manner in which all transactions occur in markets so that critical costs are not externalized. The means to achieve these things is not a matter of regulating a solution into place nor is it a matter of shutting down industry. The path forward is fomenting awareness and demand from the general public for a positive transformation in how businesses and markets function. A public value system that prioritizes sustainability can and will be reflected in both corporate policies and ultimately law. A "bottom-up" change in capitalism of this nature is the only solution that will be lasting and sincere. This is the future of capitalism.

Building Momentum

Today, sustainability has gone mainstream.[2] This is a significant point because even ten years ago (circa 2010), this would have been a difficult statement to make. A 2020 report concludes that 90% of S&P 500 companies track and pursue publicly the sustainability of their businesses [33]. A similar report from 2011 places this percentage of US Fortune 500 companies at less than 20% [34]. As Hitchcock and Willard state in *The Business Guide to Sustainability*: "in the last twenty years, the sustainability conversation has shifted from why to how, from a competitive advantage to a business imperative" [35]. While voluntary sustainability reporting tends to vary in thoroughness, sincerity, transparency, and the measurement methods used, its widespread recent growth represents enormous progress.

Larry Fink, CEO of Blackrock, the world's largest financial investment firm managing over $7 trillion in assets, releases an annual "letter to CEOs" regarded by many now as one of the mainstream barometers of big business. A theme in his letters has emerged in recent years indicating his view that global threats like climate change and inequality are threats that businesses can and must help address. In his 2018 letter [36], Fink states:

> Society is demanding that companies, both public and private, serve a social purpose. To prosper over time, every company must not only deliver financial performance, but also show how it makes a positive contribution to society. Companies must benefit all of their stakeholders, including shareholders, employees, customers, and the communities in which they operate.

Fink expresses similar views in subsequent annual letters as well [37].

An important element of Fink's recent letters is that they make the link between sustainability and climate risk to the long-term financial performance of investments. This is important as it illuminates the role of business in the problem and in the solution. If one wishes to continue to enjoy benefits and receive value created by a company but in ways that are sustainable for humanity and the planet, the company must continue also to be profitable. In part, this element of Fink's message is that sustainability and profitability are inexorably linked going forward and that a business that disregards sustainability (or profitability for that matter) is doomed one way or another in the long run.

Other high-profile leaders are now also expressing similar sentiments. In 2019, Jerome Powell, Chair of the Federal Reserve Bank, wrote in a letter to Senator Brian Schatz of Hawaii that climate change was "considered an increasingly relevant issue for the central bank" [38]. Acting US Securities and Exchanges Commission (SEC) chair, Allison Lee, announced in March 2021 that the SEC will begin to consider use of Environmental, Social, Corporate Governance (ESG) metrics in its regulation of US financial markets [39]. In February 2020, JP Morgan CEO Jamie Dimon announced plans to "facilitate $200 billion to advance the United Nations Sustainability Goals" as well as plans to discontinue advising and investing in the coal, oil, and gas industries [40].

Beyond the finance industry, many large companies have signed on to the RE100 initiative which consists of public declarations for moving toward use of 100% renewable energy. The highly influential Business Roundtable lobbying group has now also shifted away from shareholder primacy to advocating for a more balanced stakeholder-based approach which includes attention toward sustainability and social responsibility. On an international level, The World Economic Forum manifesto in 2020, titled *The Universal Purpose of a Company in the Fourth Industrial Revolution* [41], has elements overtly advocating a stakeholder management approach for business and a shift away from shareholder primacy. To quote the first section in the manifesto:

> The purpose of a company is to engage all its stakeholders in shared and sustained value creation. In creating such value, a company serves not only its shareholders but all its stakeholders – employees, customers, suppliers, local communities and society at large.

These public statements and more from leaders in the business and financial communities are emblematic of progress and a shifting awareness in society at large. No longer are these notions limited to activists and academics; the people quoted here are some of the most influential in the world and are declaring that these ideas matter and are important. The next 10–20 years will be critical in spreading awareness even further and taking action. Concerning the space industry specifically, this call for action is especially important so that a total overhaul later is avoided and the space economy forms sustainably from the start.

Business as a Solution

Academia has preceded public statements from business leaders quoted in the previous section with a similar message for several decades. In numerous cases there is an advocacy for businesses to participate directly in solving humanity's challenges through increased sustainability but while maintaining capitalist principles. Author Paul Hawken recognizes in a 1992 paper not just the responsibility but the potential sheer power of business when it comes to being a part of the solution to sustainability-related challenges. Hawken says: "Business is the only mechanism on the planet today powerful enough to produce the changes necessary to reverse global environmental and social degradation" [42]. Professor Rebecca Henderson offers similar commentary in *Reimagining Capitalism in a World on Fire* [43], but extends the notion along the lines of some of Fink's comments in that business actually stands to benefit economically by using its considerable clout to be proactive in addressing climate change and other global problems. Henderson states: "business not only has the power and the duty to play a huge role in transforming the world but also strong economic incentive to do so."

An influential book related to Hawken's 1992 paper was published in 2001 by authors Paul Hawken, Amory Lovins, and L. Hunter Lovins titled *Natural Capitalism* [44]. The biggest message from *Natural Capitalism* to highlight is that capitalism works! It works really, really well and is, in fact, the most efficient and effective system ever devised to improve lives and distribute value to as many people as possible. There is no need to abandon the best system that has ever existed for improving lives; however, there is a strong need to improve it. Hawken et al. remark on this point:

> The goal of natural capitalism is to extend the sound principles of the market to all sources of material value, not just those that by accidents of history were first appropriated into the market system. It also seeks to guarantee that forms of capital are as prudently stewarded as money is by the trustees of financial capital.

Similarly, Hawken et al. also say: "Economics cannot function as a reliable guide until natural capital is placed on the balance sheets of companies, countries, and the world" and "when natural capital is no longer treated as free, unlimited, and inconsequential, but as an integral and indispensable part of the production process, our entire system of accounting will change."

This last quote from Hawken et al. hits on the fact that, traditionally, markets only assign value to financial capital. If a market transaction does not include natural and social capital in its calculus, the full extent of relevant information is not available and the transaction participants cannot know truly if there is a win-win exchange happening. Transactions of this nature are subject to cost externalization. Recognizing this, John Elkington developed the Triple Bottom Line (TBL) concept in the mid-1990s [45] (although he famously has now "recalled" the TBL as of 2018 in favor of approaches that are more proactive and less focused on reporting [46]). The TBL is an accounting system that includes social, environmental, and economic (i.e., financial) elements of a company and has emerged as a guiding principle in sustainable businesses. Use of the TBL concept, either simply through awareness or through implementation in accounting, can be helpful toward eliminating cost externalization.

Whole Foods founder John Mackey and coauthor Raj Sisodia point out in *Conscious Capitalism* [47] that capitalism as a whole has resulted in the greatest advances in human health, happiness, and prosperity the world has ever seen. Like Hawken et al., they also suggest that there is not a need to move away from capitalism but rather hone its implementation. Further, Mackey and Sisodia emphasize prioritization of profit-seeking to support financial sustainability not as a necessary evil but rather as a critical and effective motivational method to provide a high-quality service/product and create a win-win situation for all involved.

Professor Alex Edmans expresses a similar view but frames things in terms of value [48]. Edmans explains the notion that companies should create profit only through creating value for society. Edmans is reinforcing simply why companies exist at all. They exist at the discretion of society to serve its needs, that is, create value by meeting demands expressed in a free market. In short, the goal of a company is: *maximize value creation*. Success is not despite embracing a broad definition for value, but because of it. In support of this notion, an extensive review of over 2,000 different studies stretching back to the 1970s finds in the overwhelming majority of cases a "nonnegative" correlation between corporate financial performance and attention to environmental, social, and governance goals [49].

Economist Kate Raworth advocates that instead of operating in a "growth at all costs" or "growth as fast as possible" mantra to achieve these important ends, humanity can strive for a sweet spot in between a social foundation and ecological ceiling. Above the ecological ceiling critical planetary degradation occurs and below the social foundation critical human deprivation occurs [14]. Raworth stresses the point that business, capitalism, and economics should continue to be used to uplift the lives of as many people as possible. Business should continue to be used to solve global problems like food production, producing medicine, constructing homes, the list goes on. However, there really is no point if these activities occur in ways that degrade or destroy the systems that they operate within.

Overall, there is a compelling case to continue to utilize businesses as the value creation tools of society in ways that are sustainable. The next section begins a turn in this discussion toward practicality by offering an alternative approach to shareholder primacy that supports this goal. Discussions later in Chapters 3 and 4 build on this theme further, ultimately forming guidance for value creation methods in the space industry.

Stakeholder Management

Several of those quoted in the previous section advocate for a stakeholder approach to business. Stakeholder management may well serve as the new framework for capitalism as the transition away from shareholder primacy occurs. It offers a means to embrace the power of capitalism but avoid systemic cost externalization. Stakeholder management theory was popularized as a business management approach by R. Edward Freeman beginning in 1984 [50]. At its core, it embraces two things: (1) the definition of value involves more than just financial considerations and (2) the world is complex and maximization of value creation is achieved by managing and balancing value creation for all stakeholders.

An attractive aspect of stakeholder management theory is that it is founded on core tenets of the existing free-market capitalist system including continued emphasis on the right to private property, the profit-seeking motive, and perpetual enabling of voluntary win-win transactions. Hence, it is largely compatible with existing business practices and allows for continued enjoyment of the societal benefits that capitalism brings. What makes stakeholder management distinctive from shareholder primacy though is the premise that maximizing value across all stakeholders beyond just shareholders is precisely what results also in maximum commercial success for a firm [49]. Professor David Chandler says on this matter:

> If the purpose of a firm's strategy is to build a sustainable competitive advantage that can be sustained over the medium to long term, then the best way to do that in today's complex, dynamic business environment is to create value for the firm's stakeholders, broadly defined.
>
> [51]

Over-prioritization of benefit for one specific stakeholder doesn't make sense in today's world. A world in which customers, employees, investors, regulators, and shareholders all are increasingly informed and empowered to react to results of negative externalities related to a firm's activities.

A company creating value for one stakeholder in a way that degrades critical elements of society or the environment will exist only if society permits it. Only if stakeholders remain silent. Even if a CEO or board does not care about a particular issue, they effectively have to care for the company's own good if an influential stakeholder or the general public care. As former Governor of The Bank of England Mark Carney points out in *Value(s)*: "We equate the market prices of goods, activities and labour with their worth and that worth with what society values" [52]. The acceptable nature of a company's production methods is a function of the expectations and values of the society that the company exists in to serve. Rabbi Jonathan Sacks observed on this matter in a 2009 *Times* article "Markets were made to serve us; we were not made to serve markets" [53]. It happens that, out of necessity if nothing else, the values of society worldwide today are shifting to become more cognizant of the environment and the planetary climate than ever before. This perspective is influencing demands and expectations placed on businesses and stakeholder management embraces this shifting paradigm.

Who are the stakeholders for a given company? A stakeholder is any group or individual who has a stake in the firm, can affect or be affected by the firm, or that the firm relies upon in some way to be successful. Primary stakeholders can be defined as employees, suppliers, customers, investors, and the local community. These stakeholders are so influential and important for the firm's success, in that they may (1) hold assets that are critical to the enterprise's success, (2) put their assets at risk in the enterprise, and/ or (3) have sufficient power to compel influence [54]. Secondary stakeholders may include the media, government regulators, NGOs, union leaders, consumer advocacy groups, or downstream participants in the product life cycle. Primary versus secondary classification may vary depending on the nature of the business. For example, highly regulated industries like aerospace may regard government as a primary stakeholder.

Stakeholders in the Space Industry

Stakeholder management has found its way into the space industry. National Aeronautics and Space Administration (NASA) requirement *NPR 7123.1A NASA Systems Engineering Processes and Requirements and the NASA Systems Engineering Handbook call for identifying stakeholders at the beginning of a project* [55]. While stakeholders for a space project or space company will vary depending on circumstances, the list below can be used as a guide and includes numerous examples.

Government[3]

- Executive branch of government
- Congress
- US Space Council
- Department of State
- Department of Transportation
- Department of Defense
- Department of Agriculture
- Department of Energy
- Department of Commerce
- Office of Space Commerce
- US Air Force
- US Space Force
- Space Development Agency
- NASA
- National Oceanic and Atmospheric Administration (NOAA)
- US Geological Survey (USGS)
- Federal Aviation Administration (FAA)
- Environmental Protection Agency (EPA)
- US Agency for International Development (USAID)
- Federal Communications Commission (FCC)
- Intelligence agencies
- Presidential directives

International

- World Bank
- UN
- International project partners
- Inter-Agency Space Debris Coordination Committee (IADC)
- International Telecommunication Union (ITU)

Society

- Media
- Educational institutions

- Museums
- The public
- Astronauts' families
- Local community
- Local government
- NGOs, charities, foundations
- Law enforcement
- Unions

Science and Knowledge

- Science and technology advisory groups
- Research laboratories
- Engineering disciplines
- Principal investigators
- Scientists
- Subject matter experts

Project

- Safety organizations
- Astronauts
- Project managers
- System operators
- Technical authority
- Verification team
- Project boards (flight readiness review board, engineering review board, etc.)
- System managers
- Ground facility providers
- Other nearby spacecraft
- Other users of radiofrequencies

Business

- Customers
- Shareholders
- Users
- Directors
- Corporate boards
- Competitors
- Production facilities
- Commercial data providers
- Insurance agencies
- Owners
- Employees

- Investors
- Suppliers
- Commercial enterprises
- Commercial data users

Stakeholder Management in Practice

Much of Freeman's work and that of stakeholder management practitioners is centered on the fact that this approach is easier said than done. As Freeman et al. say: "the real challenge is to determine best practices in managing stakeholders, and to determine the contexts in which those practices are most likely to lead to the best value creating results" [56]. A firm has only a limited amount of resources to use to create value and address stakeholder needs. While classification of stakeholders as primary or secondary offers some insight for a resource allocation strategy, this challenge is more complex. Part of this effort is being cognizant of which stakeholders stand to benefit and which stand to suffer the most from a firm's activities. On this point, Freeman says: "if organizations want to be effective, they will pay attention to all and only those relationships that can affect or be affected by the achievement of the organization's purpose" [57].

Company purpose, now referred to here in quotes from Fink, the World Economic Forum manifesto, Chandler, and Freeman, is central to stakeholder management. Purpose gives definition to the value being created by the organization and answers clearly the question on how a company makes the world a better place [48]. If it is well defined in the charter and well communicated by management, a compelling company purpose serves as the "north star" for the company, promotes unity among the organization, and offers guidance to the appropriate nature of stakeholder relationships. With a compelling purpose, employees want to support the company and want the company to be successful.[4] Employees are more productive, happier, and more creative [43]. Beyond just employees, company purpose also should be used to attract like-minded stakeholders across the board where all are unified in a willingness to support the purpose. Last but not least, the company purpose must be formulated such that profit is attained by fulfilling the purpose.

Even with purpose as an overall "glue" among a company and its stakeholders, the question stands: how much of the company's resources should be allocated to meeting the needs of a given stakeholder? Answering this question is the job of mangers. Due to the inevitability that numerous stakeholder needs will conflict and compete with one another, complete satisfaction among every stakeholder and the firm is all but impossible [58, 59]. The Coase theorem says that if parties are free to negotiate, private solutions can be found to negative externalities and that this will result in the efficient outcome considering net total cost versus benefit. This is a useful perspective to adopt in stakeholder management.

Even in cases where a stakeholder consensus can be achieved with regard to a business's activities, an overarching challenge exists related to the acceptability of their decision. It may be that all stakeholders agree on some compromise amount of carbon emissions, but who is to say that amount is what is actually needed to avoid externalization to the degree that sustainability is achieved worldwide among all companies? How can any one stakeholder, even one whose primary interest is limiting carbon emissions, be the arbiter as to how much a particular company or product is entitled to emit? Context-based sustainability accounting methods [60] may offer an answer, but this is admittedly a difficult issue and one that this book does not attempt to solve. Ultimately, managers must wield some degree of dictatorial power and decision-making authority that attempts a best effort solution at balancing direct needs of the firm and those of its stakeholders. The next section covers stakeholder value flow maps which can be used as a tool to aid managers in this effort.

Stakeholder Value Flow Map

A stakeholder value flow map is a practical means for managers to understand stakeholder needs and company resource allocation. Creating a value flow map consists of mapping out all stakeholder relationships and in doing so capture value flow emanating from and received by the company. A well-defined stakeholder value flow map clarifies the positive contribution that a company has toward society and helps define what value the company is uniquely suited to bring to the table. It also is an indispensable tool to understand all of the firm-to-stakeholder and stakeholder-to-stakeholder value exchanges affecting and affected by a firm. It can be complex. The Massachusetts Institute of Technology (MIT) has developed stakeholder value flow mapping tools and applied them to space exploration and Earth observation activities [61–63]. Much of the content in this section on value flow mapping is derived from the MIT work in this area.

Value flow mapping starts with modeling input and output of value for each stakeholder. Defining a given stakeholder model involves determining specifically their needs, expectations, and productivity and describing these things as input and output value flows. There are numerous types of value that can be exchanged and converted by a stakeholder, including policy, money, workforce, technology, knowledge, energy, influence, materials, goods, and services [63]. When stakeholder model definitions are complete for all stakeholders, value flows in and out of stakeholders can be connected in chains in a stakeholder value map from stakeholder-to-stakeholder [63]. Notably, since the type of value may vary within a value chain and since stakeholders can convert value types, this type of mapping is particularly useful to track value in forms other than money [61].

A useful feature of this approach is that value chains can reveal circular flows. Circular value flows, known as "value loops," can reveal how one type of value output from a stakeholder meets the needs of another stakeholder indirectly while ultimately feeding back into an input for the firm [63]. Conversely, value flow mapping can be used to identify value chains that do not form loops, value outputs that do not feed any other stakeholder value input, stakeholder expectations that are not being met, and stakeholders that do not produce a value output for any other stakeholder. In theory, if all stakeholders are included in a stakeholder map, then all conceivable negative and positive impacts of a firm's actions are captured. Or put in a different way, all possible value creation opportunities and value loss risks are captured.

Once a comprehensive stakeholder value flow map is created, weight factors can be applied to value flows and the map can be used by managers in studies to find optimal value creation strategies. How to define the weight factors? Two options are: (1) formation of bilateral agreements between informed third parties and (2) use of Kano's Methods for Understanding Customer-Defined Quality [64] to discern perceived stakeholder value [61]. A weighted value flow map can be used to assess a company as a whole, a business model, a product, or even the impacts of a single decision.

An example of a stakeholder value flow map for a hypothetical remote sensing satellite company is shown in Figure 2.1 (adapted from Cameron et al. [63]). In this example, the remote sensing company produces satellites, operates them, and provides value-added products using the raw data. Customers include the public and the government. This value flow map is simplified for illustrative purposes. An actual value flow map for a satellite company such as this would have more stakeholders and more value flows than are shown. For example, employees, individual regulatory agencies (ITU, FAA, FCC, NASA), the media, NGOs, investors, the local community, and other users of orbital space are all additional stakeholders not shown in Figure 2.1. Examples of additional value flows not shown in Figure 2.1 are regulations and compliance between the government and all stakeholders, services from the government to all stakeholders, and taxes from the industry to the government.

The stakeholder value flow map in Figure 2.1 is shown in such a simplified form for several reasons. First, a complete value flow map would reach a complexity level where it no longer is useful to visualize it in a single demonstrative figure. In practice, computational tools tracking the complex web of value flows and interconnected relationships are needed. Second, several features of this flow map are intentionally imbedded to highlight points of this discussion. It is evident that suppliers and the satellite company both produce material waste (e.g., scrap material, emissions, processing chemicals, etc.). A more detailed value flow map can break the waste flow into specific components and include additional stakeholders that may utilize them as system inputs. Also shown in the simplified value flow map are several value loops. For example, the exchange between the satellite company and educational institutes. The satellite company flows money and raw data to academia and in return gets a skilled workforce and R&D.

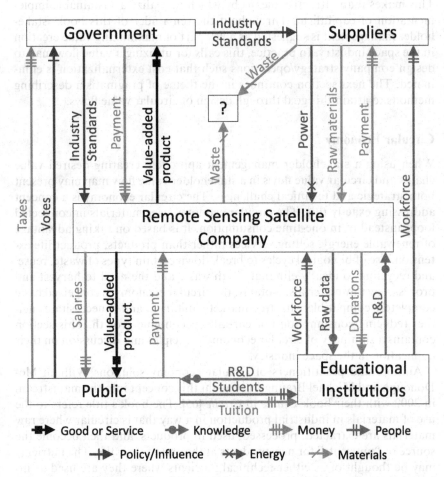

Figure 2.1 Stakeholder value flow map for a remote sensing company. Adapted from Cameron et al. [63].

Insight into stakeholder needs and value flows helps managers design company strategy and operational practices related to products, investments, community impacts, supplier selection, pricing, manufacturing infrastructure, use of resources, waste disposal methods, internal organization functionality, and more. The goal of managers in this context is designing strategies that prioritize all primary stakeholder needs to appropriate levels where other stakeholders' needs are not sacrificed below an acceptable level. If executed effectively, this should result in a maximization of value creation.

Stakeholder management as described here is not a new idea. It's been around for decades and seen some degree of implementation and success.

This makes it an attractive means by which to realize a sustainable implementation of capitalism. Throughout the remainder of this book, stakeholder management is suggested as a key part of maximizing value creation in the space industry. In practice, this calls for utilizing a value flow map to design company strategy/operations such that cost externalization is eliminated. The next section continues in the theme of pragmatism describing methods to attain this goal through design of circular value flows.

Circular Economy

When using a stakeholder management approach, creating desired value chains and circular value flows in a stakeholder value flow map may present both strategic and technical challenges. The circular economy is a concept addressing exactly this. The circular economy uses materials in connected loops instead of in one-time consumption. It is based on taking advantage of renewable energy, selling services rather than products, product life extension, use of biological cycles to break down certain types of waste, reuse, and recycling to ideally eliminate both waste and the need to harvest and process new raw materials. Notably, the circular economy is conceived to be completely compatible with free-market capitalism and it necessitates neither reducing consumption nor curtailing economic growth. This section contains a summary of circular economy principles and discussion on their application in the space industry.

Authors and practitioners of circular economy solutions William Mc-Donough and Michael Braungart brought this concept into the mainstream in 2002 with their book *Cradle to Cradle* [65]. The book's title refers to the use of materials in industrial production in a way that is circular where raw materials are extracted, processed, used in products, and then become the source or "nutrients" for new products at the end of their life. The nutrients may be thought of as either technical nutrients where they are used as inputs to an industrial system or biological nutrients where they are used as inputs to an environmental system. If a production process does not adhere to these rules, it can be said to be "unnatural" or disruptive to a symbiotic sustainable system. An unnatural process could not exist permanently in nature by definition, as it would ultimately destroy itself through waste accumulation and/or exhausting input resources.

The "linear economy" is the more traditional model that has been used historically in capitalism. It follows a "cradle-to-grave" flow of materials from raw material harvest to products and ultimately to waste. One of the reasons this system came to be in today's world is that economically it often is simply cheaper and more profitable for owners of capital to extract raw materials, leverage the now highly optimized industrial infrastructure to produce products, dispose of them at some point, and then sell a replacement. This is a continuous cycle of profits and employment and economic benefit to all involved including the consumer. Upon closer examination though a linear economy approach may not actually not be "cheaper" over-all. The previous section on externalization described how this pattern is economically inefficient and prone to production levels that are higher than socially desirable (i.e., create more harm than good in the long run). The circular economy essentially internalizes all costs but still promotes continued consumption, innovation, competition, and economic growth.

Zero-Waste

The circular economy at its core is based around the notion of closed technical systems. That is, industrial processes that eliminate or minimize raw material harvest and waste. This is achieved through circular value flows where inputs for one system are sourced only from renewable energy and the outputs of another system. System outputs used in this manner would be simply waste if not for their use as technical nutrients. In sourcing technical system inputs from outputs of other processes, negative environmental impacts associated with waste disposal and with raw material harvest are avoided. Raw material harvest negative impacts include ecosystem destruction, creation of polluting byproducts, depletion of nonrenewable resources, and expending energy on an activity that may be unnecessary if the same resource can be obtained by other means. Companies that operate in ways that avoid these impacts can be described as zero-waste.

In addition to reducing environmental impacts, there is also a compelling economic argument for zero-waste. System outputs that are nutrients for another system constitute a commodity with economic value. Maximum economic efficiency of an industrial process entails only system outputs that are financially valuable. Anything less effectively leaves money on the table. Is elimination of waste in a technical industry achievable though? Examples of zero-waste manufacturing companies include the likes of Subaru, Toyota, General Motors, Unilever, and Proctor & Gamble. The zero-waste goal was achieved in these cases simply by removal of the option to use a perceived hidden subsidy in the form of an infinite waste sink. In doing this, the cost of waste disposal is no longer externalized and company processes are forced to be configured accordingly. The remainder of this section continues this theme describing practical means to achieve zero-waste in the space industry.

Value Management

Reduction or elimination of waste is a win-win-win in terms of business, environment, and society, but what does this actually entail? How does a manufacturing company in the space industry, for example, reduce or eliminate waste? Some of the means to achieve this goal include recycling, re-use, elimination of toxic chemicals and byproducts, product longevity, and service business models. This is getting at perhaps the most central tenet of the circular economy and that is value management. Businesses have been creating value for centuries, but managing it in products beyond the point of sale for recovery later is less common.

Rather than disengaging with a customer after the point of sale, the seller/producer can track and manage the value embedded in a product such that it can be recaptured at the end of its useful life. Sometimes, this is described as activating a two-way value chain associated with a product, the "supply chain" and the "return chain," both of which can be designed using a stakeholder value flow map. There often can be a strong business case for activating the return chain. If a product is thrown away at the end of its useful life, 100% of the energy, expertise, time, and labor to produce it, all of the embedded value, go into the landfill. In this case, the manufacturer in theory must then repeat these same expenditures in resources, energy, effort, and time to make a replacement product. Walter Stahel notes in *The Circular Economy: A User's Guide* that "waste prevention is also a prevention of economic and resource losses" and "if producers retain ownership of their goods, the goods of today are tomorrow's resources at yesteryear's commodity prices, and increase the resilience of society through a future resource security" [66]. Essentially, products in use can be treated as a reserve stock of material for future products. For example, a spacecraft is not just an asset for current revenue but also simultaneously is a source of raw material and specialized components for future revenue-generating assets.

Tracking and managing product value to the benefit of a company past the point of sale is simultaneously a direct contribution to both profitability and sustainability. In the space industry, where products are highly specialized and quality control is emphasized more than most other industries, embedded value is significant. For example, a hypothetical piece of structure on a spacecraft may be made from relatively cheap aluminum, but the resources required for its engineering, inspection, machining precision, and acceptance testing may be considerable. In a case like this, recovery of the raw material at the end of the part's life (i.e., recycling) is worth something, but retaining the embedded value in the part itself by reusing or refurbishing it may be worth much more.

One may begin to see how a long-term value management view could influence product design. For example, prolonged fatigue loading exposure or corrosion issues associated with hardware reuse/life extension can be mitigated with geometry or alloy choices in the design. The design choices may be more expensive, but not so overall if the component is reused and the recovered value is factored in. This example highlights the notion that the finished product has more value than that of the materials in it. This would suggest also that in specialized parts and components, more value stands to be recovered through reuse and refurbishment compared to recycling.

Whatever the method of value management is, a company taking this approach has a financial incentive to design and produce products that retain value. This is a stark contrast to a linear economy approach where the financial incentive is simply to produce and sell as many products as possible. Value management also is not necessarily limited just to recovery at end of life. It also can involve continuous revenue beyond the point of sale. For example, an aerospace producer may enable both long-term revenue and end-of-life value recapture by planning to participate in operation, regular upgrades, maintenance, and repair services of their product. An example of this type of relationship can be found in the sale of military aircraft to the United States. Some aircraft like the US Air Force B-52 bombers are decades old. Industry continued revenue capture long after the point of sale through maintenance and technology upgrades. By producing military aircraft that last for decades, industry creates literally a physical revenue platform (the airframe) that forms the core of a long-term business relationship. Spacecraft are not the same thing as aircraft, but extending this concept to space hardware is not altogether impractical.

Recycling

Recycling hardware materials is one option for value management, though it does not come for free. Recycling costs money, it takes energy, and it creates waste from associated activities like sorting, remelting, cleaning, and machinery operation. Designing products and parts to be disassembled, reused, or repurposed typically is preferable and can make more sense economically [23]. If disassembly, reuse, and repurpose are not possible, then it is preferable to utilize recycling for value recapture compared to doing nothing at all.

The data in Table 2.1 indicate that sourcing common recycled aerospace materials requires orders of magnitude less energy compared to extraction and processing raw materials [67]. Additionally, data for silicon wafers, lumber, and cement are included in the list to offer a comparison to materials in other large industries. This comparison highlights the high energy cost of materials for space compared to construction industry and the relatively low cost of materials for space compared to the microchip industry (though microchips are used in space systems). Overall, the energy savings between recycled materials and raw materials shown in Table 2.1 is considerable, in the range of 67%–97%.

As Table 2.1 implies, the positive impact on greenhouse gas reductions from using recycled metals like steel and aluminum instead of raw materials can be significant [69–71]. This is relevant given that steel production and aluminum production account for 9% and 1.5%, respectively, of all greenhouse gas emissions worldwide [72]. Aluminum, the most common aerospace material, is highly energy-intensive to produce from raw Bauxite ore compared to other materials. Four tons of ore yield one ton of aluminum and in doing so produce the toxic and radioactive "red mud" byproduct

Table 2.1 Energy required to produce common materials and savings associated with using recycled material.

Material	Energy to Produce from Raw Material (MJ/kg)		Energy savings to produce from recycled material	
Carbon fibers	200–600	[68]	95%	[68]
Carbon fiber composite	770	[69]	—	—
Plastic	80	[69]	80%	[70]
Aluminum	190–230	[70]	90–97%	[70]
Titanium	360–750	[70]	67%	[70]
Nickel	180–200	[70]	90%	[70]
Stainless steel	57–68	[70]	68%	[70]
Steel	20–25	[70]	60–75%	[70]
Silicon wafer	22,000	[69]	—	—
Lumber	2.8	[69]	—	—
Cement	3.1	[69]	—	—

that must be stored. If faced with raw material extraction, there is a strong environmental motivation to source as much metal from reused or recycled sources as possible.

One challenge area, particularly for high-performance products like aircraft and space hardware, is that recycling specialized materials can be difficult or even impossible. Some alloys or polymers simply are manufactured into an irreversible chemical state. In other cases, it is difficult to avoid contamination and mixing from coatings, multiple welded parts, and various different alloys. For example, recycling of the common aerospace aluminum alloy Al 7075 is possible but only if the scrap material is strictly controlled to include only Al 7075. Mixing in even small amounts of other aluminum alloys will contaminate the alloy and reduce mechanical properties. The same is true for recycling other common aerospace alloys such as the titanium alloy Ti-6Al-4v. Overall, contamination of recovered material has been the greatest challenge preventing widespread recycling of specialized high-performance aerospace alloys [73].

If contamination cannot be avoided, recycled alloys may still be "downcycled" and used either for cast parts where mechanical property requirements are less demanding or for extracting limited individual metals in element form to use in other new alloy formulations [71, 72]. The latter can be complicated because only certain elements can separate from the base metal and be extracted in isolation during a melting process. Downcycling, though, is actually the most common use of recycled aerospace alloys. In this case, new material still must be sourced to replace the original high-performance alloy part, but other less critical parts benefit from sourcing recycled material. Given the limitations with recycling certain high-performance alloys, designing for long-term value management in some cases may entail the use of lower-performing materials that can be recycled and therefore better retain their value. Trade studies using a stakeholder value flow map can help assess options like this.

Aside from metal alloys, another common material system used in the aerospace industry is carbon fiber-reinforced polymer composites. The main component in composites to recover during recycling is the carbon fiber. The polymer matrix material encapsulating the fibers is much cheaper and easier to reproduce. Recycling carbon fibers can occur either during fabrication when material scraps are generated or at the end of life. Beyond just the carbon fibers and polymer matrix, composite structures usually consist of numerous additional materials such as metallic or foam sandwich core, metallic fasteners, metallic inserts, and adhesives, all of which can make recycling more challenging. Table 2.1 indicates a 95% energy reduction for recycled carbon fibers compared to the raw material production making recycling well worth it if it is possible. In some cases, recycled carbon fiber quality may be near pristine and appropriate for use in high-performance parts [68, 74]. In other cases, reduced quality recycled fibers can be downcycled and used in products with lower performance requirements.

In addition to raw materials, recycling complete aerospace vehicles has been studied for some time as well. Recycling a decommissioned aircraft was undertaken in 2005 by the Airbus-led PAMELA-LIFE project. Airbus dismantled an A300 aircraft and was able to recover 70%–80% of the total material in the aircraft by mass. Later, Airbus implemented the process developed on the A300 on an A380 and was able to recover 90% of material for reuse [75]. In 2015, Boeing successfully dismantled a retired 757 aircraft and, like Airbus with the A380, was able to recycle or reuse 90% of the aircraft. These efforts involved more than just raw material recycling, including also recycling of wires and electronics [68] along with reuse and refurbishment of everything possible like the landing gear, engines, avionics, and even the seats [76]. It is not a stretch to see how this concept could be extended to space vehicles such as reusable rockets.

Service Business Model

An often used and entirely different approach from recycling and reuse for value management is adopting a service business model. A big advantage of a service-based product is that the service provider benefits financially directly from efficiencies related to product manufacture, use of materials, use of energy, and longevity. The service companies that are most efficient, that is, those that offer the most value to customers while consuming the least, are the most successful. This is in contrast to a product-based business where the provider benefits financially the more expensive the product is and the more frequently it has to be repurchased and reproduced. Common everyday examples of service businesses are voicemail, office supplies, carpets, pool maintenance, climate control in buildings, car sharing, tool rental, cloud data storage, and light bulbs. Service-based products can be especially attractive also for items that are complex and high cost (like spacecraft).

In many cases, the service business model allows multiple customers to obtain the same value from a single product. This constitutes increased consumption and revenue with a neutral use of resources. Benefits to the customer as a result include lower price, more convenience, better quality product, and access to a product or service that would otherwise be financially out of reach. Overall, a service business allows for growth in consumption, employment, and GDP, but while reducing environmental impacts. The next section examines more closely application of the service business model and other circular economy principles in the space industry.

Service Business Models in the Space Industry

A study by Lacy and Rutqvist (not specific to the space industry) suggests four general areas for value creation using circular economy principles: (1) elimination of wasteful resources, (2) life cycles, (3) capacity, and (4) embedded value [23]. Resource waste may be reduced by things like product optimization, renewable energy, and manufacturing efficiency. A product life cycle may offer more value through upgrades, refurbishing, maintenance, reuse, and product longevity. Wasted capacity may be eliminated through increased sharing, co-owning, co-using, and resource pooling. Finally, eliminating wasted embedded value can be achieved by increased recycling, upcycling,[5] downcycling, and component harvesting. Among the strategies within these four categories, the space industry stands to most effectively adopt circular economy principles using the service-business model and hardware value recovery.

The most prominent examples of product value management today in the space industry are reusable rockets and launch services. A single heavy-lift rocket launch traditionally costs hundreds of millions of dollars. In part, this high cost was due to the fact that space hardware is energy-intensive to produce because of demanding performance requirements, manufacturing quality control, and extensive certification test activities. In fact, it may be difficult to find anything created by humans that is more of a contrived, complex, and intensive use of energy for a single product. In the past, all of this manufacturing energy and effort was wasted immediately after the launch as spent rockets would fall into the ocean as waste.

In the modern launch service business model, access to orbit is offered by a provider who retains ownership of the rocket and reuses it with a new customer after each flight. This approach, pioneered by SpaceX, embraces circular economy principles and notably is also in complete alignment with free-market capitalism. It offers constant revenue to the launch provider while saving costs to the environment and the customer by avoiding constant remanufacturing of the same product. Use of capitalism in this way in the rocket launch industry has resulted in orders of magnitude increases in efficiency, access, and social benefit from space systems. Now in 2022, SpaceX Falcon 9 rocket costs are as low as approximately $60 million to launch a dedicated payload [77] or as low as $1 million for a rideshare payload [78].

As with launch vehicles, technical innovation and cost reduction can be realized across the space industry using the service business model. Space "data-as-a-service" is a case where customers pay a commercial data provider to supply data collected in space. Data may consist of any number of things, including Earth imagery, scientific measurements, telemetry, or situational awareness. The list of growing space service businesses goes on and includes cargo delivery, platforms for science experiments, platforms for applied research, and any number of consulting roles covering engineering, management, planning, or industry analysis. Even specific hardware components or subsystems integrated within a larger vehicle may be provided as a service. For example, thrusters, avionics, consumables (breathable air, food, water, propellant), robotics, or thermal control. Industrial processes are also able to be provided as a service such as maintenance and operations. All of these examples are used to emphasize that it's not just the high-profile space companies like launch providers that can engage in the circular economy. Component and industrial process providers, big and small, can adopt the same principles and become participants in a sustainable value flow loop on a space company's stakeholder map.

Space Vehicle Value Recovery

Options for value recovery at the end of a product's life are reuse, repair, recycling, or life extension. Reuse can be enabled by including intentional design features such that a product can be disassembled, can be inspected to support life extension certification, and is suited to resist issues resulting from prolonged fatigue, corrosion, and risk of damage. Enabling recycling may entail design specifically using only recyclable materials. This potential design limitation plus the environmental impact associated with recycling make it the last choice among the value recovery methods.

With reuse, the components of a larger assembly that will tend to wear out first are limiting factors in the value return chain. These components therefore should be modular and replaceable in order to enable value recovery for the rest of the system. An example of this is thermal protection. Given the criticality and high demand placed on thermal protection systems, this is an ideal example of hardware that if planned for replacement and refurbishment, can enable repeated flights of the same vehicle. As the space industry grows, the costs of not moving to reusable hardware systems include, in addition to environmental impacts and higher costs, the risk of damaged brand value caused by public displeasure of wasteful and unsustainable activity.

SpaceX CEO, Elon Musk, has a particularly illuminating quote on launch hardware recovery and reuse. In considering a reuse strategy for the Falcon

9 rocket, one may easily overlook recovery of the ejected cargo fairings. At
$6 million, the fairings are a *relatively* low-cost component compared to the
rocket itself and much less complex to remanufacture. Still, as Musk points
out in a 2017 press conference: "Imagine you had $6 million in cash in a
palette flying through the air, and it's going to smash into the ocean. Would
you try to recover that? Yes. Yes, you would." Since 2017, SpaceX has successfully managed to repeatedly recover the $6 million Falcon 9 fairings at
sea after falling back to Earth attached to a parachute. The Falcon 9 fairing
recovery is a prime example of a case where what's good for the financial
bottom line is simultaneously good for the environmental bottom line.

Another prominent example of reuse in the space industry can be found
in NASA's Orion spacecraft [79, 80]. The Orion crew capsule is designed
to be disassembled and refurbished so that as much hardware as possible
can be used in a future vehicle. At first, this will include limited high-value
items like computers as well as other interior cabin features like crew seats.
The degree of reuse is planned to increase though. The long-term reuse concept for Orion is based on an indefinite launch cadence where a given crew
capsule gets reused after refurbishment three Artemis missions in the future. Similarly, the crew capsules in NASA's Commercial Crew program are
planned for refurbishment in between flights and reuse.

Value retention can also be approached through vehicle life extension. In
the aircraft industry, air shipping companies use old converted passenger
aircraft for cargo flights. These aircraft are still flightworthy but past their
passenger certification. The requirements for a spacecraft human rating
are considerably more onerous than for an uncrewed space vehicle. Crewed
space hardware may have a life performing uncrewed missions after a human rating has expired. Life extension in any case (crewed or uncrewed)
may be enabled also by a reinspection of hardware and/or update to design
analyses. Spacecraft servicing is another means of life extension. Approximately, 20 functional satellites are retired each year because they run out of
fuel [81]. This is not just a problem of increasing space debris; it has an effect
on Earth's environment. The need to perpetually reproduce new satellites to
replace others that still function but are out of fuel drives a continuous high
energy, resource-intensive, and waste-intensive production line on Earth.
Satellite refueling services can effectively solve this problem.

Circular Economy: Summary

Circular economy principles internalize environmental and social costs
associated with a particular good or service transaction by creating circular value flows and eliminating waste. This is a natural approach to adopt
within stakeholder management, given that cost internalization is inherent
in balancing needs across all stakeholders. In practice, this entails the need
for business managers to devise strategies for service business models and
product value management. In the space industry, ultimate value recapture

can occur through product designs that include features for longevity, reuse, disassembly, use of modular components, and material recovery. Overall though, for space industry professionals to implement intelligent circular economy strategies, a precise definition for "value creation" is needed to guide an organization. Once value creation at a high level is well understood, this understanding can be applied to define core features of a company like its purpose, its business model, and the nature of its products/services. The details of circular economy and stakeholder management strategies can then follow. The next two chapters explore the topic of value creation.

Notes

1 The legal notion of "promissory estoppel" in contract law says that if a company has made clear to the public and to potential investors (i.e., in their corporate charter) what its purpose is and how it plans to pursue it, there can be no legal claim from an investor later that this activity is not lawful. Promissory estoppel has been recognized by the US Supreme Court as a state law doctrine [268].
2 This section takes a decidedly optimistic view on progress related to sustainability awareness. A more cynical view pointing out instances of insincerity, insufficient action, and slow progress is certainly possible. An optimistic presentation is chosen intentionally, as this must be the attitude if success and teamwork are to be achieved. Everything that is done to further the sustainability of humanity is done so through an optimistic view that it matters and is worthwhile. There is no utility in adopting a pessimistic perspective if progress is the goal!
3 Several examples of government agencies are listed from the United States. Analogous agencies in other countries should be considered as well.
4 Note how far this has come from the days of feudalism described previously where the primary motivation of production was the threat of physical violence to workers!
5 Upcycling is where a product is reused in a way that is different in nature than the original use for the product but still of distinctive value. For example, use of a recovered human spacecraft as a museum piece where a fee for entry is charged would constitute upcycling the spacecraft.

3 Value Creation

This book is about value creation in the space industry. Value is somewhat of a nebulous subject though after this chapter it should be clear as to exactly what is meant by "value creation," at least in this book. Consider first the concept of value of exchange. Aristotle said that in an exchange of goods, each party should recover from the other "what is equal in accordance with proportion" [82]. From this high-level view, value may be manifest by something, anything, that can be exchanged for something else. If one wants a bottle of water, they need something to exchange that someone already possessing a bottle of water deems is minimally "equal in proportion." If one can create something like that, they can create value. This is the concept of exchange value.

How though to gauge if something is equal in proportion? Is this referring to money and market price? After all, market price fluctuations can occur rapidly and are caused by all sorts of factors like production efficiency changes, weather, politics, public trends, and supply chain disruptions. Additionally, in today's world, social and environmental costs often are not considered at all in determining market prices. These things clearly are important to humanity; so if the premise is adopted that value is defined by price, one can at least observe that price is often being determined incorrectly. While admittedly there is some compelling logic to defining value in the context of price in an exchange, the concept appears to be more complex. This topic is clarified further in the following sections so as to better inform on what it really means to maximize value creation in the space industry.

History of Value Theory

Value theory has roots in economics. Before widespread stability and prosperity began to spread through industrialization, as discussed in Chapter 2, the primary motivations of capitalism were slightly different. The 18th century saw the study of economics rising in Europe as a powerful force that would become increasingly relied on to guide nations toward the prosperity of their populace. The prosperity of nations was viewed by nobility in this

DOI: 10.4324/9781003268734-3

era as measured, not yet by the engagement of the population in the value creation system, but by the state's ability to finance wars and expansion. A prosperous nation was one that had the ability to finance a great military which could then expand that nation's borders and help to spread its influence around the world. To enable this form of prosperity, there was a need to increase national financial resources and so the study of economics was born.

French thinker Francois Quesnay was among the first influential people to study economics in the context of national prosperity. In the mid-18th century, he embarked on a study of economics with the support of the French court with the simple, high-level goal of increasing his nation's prosperity. Quesnay's starting point was to develop some understanding and criteria for what types of activities constitute a productive, value-creating, economic role. If this could be understood better, a national economy could be shaped deliberately around these activities and become more prosperous (this is essentially the same goal at hand in this book, but the target is the space industry). Quesnay's view, which represented the position of his contemporaries known as the physiocrats, was that the only productive activities are those that extract products from the earth like crops, minerals, or lumber [83]. Notably, this view suggests that, aside from resource extraction perhaps, value cannot be created in space. Following Quesnay's work, value theory continued to evolve and become more sophisticated.

What Quesnay was to the physiocrats, Adam Smith was to the classical economists. Smith's view, described in 1776 in *The Wealth of Nations* [27], was that value can be created along the production chain of a product and is increased as more skill and labor are required. Therefore, in Smith's view, the path to a more prosperous nation is to create more and more value by continuously expanding the size and complexity of manufacturing processes. This will result in more products that are higher in value due to the greater amount of effort and expertise needed to create them. One cannot help but to see parallels between Smith's view and the space industry, which involves a highly specialized and complex production line.

Other classical economists of this era had a similar view on value. David Ricardo observed that the value of a good in exchange is based both on utility and scarcity, though, like Smith, Ricardo distinguishes actual value from exchange value in that the former is based on the amount of labor required to produce the good. Similarly, economist John Stuart Mill said that value in economics refers to value in exchange but value of a good relative to other goods can only be possible if a good is useful and difficult to procure [84]. Mill noted that effectual demand (demand only from those with the means to act on it) also influences value. Ricardo and Mill both said that value is always grounded by the cost of production. On this point, Mill said: "the natural value of some things is a scarcity value; but most things naturally exchange for one another in the ratio of their cost of production, or what may be termed their cost value" [84]. Not exactly a classical economist, but with a similar view in this area, Karl Marx said: "we see then that that which determines the magnitude of the value of any article is the amount of labour socially necessary, or the labour time socially necessary for its production" [85]. This view would suggest that things like water and air have no value because they are plentiful and require no labor to produce. Ricardo, Smith, Mill, and Marx all recognize two apparent forms of value: one related to utility and the other related to exchange.

Building on the work of the classical economists, Jules Dupuit had similar views, particularly on the role that utility plays in value. Dupuit made a distinction between value of utility and value of exchange, where utility is the degree to which something can bring pleasure. Dupuit said that utility can be measured by the maximum price somebody would need to be paid to give up enjoyment of a certain good. Note this price may be much higher than the market price [86]. Hermann Gossen also framed things in terms of pleasure to explain value [87]. He said therefore that in the pursuit of pleasure one will experience less and less pleasure from the same activity the more times the experience is repeated. He said that value is a measure of how much pleasure something can enable. Also, value is reduced by the amount of pain that is required to create the thing. Naturally, if the amount of pain exceeds the amount of pleasure, the thing is no longer valuable or desirable.

Contributions in the field of value theory continued, but it wasn't until the marginal revolution in 1871 that a new, broadly influential economic paradigm emerged. The marginal revolution was marked by three independent simultaneous publications: (1) William Stanley Jevons published *The Theory of Political Economy*, (2) Léon Menger published *Principles of Economics*, and (3) Carl Walras published *Elements of Pure Economics*. Author Burt Mosselmans describes the shift in thinking as follows:

> The authors of the marginal revolution wanted to set up a universal theory that would treat land, labor, and capital simply as factors of production that would be rewarded following the same principles. The amount paid to each factor of production would be determined by its scarcity, in relation to consumers' wants for the products that these factors could produce. This implies that consumer demand, and therefore utility, received a more prominent place in economic theory [than in classical economics].
>
> [88]

In practice, marginalism influences how market pricing works through the concepts of marginal utility and supply. In terms of demand, marginalism says that the market price will reflect value based on the final purchase of a good. For example, if on average people buy two cars, then the market price of a car is based on the utility of that second car, which presumably may be less than the first. The concept of marginal returns also applies on the supply side from continued activation of capital for production. The means of production that are most efficient will always be activated first. As production increases, efficiency decreases and diminishing returns are seen. The marginal cost of producing something is defined according to the last and least efficient unit that is produced. In summary, marginalism defines value as anything that fetches a price in the market. The amount of value is governed by utility, scarcity, marginal demand, and marginal supply. Modern markets function largely according to marginalist principles.

Building on Multiple Value Perspectives

The appearance of value changes dramatically, depending on one's perspective and knowledge of value theory. Mariana Mazzucato remarks on this challenge in *The Value of Everything*: "...the distinction between productive and unproductive activities has rarely been the result of 'scientific measurement'. Rather ascribing value, or the lack of it, has always involved malleable socio-economic arguments which derive from a particular political perspective..." [89]. Consider the two partially conflicting definitions of value from the classical economists and from marginalism. On the one hand, it makes perfect sense that to create value involves some form of work, be it intellectual or physical, aimed at production of something that is in demand. The harder the commodity is to produce, the more valuable it is and so products and services that are difficult to create appear to have some distinctive type of value related to this fact.

Now consider a definition of value according to marginalism where provision of any product or activity placed in the market fetching a price constitutes creation of value. No matter where the commodity came from or how difficult it was to produce if when placed in the market a price is fetched, it is valuable by definition. The level of value created by introducing this commodity in the market is driven by scarcity and utility. This appears to be a different form of value than that defined by the classicalists, though still valid for different reasons.

Finally, consider a third perspective. A hypothetical company produces a commodity in a free-market context that fetches a price. For a moment, forget about production complexity and the force of scarcity that helps determine the price. Focus on the degree and nature of importance that the commodity has. Is the commodity a luxury item or a life-saving item? Is the commodity an optional service or a critical service? It could be that many different commodities fetch the same market price, but objectively one can assign greater importance to one over another. Marginalism avoids this type of grading. It's true that one product may have greater utility, but if it is sufficiently available, its value (i.e., price) will be low. While this assignment of value makes sense in the marginalist perspective and is somewhat intuitive to many today, clearly a critical item would seem to many people to be more important than an optional luxury item available for the same price. Here, a third perspective on what defines value emerges and that is a commodity's importance to humanity. Value reflecting importance and benefit to humanity is labeled "true value", for now, in this discussion as a placeholder term. Several of the quotes from economists in this section make reference to this form of value.

Which perspective is correct? The classical perspective where value is defined based on production complexity? Marginalism, where value is defined by market exchanges based on scarcity and utility? Or is value best thought of as the degree of importance to society? The better question for this book is: *what perspective is the most useful?* The purpose of any company is to meet a demand of society. Companies do this using profit-seeking as a foundational motivation, but profit is not why they exist. Companies exist to meet the demands of society, or in other words, to benefit humanity. Successfully meeting a demand of humanity is what defines value creation from the perspective of a company. This view is closely aligned with the concept of true value. The profit-seeking motivation introduces a complication though. By definition, a company is only capable of creating true value (i.e., benefiting humanity) if a profit occurs. Companies cannot create true value without also creating exchange value.

It is preferable that the collective outcome of all activity in the space economy consists of the maximum benefit to humanity that is possible. Maximizing value creation in the space industry is an intuitive goal. However, if proactive efforts are not made to embrace the dual necessity of both exchange value and true value in this endeavor, there is a risk that transactions and even companies as a whole run counter to humanity's prosperity. Really, there should not be even a single market transaction that occurs that has the effect of degrading human prosperity. A system that permits this kind of self-destruction is illogical, unnatural, and there is no need for it. A unified value theory that includes considerations of both exchange and true value can be used to avoid this and to guide optimal outcomes for humanity from businesses. The concept of exchange value is widely understood through mature practices of finance and accounting. The concept of true value needs further discussion.

Intrinsic Value

A close match from philosophical discourse to the concept of true value, as introduced here, is intrinsic value. Philosopher G.E. Moore introduced the concept of intrinsic value circa 1903 [90] to help articulate the notion of the inherent value of something unrelated to its value in an exchange. Utilization of the concept of intrinsic value in this discussion however is a non-trivial task as it has received numerous perspectives on its definition over the years. Furthermore, there are varying interpretations on the relevance or utility of the concept of intrinsic value in the first place. Chelsea Batavia remarked on the many "dimensions" of intrinsic value that have been discussed: "Philosophers have characterized these dimensions differently, and it would be misleading to suggest any one, monolithic concept of intrinsic value emerges from the literature" [91]. Emrys Westacott points out that defining and understanding intrinsic value is all well and good, but there is a dilemma of "subjective" judgments of intrinsic value and that "in the absence of criteria for deciding which things fall under it, the concept itself is empty, and its application blind" [92]. Elliott Sober also described advice to use or employ the concept of intrinsic value as "empty" without a useful criterion [93]. With these challenges in mind, the following discussion ultimately distills the concept of intrinsic value into pragmatic features for application in a unified value theory to apply in the space industry.

Moore defined intrinsic value according to the isolation test. He said in *Principia Ethica*:

> We can consider with regard to any particular state of things whether it would be worthwhile that it should exist, even if there were absolutely nothing else in the Universe besides...we can consider whether the existence of such a Universe would have been better than nothing, or whether it would have been just as good that nothing at all should ever have existed.
>
> [90]

Moore emphasized later in his 1922 paper titled *The Conception of Intrinsic Value* [94] that this consideration and the existence of intrinsic value must be objective and that goodness is a type of intrinsic value.

Scott Davison describes intrinsic value as "something is intrinsically valuable only if it is good in itself, independent of other things" [95]. Davison elaborates further, saying: "something is intrinsically valuable to a certain degree if and only if its intrinsic structure would lead fully informed, properly functioning valuers to value it for its own sake to that degree." Thomas Scanlon has a similar view declaring that something intrinsically valuable would be declared so by any fully informed valuer [96].

James Schwartz acknowledges a variety of uses of the term "intrinsic value" in philosophy; however, he defines it broadly as something that "... adds value to the world simply by existing. In practice, that something has intrinsic value is a *prima facie* reason for adopting 'pro-' attitudes toward it (e.g., for preserving or protecting it, or for thinking it is the kind of thing that ought to exist)" [13]. On struggling to pin down proof of the concept or find a universally precise definition for intrinsic value among philosophers, Michael Zimmerman offers "isn't it clear, on reflection, that a morally sensitive person will favor certain things, but not others, for their own sakes? If so, that's basically all you need to accept that some things have intrinsic value" [97].

Most interpretations and definitions for intrinsic value share some commonality described so far by these examples. There is more or less agreement that intrinsic value refers to something that can objectively be determined to be good and preferred. Details beyond this high-level view of the definition begin to get more complicated.

Intrinsic versus Instrumental

To better understand intrinsic value, one can consider its conceptual opposite, instrumental value. "Intrinsic" is a descriptor of a property that is innate to something. A property that is part of the natural state of something and is not dependent or influenced by any outside factor. For example, a particular apple is red no matter what. No outside opinions or uses or thoughts otherwise change the fact that light from the Sun reflected off of this particular apple corresponds to the wavelength that is defined as red. The red color is an intrinsic property of the apple. On the other hand, a particular apple is nutritious only if consumed by an animal in need of chemicals contained in the apple and able to digest them for this use. If this never occurred or no such animal existed, then the potential nutritional value would never exist. Therefore, nutrition is an instrumental property of the apple. An instrumental property is one that depends on an external relation.

In addition to intrinsic versus instrumental properties, another related and important concept is whether something is an end or a means to an end. Can a means to an end ever be said to have intrinsic value if its very purpose is to provide instrumental value in order to achieve the end? What about countless suppliers, supporting activities, and other means that must exist for a particular instance of intrinsic value to be created by a company as an end? On the one hand, it seems clear that a means purely created for its instrumental properties needed in order to achieve a greater and more complex end cannot be said to itself have intrinsic value. On the other hand, if this means is an indispensable part of a complex end that is intrinsically valuable, is it completely detached from the concept?

Shelly Kagan addresses this same question. While avoiding any firm conclusion, Kagan presents an argument that "intrinsic value need not depend solely upon intrinsic properties" and similarly that "value as an end need not depend solely upon an object's intrinsic properties" are compelling enough that Kagan wants "...to leave open the possibility that the intrinsic value of an object may be based (in part) on its instrumental value" [98]. Kagan states: "We should allow for the possibility that someone might value an object intrinsically – that is, as an end – even though what they value about the object is not simply a matter of its intrinsic properties." At a high level, the thought behind this argument is that when any creature values something it is according to some relation that they have with it. If somebody values a painting because it is beautiful, its beauty may be an intrinsic property (some would argue), but the value placed upon the painting by the viewer is based on their relational experience when they see it, which is not something that exists innately within the painting.

This perspective is shared also in part by Christine Korsgaard, who says in *Two Distinctions in Goodness:*

> To say that something is intrinsically good is not by definition to say that it is valued for its own sake: it is to say that it has goodness in itself. It refers, one might say, to the location or source of the goodness rather than the way we value the thing. The contrast between instrumental and intrinsic value is therefore misleading, a false contrast.
>
> [99]

This invokes now a similar theme to the previous discussion on Kagan's work and the notion of instrumental value being a possible component of intrinsic value.

Korsgaard goes on to state:

> The natural contrast to intrinsic goodness-the value a thing has in itself-is extrinsic goodness, the value a thing gets from some other source. The natural contrast to a thing that is valued instrumentally or as a means is a thing that is valued for its own sake or as an end.[1]

Korsgaard also remarks that:

> No matter how much the philosopher wants to insist that the value of a good thing must be intrinsic and so nonrelational, the sense remains that the goodness of a good thing must have something to do with its goodness to us.

Korsgaard's comments are helpful to further stitch together the discussion here. Consider a hypothetical means, X, and an end, Y. X has intrinsic properties that result in instrumental value that it can contribute to realization of the end, Y. Y is intrinsically good. Therefore, it cannot be beyond consideration that the instrumental value of X contributes to intrinsic value of X. In other words, because X is instrumentally valuable in realizing the larger more complex good, Y, X may be considered a component of Y and therefore be intrinsically valuable itself.

Emmanuel Kant used the terms unconditional value and conditional value for intrinsic and instrumental, respectively [100]. Conditional value implies that something may be good in certain conditions. This ties back to the concept discussed that something may be intrinsically valuable as an end if that end is to provide instrumental value toward another more complex good. As Korsgaard says "...the goodness of the end to which it is a means will be a condition of its goodness" [99]. Kant makes a distinction that something can have objective value but not intrinsic value. Kant says an object's goodness is relational, but for it to be unconditionally good, that is, intrinsically good, it must trace to goodwill imposed by a rational human being.

J.B. Callicot also supports a similar view where intrinsic value is a function of its relation with a human valuer, thereby highlighting that the "source" of value is human [101]. Scott Davison says on this matter: "there is no noncircular way to show that any particular experience of intrinsic value is correct; instead, we must appeal to other value experiences and general principles derived from them" [95]. These views all suggest that something may have intrinsic value based, at least in part, on an external relation.

Consider some conclusions from this section. The premise going in was that the space industry should produce things that are intrinsically valuable as this is a reflection of importance or "true value." What is gleaned from the numerous views on intrinsic value that have been presented is this: things are preferable that are inherently good as an end or as a means to another inherently good end. This statement notably establishes the concept that means to an end are good themselves if the end is also good. This is important because a unified value theory must be applicable to all points in a value chain, not just the end point. Overall, this concept suggests that doing things that are good in the space industry is a core component of maximizing value creation. Straightforward enough, but this introduces a new challenge and that is how to define goodness.

Goodness

Goodness can be a challenging concept to articulate and apply in practice. Nevertheless, it has a distinctive prerequisite role in a unified value theory that draws from the concept of intrinsic value. What does it mean exactly that something is inherently good and how can such a seemingly subjective concept ever be pragmatic in a business? Historical debate has seen numerous perspectives on the question of what is good. These can be divided into different categories such as hedonism, non-hedonism, virtue ethics, consequentialism, and deontology. A unified value theory must consider all perspectives.

Plato describes two definitions of good in the Socratic dialogue *Philebus* written in the 4th century B.C. Pleasure is good according to a hedonist perspective and knowledge is good according to a non-hedonist perspective. Aristotle, associated with the virtue ethics perspective, said that good may be defined as that which all things aim (virtues), and for people, this always is happiness but not necessarily pleasure. Similarly, Henry Sidgwick and G.E. Moore said that pleasure is not a necessary criterion for goodness, and may argue that there are some intrinsically good things that do not involve pleasure such as knowledge and virtue. Others had definitions for good not directly involving pleasure at all. Nietzsche said that good is power in terms of all kinds of excellence in the human spirit. St. Augustine and Thomas Aquinas said that good is communion with God. All of these views are largely in line with non-hedonist and virtue ethics perspectives.

As noted, the hedonist perspective is entirely framed around pleasure as the criterion for good. A hedonist would say that any end desired by a human is so desired because it ultimately somehow leads to pleasure. Jeremy Bentham expresses this view in *An Introduction to the Principles of Morals and Legislation*: "Nature has placed mankind under the governance of two sovereign masters, pain and pleasure. It is for them alone to point out what we ought to do, as well as to determine what we shall do" [102]. John Stuart Mill supported the hedonist view as well and wrote in *Utilitarianism*:

> ...if human nature is so constituted as to desire nothing which is not either part of happiness or a means of happiness, we can have no other proof, and we require no other, that these are the only things desirable.
>
> [103]

Both Mill and Bentham are associated with hedonist and consequentialist ethical perspectives where morality is judged according to pleasure deriving from the consequences of an action.

Immanuel Kant is most famous for the deontological perspective on ethics and what is good. A Kantian view takes the position that there are moral imperatives that one must live their life by that cannot be violated. Some refer to this as listening unquestionably to one's conscience in order to know what is right. Kant would describe that which is good is what adheres to moral imperatives.

According to the numerous perspectives described, the historical definition of good is either some form of happiness or pleasure or some form of excellence or knowledge. A unified value theory for the space industry can adopt a broad enveloping perspective. In an analysis of philosopher Franz Brentano's work, R.M. Chisolm remarked:

> ...we may make two lists—a list of things that are intrinsically good and a list of things that are intrinsically bad. The good list would include such things as these: pleasure, happiness, love, knowledge, justice, beauty, proportion, good intention, and the exercise of virtue. The bad list, on the other hand, would include such items as these: displeasure, unhappiness, hatred, ignorance, injustice, ugliness, disharmony, bad intention, and the exercise of vice.
>
> [104]

Chisolm's list is useful as it represents a summary of sorts of the history of philosophical discussion on goodness. The definition for good in a unified value theory for the space industry can be based on Chisolm's list. For simplicity, it is condensed down to the following virtues: harmony, pleasure, knowledge, justice, beauty, and benevolence. Note that this view on defining good resembles a non-hedonist virtue ethics perspective.

Harmony in particular in this list (which is relabeled from "proportion" compared to Chisolm) refers to balance and optimized mutual relationships between things like humans-to-nature, humans-to-humans, and social-economic-environmental systems. In *The Land Ethic*, Aldo Leopold states:

"a thing is right when it tends to preserve the integrity, stability, and beauty of the biotic community. It is wrong when it tends otherwise" [105]. Natural "rules" of animal communities have evolved, according to Leopold's view, to preserve life, procreation, and prosperity. A natural system could not exist in any way but harmony with itself and its surroundings and so this must be a component of goodness. A lack of harmony may specifically help create the opposite of good as described by Chisolm in his bad list and similarly defined by William Frankena as "what is bad in itself is so because of the presence either of pain or unhappiness or some kind of defect that lacks excellence" [106].

Harmony is so important in avoiding creation of the bad; it must be considered as a prerequisite of the good held above the other virtues listed. In practice, harmony may be achieved through support of sustainability goals, circular economy principles, and/or maintaining a TBL balance. Achieving harmony in the space industry according to these means is discussed in later chapters.

Intrinsic Value in Practice

Some may feel that traditional definitions of intrinsic value and/or goodness are being stretched in this discussion. The goal here is to merely draw from these concepts to help build a unified value theory for the space industry. Intrinsic value offers a rich history of thought and analysis to help define in more precision the concept of true value. The historical debates on intrinsic value and goodness need not be impediments to using their concepts to this end. To avoid any misconception or confusion, the term *stakeholder intrinsic value* is introduced as a more specific descriptor of value according to the definition developed in this book for application in the space industry.

The concept of stakeholder intrinsic value is defined in its entirety in the next chapter as a unified value theory that considers both exchange value and true value. Concerning true value, this chapter established two elements of the definition. First, for something to constitute stakeholder intrinsic value, it has to have inherent goodness. Second, stakeholder intrinsic value may be assigned to either things that are inherently good ends in themselves or to things that are means to an end that is inherently good. Goodness is defined as the presence of harmony plus optionally one or more of the following additional virtues: pleasure, knowledge, justice, beauty, and benevolence. The list of virtues is limited to familiar concepts involving some level of consensus in historical debate. While declaring a "settled" definition for what is good may seem presumptuous, a settled definition is exactly what is required to support an actionable unified value theory.

Note

1 The terms "extrinsic" and "instrumental" are used interchangeably here.

4 Stakeholder Intrinsic Value

Stakeholder intrinsic value is a unified value theory that pairs inherent goodness (i.e., true value[1]) and profitability (i.e., exchange value) as complimentary elements that describe the value of something. This concept embraces the simple preference that companies do good things, not bad things, and among the good things that are possible, there is a focus on those which are most important. The concept also embraces the view that profit-seeking is the most effective means to realize this preference consistently on a large scale. Building on the previous chapter, this chapter serves to condense the value theory concepts discussed so far into succinct and actionable criteria. Space industry professionals should use the stakeholder intrinsic value criteria to help guide the definition and operation of their organizations. The intent is that doing this results in the maximum value creation from an organization that is possible. In practice, this involves using the criteria to assess numerous value creation schemes and proceeding only with those that rank the highest.

The stakeholder intrinsic value definition is shown below. Items 1 and 2 in the definition are discussed in the previous chapter. Explanations of items 3 and 4 in the definition plus some additional commentary on the formulation are provided in the following sections.

SOMETHING HAS STAKEHOLDER INTRINSIC VALUE IF:

1 It is inherently good by way of embodying harmony plus optionally one or more of the following virtues: pleasure, knowledge, justice, beauty, and benevolence.

2 Item 1 is true as a result of one or both of the following:

    a Innate properties that are unaffected by external influence.

    b Instrumental value that is based on an innate property where the instrumental value is a means to enable an external bearer of the criteria in item 1.

3 It is profitable in a free market.

4 Conclusions on items 1 through 3 are determined collectively by a company and all of its stakeholders.

DOI: 10.4324/9781003268734-4

Degrees of Stakeholder Intrinsic Value

Ranking multiple options in a value creation assessment naturally calls for the notion of degrees of value. Given two variations of a value creation scheme, which one produces more value than the other? This is a question that managers are likely to confront. The degree of stakeholder intrinsic value can be determined for something according to (1) applications of its instrumental value, (2) alignment with the goodness virtues, and (3) profitability. Having multiple stakeholder views will help determine the most accurate answer possible to questions related to degrees of value. This book does not present a scoring methodology to use with stakeholder intrinsic value, but something to this effect is likely needed by managers in practice.

One way to help focus a stakeholder intrinsic value ranking activity is for managers and the stakeholder group to take an anthropocentric perspective. This is known as an "ecosystem services" view where the health of the planet and biosphere as a whole is considered important primarily for the benefit of humanity. Specifically, ecosystem services include things like food, fresh water, clean air, timber, fibers, pollution filtering, flood mitigation, a livable climate, regulation of disease, recreation, aesthetic value, and spiritual value. Other perspectives on grading value of nature exist such as egalitarianism where humans have "excellence" [107], sentience [108], or life itself as a defining criterion [109, 110]. These alternative views are not suggested here as wrong, but merely less practical than the ecosystem services view in terms of resonating with the greatest number of people possible.

The modern movement to consider environmental capital in monetary terms within economics and business operations was popularized by the Millennium Ecosystem Assessment in 2005 and by Fischer et al. in 2008 [111]. There was a recognition that ecosystem services described a type of value for nature that is compatible with free-market capitalism. Arguing for preservation of nature for its own sake has struggled to gain broad appeal and to achieve its primary goal [112]. Good or bad, right or wrong, it has struggled simply because it is not a compelling argument to enough people and therefore is not a useful tact (apparently). Taking an anthropocentric perspective is a pragmatic means to assist in determining degrees of stakeholder intrinsic value. This perspective offers a common reference point (i.e., impacts to human prosperity) to compare performance related to creating both exchange and true value.

Role of Profitability and Stakeholders

Item 3 in the stakeholder intrinsic value criteria is profitability. This is an important nuance in the definition because it imposes a rigid requirement that true value be created in ways that also create exchange value. Of course, there are other ways to create true value that do not necessitate profit. Charities, governments, NGOs, nonprofits all have value-creating roles in society and in the space industry that do not involve profit-seeking.

The roles of not-for-profit organizations include acting as a safety net, acting as a watchdog, offering accountability to those in power, compassionately providing for those most in need, defending those who cannot do so for themselves, managing production/use of public goods, managing common resources, setting universal industry standards, the list goes on. It should be obvious that these roles are important and should continue. That said, use of capitalism stands to increase value creation for society beyond important not-for-profit activities through efficiency, innovation, and resonance with human nature. For this reason, it is preferable to create value using the profit-seeking motive and markets whenever possible. The stakeholder intrinsic value criteria adopt the position that when profitability and goodness occur simultaneously, value creation is maximized.

Item 4 in the stakeholder intrinsic value criteria calls for stakeholders to collectively assess value creation schemes. Stakeholders are necessary because goodness and profitability are hollow concepts if not rooted in a complete context that contains all perspectives and sources of information. To rate something of value according to just one perspective and one source of information is potentially so subjective, lacking in rigor, and inconsistent case-to-case, that the credulity of any unified value theory depends on addressing this issue. The group of stakeholders adopts the role of fully informed valuer in a stakeholder intrinsic value assessment. This level of insight is one that no law or regulation could ever hope to achieve, given the need for case-specific considerations.

The collective role of stakeholders is important in the assessment of both goodness and profitability. Regarding profitability, a perfectly functioning free market at maximum efficiency requires buyers and sellers to be fully informed of all relevant information in a given transaction. Full availability of relevant information about a market transaction is what ensures a win-win exchange between supplier and customer. Anything less is in opposition to free-market capitalism itself and may lead to merely the appearance of value creation through cost externalization.

Regarding goodness, it is inevitable that numerous items from the goodness criteria will be embodied simultaneously in different degrees and/or even in conflict with one another case by case. Furthermore, while stakeholder intrinsic value is rooted in a virtue ethics perspective, to some degree there is not one but three ethical themes in the criteria seemingly at a tug-of-war with one another: deontology, consequentialism, and virtue ethics. These three ethical themes manifest in the stakeholder intrinsic value criteria as harmony, profit, and goodness, respectively. Given these challenges, it is all but impossible for a single person to conduct a value assessment that is credible in terms of being subjective and thorough.

The glue that makes these potential conflicts and differing ethical perspectives function together in stakeholder intrinsic value is the stakeholders themselves. This may be no easy task though. All three ethical perspectives embedded in the stakeholder intrinsic value criteria are fallible and subject to contradicting one another. For example, a consequentialist approach enables realization of benefits from capitalism, but as Tony Milligan observes: "consideration of the consequences of action may be an indispensable requirement for ethical deliberation but an *unconstrained* consequentialism does not seem at all like the right kind of ethic to shape our attitude towards the emerging space frontier" [113]. Saara Reiman also points out that consequentialism ethics may be challenging when it comes to space exploration because one cannot always easily tell the consequences of actions [114]. In other words, it may be impossible to have a fully informed transaction. The space environment is inherently unknown, communication is hard and delayed, lives hang in the balance, and there is a relative lack of information compared to more familiar settings. Reiman stresses that consequentialism is difficult to earnestly implement in "poor epistemic conditions." It is left to the stakeholders to wrestle with any limitations case by case related to adopting a consequentialist perspective.

What about the deontological constraint of harmony in the stakeholder intrinsic value criteria? Hans Jonas proposed that Kant's categorical imperatives must extend to considerations of the natural environment and of humanity's future as a species [115]. The inclusion of harmony in the stakeholder intrinsic value criteria effectively resembles this same view; however, the inclusion also of stakeholder deliberation may be seen to effectively soften the "categorical imperativeness" of harmony by allowing additional also important factors to be considered. The necessity of harmony in the criteria has the appearance of a rigid requirement, but it is left open to the stakeholder deliberations as to the nature and degree of enforcement case by case.

Allowing for multiple ethical perspectives permits room for discussion, entertainment of diverse views, and case-by-case consideration of context, all of which are critical in determining a collectively optimal value creation scheme. Stakeholder intrinsic value embraces this challenging array of ethical views head-on and so may be described as a virtue-ethics-based concept with deontological and consequentialist constraints placed on it. Practitioners of the stakeholder intrinsic value concept need not be explicitly aware of this theoretic background which helps make use of the criteria broadly compatible with capitalism.

The means by which value creation is pursued in the space industry should be assessed by managers using the stakeholder intrinsic value criteria. This presumably would involve consideration of numerous options where only those that maximize the harmony and goodness criteria while remaining profitable would be selected. In other words, only those that maximize value creation are selected. The subject of an assessment must be a bearer of stakeholder intrinsic value. Bearers can be diverse and include physical objects, information, algorithms, activities, services, actions, tasks, decisions, choices, organizations, processes, and states of affairs.

Stakeholder Intrinsic Value: Defined

The purpose of this chapter is to define stakeholder intrinsic value. In formulating the definition, certain unilateral decisions were made for the sake of pragmatism. Elements of the concept that may be unsatisfying to experts in the field of philosophy or at least considered unsettled matters include:

- Goodness is defined as something that embodies at a minimum harmony alone but may also include one or more of the following virtues: pleasure, knowledge, justice, beauty, and benevolence.
- There is little restriction to bearers of stakeholder intrinsic value other than that the bearer must be something that can be assessed relative to profitability. Bearers of stakeholder intrinsic value may include the following: physical objects, information, algorithms, activities, services, actions, tasks, decisions, choices, organizations, processes, and states of affairs.
- Something may be intrinsically good despite the fact that the good may be based on a relational property. Something may gain intrinsic value from its inherent instrumental value that is being used toward another intrinsically valuable end.
- Degrees of stakeholder intrinsic value is a valid concept and may be determined for something based on (i) applications of its instrumental value, (ii) alignment with the goodness virtues, and (iii) profitability.
- The term "value" envelops two things: goodness and profitability (i.e., reflecting true value and exchange value).
- The role of a fully informed valuer is filled collectively by the stakeholder group.

The definition for stakeholder intrinsic value is shown below, repeated from the beginning of this chapter. Much of the remaining discussion in this book is framed around opportunities to create stakeholder intrinsic value in the space industry. A final comment on stakeholder intrinsic value is that this book is limited to formulation and presentation of the concept. Case studies on its application are considered future work at the time of this publication.

SOMETHING HAS STAKEHOLDER INTRINSIC VALUE IF:

1 It is inherently good by way of embodying harmony plus optionally one or more of the following virtues: pleasure, knowledge, justice, beauty, and benevolence.
2 Item 1 is true as a result of one or both of the following:
   a Innate properties that are unaffected by external influence.
   b Instrumental value that is based on an innate property where the instrumental value is a means to enable an external bearer of the criteria in item 1.
3 It is profitable in a free market.
4 Conclusions on items 1 through 3 are determined collectively by a company and all of its stakeholders.

Stakeholder Intrinsic Value Creation in Space

Efforts toward establishing frameworks similar to stakeholder intrinsic value for the space industry have occurred in the past. *The Ethics of Space Policy* was released by the European Space Agency (ESA) and the UN Educational, Scientific and Cultural Organization (UNESCO) in 2000 [116]. This document considers specific ethical risks in the space industry related to use of nuclear energy sources, electronic surveillance, encroachment of individual freedoms, encroachment on identity and cultural diversity, and acceptability of messages transmitted by satellites. While not a central feature, the document also permits commercial activity in space in certain conditions.

In 2003, David Livingston released the *Code of Ethics for Off-Earth Commerce* [117]. Livingston suggests that "[Space] Companies would find it advantageous to balance the goal of wealth maximization with ethical principles if such a strategy enhances the long-term prospects for success." Livingston's code includes several features in common with stakeholder intrinsic value such as promotion of capitalist principles, promotion of the importance of sustainability, preference toward voluntary action rather than rigid regulations, and a realization that the space industry is best positioned for success and value creation if these themes are prioritized. Similarly, in *The Value of Science in Space Exploration*, Professor James Schwartz frames justification for a space exploration activity according to three criteria: (1) it must be good in principle, (2) it must be possible, and (3) it must be good in balance (i.e., worthwhile in the context of other resource demands) [13].

Compared to the frameworks offered by ESA/UNESCO, Livingston, and Schwartz, stakeholder intrinsic value adopts similar principles for the space industry. All frameworks include both a need to produce that which is inherently good and a need for sustainability or balance. The amount of emphasis on commercial practices varies more. Stakeholder intrinsic value adopts these same principles overall but approaches implementation differently. Stakeholder intrinsic value is designed to be grounded in philosophy and economics but at the same time usable for those less interested in the theoretic background. The features thought to best realize pragmatism in stakeholder intrinsic value are emphasizing the need for profitability, defining briefly but clearly goodness, and fully integrating implementation with the preexisting practice of stakeholder management.

Remote Sensing, Telecommunications, and GNSS for Value Creation

Space systems currently offer the most value to humanity in three areas: remote sensing, telecommunications, and Global Navigation and Satellite Systems (GNSS). These three areas do not envelop the total sum of value created in space for humanity, but these are the three main categories today.

Other sources of value to humanity include science, exploration, R&D, tourism, inspiration, and more to be discussed in coming chapters. This section serves to introduce discussion on stakeholder intrinsic value creation in space.

Remote Sensing: Campbell and Wynne define remote sensing as "the practice of deriving information about the Earth's land and water surfaces using images acquired from an overhead perspective, using electromagnetic radiation in one or more regions of the electromagnetic spectrum, reflected or emitted from the Earth's surface" [118]. While not a universally applicable definition, it does envelop the concept for the purposes of this book. The first instance of a dedicated remote sensing satellite traces back to 1959 when the weather satellite Vanguard 2 was launched. Remote sensing data includes commonly visual images, but much more is possible through instruments like radar, lidar, and hyperspectral imagery. While remote sensing data has many applications, the 2018 Earth observation decadal survey described several main areas of recent and expected progress in the field [6]. These areas are listed below. The degree to which stakeholder intrinsic value creation is possible relative to each item is described in Chapters 5 and 6.

- Improving weather forecasts
- Protecting against solid earth hazards
- Ensuring water resources
- Maintaining healthy and productive oceans
- Mitigating adverse impacts of climate change
- Protecting ecosystems
- Improving human health

Telecommunications: Telecommunications refers to any transfer of data using satellites. The first instance of this was in 1960 when the satellite Echo transmitted a speech from US President Eisenhower from the Jet Propulsion Laboratory's Goldstone facility in California to an AT&T station in Holmdel, New Jersey. Today, this type of data transfer is ubiquitous and includes commonly television, phone, internet, radio, and fixed point-to-point data links. Telecommunications is the most established realm of commercial activity in space and has enjoyed profitability for decades.

Global Navigation and Satellite Systems (GNSS): GNSS refers to what is commonly known as Global Positing Service (GPS) navigation services. The first GNSS system was created by the US Army and completed in 1993 solely for government use. Today available to the public, navigation services using GNSS extend well beyond the familiar private vehicle and smartphone applications to a wide array of commercial, industrial, and government uses. GNSS also offers time synchronicity services, which are important in global choreographed data systems such as international finance and public utility management. More details on how GNSS is used to create value are included in Chapters 5 and 6.

Table 4.1 Stakeholder intrinsic value goodness virtues relative to remote sensing, telecommunications, and GNSS.

	Remote Sensing	Tele-Communications	GNSS
Harmony	✓	✓	✓
Pleasure		✓	✓
Knowledge	✓	✓	✓
Justice	✓	✓	✓
Beauty		✓	
Benevolence	✓		

Consider now remote sensing, telecommunications, and GNSS in the context of the stakeholder intrinsic value criteria. To aid this discussion, elements of the criteria can be broken down into four areas: harmony, stakeholders, profitability, and goodness. Each of these areas is discussed at length in this book relative to activities in space. Regarding harmony, remote sensing; telecommunications; and GNSS can all occur sustainably and support sustainability initiatives in different ways. Chapter 6 covers this topic extensively. Regarding stakeholders, Chapter 2 covers practical management strategies to create value using profit-seeking and markets while supporting sustainability. An earlier section in this chapter discusses the role of stakeholders in stakeholder intrinsic value creation. Regarding profitability, remote sensing; telecommunications; and GNSS can all be profitable; however, there is some nuance to this. Commercialization of space systems is discussed at length in Chapter 5. Regarding goodness, remote sensing; telecommunications; and GNSS can all be applied in various ways to realize the goodness virtues in the stakeholder intrinsic value criteria. Table 4.1 presents a preliminary assessment on goodness of remote sensing, telecommunications, and GNSS. The following chapters highlight this topic in greater detail and Chapter 8 contains an expanded version of this table.

Increasing Value Creation in Space

Remote sensing, telecommunications, and GNSS are established sectors of the space industry. Value creation in these three areas has already been occurring for decades, but how can value creation be *increased*? One way is using the stakeholder intrinsic value criteria to guide incremental improvements to value creation methods. Space industry professionals can assess variations of value creation strategies, some preexisting and some new, and proceed only with those rating highest according to the stakeholder intrinsic value criteria. These value assessments can delve down to details as fine as a single decision, an action of a supplier, or design features of a product.

Essentially, the stakeholder intrinsic value criteria offer a roadmap for maximizing value creation. Specifically, remote sensing; telecommunications; and GNSS all stand to realize increases in value creation through:

1 More capacity
2 Innovation on value-added data processing and application tools
3 Value chain innovation

More capacity is in support of a goal to serve both more customers and smaller customers going forward. This involves more satellites, more computational power, and more services made available. It involves greater data transfer bandwidth, easier access to tools and products for customers, and higher-performing hardware systems. The potential customer base out there that could benefit directly from space systems is enormous if product availability is extended to individual people. More capacity in differing forms to engage with and meet this need is a clear means to realize increased stakeholder intrinsic value creation from remote sensing, telecommunications, and GNSS.

The second opportunity listed for increased value creation is innovation on value-added data processing and application tools. This opportunity is based on the premise that one already has access to either raw data (like Earth imagery) or some basic space system functionality (like GNSS). The value added comes by leveraging these free resources in products or services for innovative applications. Other value-added product and service innovations can include new software tools, new artificial intelligence (AI) algorithms for data processing and modeling, new system management techniques, and new applications in industries that previously did not use space systems. A prominent example of a value-added tool is packaging remote sensing data and GNSS services into personal navigation software. Value-added tools to come may be less obvious. For example, the Lightning Image Sensor (LIS) on the International Space Station (ISS) records time and occurrence of lightning, day and night, and offers this data up for free. It is up to the next entrepreneur to determine what value-added tools can be created and monetized, if any, to create stakeholder intrinsic value using LIS data. LIS is given as an example, but the same mentality applies to any preexisting open-source data.

The potential for additional value-added data processing tools may be virtually limitless. Diverse industries like real estate, insurance, investment banking, education, transportation, security, manufacturing, shipping, agriculture, and more all can leverage space systems to increase efficiency, production, and sustainability (more on this in Chapter 6). Satellite remote sensing systems now have petabytes and decades of data, and this enormous repository is growing at an increasing rate. Simply put, there are more remote sensing data that exist than can be processed and utilized. Data mining remote sensing data of the Earth to extract patterns and correlations with human and planetary interests is a value-added activity of which the full extent of commercial opportunities cannot yet be known.

The third opportunity listed for increased value creation from remote sensing, telecommunications, and GNSS is value chain innovation. Each of these three types of space systems drives an independent value chain. Other existing areas in space that independently drive value chains are exploration (human and robotic), science, space tourism, and security. These seven categories in total are notable, in that in theory they do not depend on one another for their supporting value chain. That is, a stand-alone value chain could exist solely in support of each (though in reality there is overlap and no need for "stand-alone value chains").

These value chains are boundless areas for innovation and increased value creation. For example, activities leading to provision of a physical product include product R&D, market research, raw material extraction and processing, system manufacturing, testing, marketing, sales, operations, value management, disposal, and value recapture. There are countless points of access for innovative companies or new ideas to increase stakeholder intrinsic value creation in this series of activities. Pursuit of stakeholder intrinsic value need not always create a new value chain, but rather can involve improving an existing one.

The three top areas for increased stakeholder intrinsic value creation from space systems are described here as (1) more capacity, (2) innovation on value-added data processing and application tools, and (3) value chain innovation. These three areas will continue as recurring themes throughout the remainder of this book as discussions on stakeholder intrinsic value creation in space continue.

Spin-off Technology

Spin-off technology is often presented as a way in which the space industry creates value. It's true that there are numerous spin-off technologies from space that have benefits beyond the space industry. Examples of spin-off technologies include advanced water filtration systems, miniaturized ultrasonic scanners, laser eye movement tracking, sleep science, bone loss and kidney stone prevention, robotics advances, agriculture technology, radiation and cancer research, microgravity material processing (proteins, silicon, fibers, metallurgy), scratch-resistant glass, memory foam, structural analysis software, the list goes on much longer [119].

While spin-off technology seems to fit in the context of creating value for humanity, it must be considered as a fortunate bonus which cannot be a part of any core stakeholder intrinsic value creation scheme for a business. Consulting firm Navigant performed a study on the benefits of the ISS for humanity and offered some useful perspective in this area, saying: "While a better understanding of the universe is intrinsically valuable, the sum total 'payoff' of that knowledge is impossible to predict and likely to take a long time to reveal itself" [119]. The prospect of spin-off technologies is best considered as a motivating factor by governments developing say a large space program spanning decades, involving no requirement to turn a profit, and intended to benefit an entire nation in the long term. The discussion in this book on stakeholder intrinsic value creation is better served by focusing on methods, capabilities, and assessment of direct value creation activities. Fortunate spin-off technologies that come from the space industry will no doubt continue, but this cannot be part of the calculus for stakeholder intrinsic value.

Note

1 Recall from Chapter 3, exchange value refers to market price and "true value" refers to the utility or importance of something.

5 Commercialization of Space Systems

Stakeholder intrinsic value creation in the space industry necessarily involves commercialization. In this approach, value creation is maximized through familiar features of capitalism such as efficiency, innovation, profit-seeking, and provision of value to the greatest number of people possible. However, some types of goods and services are most efficiently produced by markets and some are not. Reasons that markets may not be ideal in certain cases include low demand, high production costs, risk, technical gaps, or the very nature of a particular product or service. Stakeholder intrinsic value is proposed as merely the *best* means to create value, not the only means. If a commercial approach is not an option but the good or service under consideration is desired by society nonetheless, provision by government or some other not-for-profit organization is required. This chapter explores the history of space system commercialization along with an analysis and set of guidelines related to what can and cannot be commercialized in space.

Government versus Commercial

Governments have demonstrated that they are fully capable of developing and operating space systems. Why not continue with this proven approach to creating value in space versus shifting toward commercial means? There are three reasons: (1) governments have limited resources and so a cap on value creation is eventually reached; (2) government-funded projects and initiatives are subject to inconsistencies and cancellation from politics, optics, and national budget cycles; and (3) government projects often struggle with efficiency. Capitalism on the other hand is only capable of producing value that is in demand and it is only capable of doing this in ways that are self-sustaining and efficient. This occurs through profit-seeking and competition and is less restricted in terms of a cap on total value creation.

Consider an example. Tremendous value was created by the US government through sending people to the Moon in the Apollo program. However, as Ozgur Gurtuna points out, Apollo was canceled in the end

DOI: 10.4324/9781003268734-5

because the primary forms of value, prestige and political power, had already been obtained, and "without an economic basis for sustained flight to the Moon, there was little reason to keep the Apollo program running" [120]. One can conclude that for a given value creation activity in space (landing a human on the Moon in this example) if it were executed in the context of stakeholder intrinsic value creation (i.e., using the profit-seeking motive), more net value would be created and it would be created consistently over a longer period of time compared to if it were executed by the government. The catch is that only certain types of things are suitable for commercialization.

Examples highlighting these points were described in Chapter 1, namely, NASA's commercial crew and commercial cargo programs. The result of these programs which transitioned provision of low Earth orbit flights to a commercial market resulted in flights that are both cheaper and available to more customers beyond just the government. Here, commercialization was successful in creating more value overall, but this is not to be expected universally in every instance of value creation in space. How can one identify and understand systematically which activities in the space industry are suitable for stakeholder intrinsic value creation and which are best left to governments? Also, which existing government-led activities can reasonably be expected to become commercialized in the near future? Basic principles of economics can help to begin to answer these questions.

Commercialization Criteria

The economic concepts of excludability and rivalry can be applied in the context of the space industry to assess commercialization potential at a basic level. Goods that are excludable and rival, private goods, are best suited for production using capitalism. Something is excludable if someone can be prevented from using it. A company can produce a physical product and then decide whom they sell it to. Or they can choose to sell it to nobody. A product like this is excludable. If a street performer plays a song for tourists, it is impossible to exclude anyone from enjoying the product. A song from a street performer is non-excludable. Something is rival if one person's use of the good inhibits another person's use of the same good. A physical product may be rival because once in use or once consumed, another person cannot use it. Or to a further extreme, if only one of those items exists and replication is difficult or impossible, one person's use inhibits all other uses. A song from a street performer on the other hand is non-rival because one person's use has no effect on another's. A street performer's product is non-excludable and non-rival and therefore is not efficiently produced using capitalism and markets.

Degrees of excludability and rivalry do not define if something has value or worth, but they do indicate if it is something suited for capitalism and markets to provide. Various permutations of excludability and rivalry are listed below:

- Rival + Excludable = Private goods (physical products, services)
- Rival + Non-excludable = Common resource (air, fish in the ocean, freshwater aquifer)
- Non-rival + Excludable = Natural monopoly (fire protection, cable TV)
- Non-rival + Non-excludable = Public goods (national defense, knowledge)

Markets are the most efficient manner in which to manage and produce goods if they are rival and excludable. These are private goods. Public goods and common resources, on the other hand, are non-excludable and not conducive to production and management by markets. They have value to society but not market value as it is difficult to prevent someone from using them. As a result, public goods and common resources are prone to externalities because there is no market price attached to them. Even if one consciously tries to avoid cost externalization in these cases, it is challenging because the market cannot say what price to assign it in a transaction. Note that stakeholder management and circular economy principles address this challenge in part by designing value flows that consist of more than just money.

If a good is non-excludable, often there is an incentive for free riding. Potential users know they can access the good without paying since they cannot be excluded. For example, disposal of waste into the environment. This is a need for many and some will choose to treat the environment as an infinite waste sink and free ride by exploiting this function without care for the costs to others. This is a case where a market is not the answer; there's nothing to commoditize and there's no way to restrict access (globally) to the waste sink. Government regulation in this case would be the better solution for provision of a waste sink. If a market solution drives or cannot prevent free riding for a non-excludable good, then provision and management by the government may be the *economically efficient* approach. For example, general scientific research falls into the category of non-excludable non-rival and is considered a public good. Profit-seeking companies free ride on use of this good, and it is often produced by governments. This is one way that governments can deliberately support industry. Alternatively, companies may decide to produce specialized knowledge internally for their products, and if so, this specialized knowledge becomes excludable.

Common resources are non-excludable but unlike public goods they are rival. One person's use of a common resource inhibits or diminishes others' potential use. Some space-related examples of a common resource are an orbital position and a radiofrequency bandwidth for a satellite to use. Other generic examples are clean air and water. Use of markets would result in inefficient management and production of common resource goods through a tendency toward cost externalization. In cases like this, establishing private property rights is a way to deliberately create conditions of excludability and rivalry. Refer to Chapter 2 and the advent of private property in the form of real estate parcels in 17th-century England which helped the formation of capitalism in the first place. If private property rights do not exist or are poorly defined, a market will not allocate resources efficiently.

Use of capitalism to produce value for humanity in space requires private property rights and enforcement of those rights. A hotel on the Moon or a precious metal extracted from an asteroid is of no value if these things are non-excludable and non-rival. Expanding on this concept, say a company is allowed to "own" a particular orbital slot or region at a Lagrangian point and their ownership came at a market price similar to as in the real estate market. On this notion, authors Nelson and Block speculate in *Space Capitalism* "...when debris and clutter choke the trail, these problems can be best solved with private owners who will have direct personal interests in maintaining and upgrading the path by removing the trash and limiting over-use by interlopers" [121]. This concept is similar to the notion of a carbon cap and trade system where manufactures "own" a certain allowed allotment of carbon emissions. In this case, market forces are driving efficient use of the common resource (i.e., Earth's atmosphere as a waste sink) and externalities are effectively removed from transactions involving production of carbon emissions. These scenarios depend on the government to install and enforce private property rights.

Note that some non-rival goods like software are still placed in functioning markets. Goods like software, a feature film, or intellectual property are inherently non-rival because the cost of reproduction or provision to users beyond the first user is essentially zero. Additional users in no way inhibit the first user assuming each has their own copy of the good. Many are familiar with piracy issues related to software and feature films and these problems come about in part due to their non-rivalrous nature. In this case, unregulated markets will tend toward monopoly and inefficiency. Regulation is required for use of markets here and this involves things like licensing, intellectual property protections, and anti-distribution laws.

Excludability and Rivalry of Space Industry Activities

Consider now goods specifically related to the space industry. What are the ideal areas for commercialization and stakeholder intrinsic value creation? A list is given below highlighting which types are and are not suited for production using markets based on considerations of excludability and rivalry:

Suitable for production in markets:

- Specialized remote sensing data not available from government systems
  - Excludable because a company can withhold data
  - Non-rival because one person's use of the data does not affect another's use of that same data; licensing and regulation are required for commercialization

- Satellite telecommunications services (TV, radio, internet, point-to-point)

  - Excludable because a provider can withhold service from users through data encryption or geographic offering
  - Non-rival because one person's use of the data does not affect another's use of that same data; licensing and regulation are required for commercialization

- Value-added software related to application of remote sensing, telecommunications, or Global Navigation and Satellite Systems (GNSS) services

  - Excludable because a company can withhold a copy of the software
  - Non-rival because one person's use of the software does not affect another's use of that same software; licensing and regulation are required for commercialization

- Value-added consulting related to development, operation, or end uses of space systems

  - Excludable because a company can withhold consulting services
  - Rival because a consultant occupied by one client is unavailable to serve another

- Access to space (human and robotic spaceflight, exploration, tourism)

  - Excludable because someone can be prevented from occupying a seat or payload bay on a spacecraft
  - Rival because an occupied seat or payload bay is unavailable to others

- Space cargo delivery

  - Excludable because someone can be prevented from accessing the cargo delivery system
  - Rival because cargo space used is unavailable to others

- In-space research – specialized knowledge

  - Excludable because data can be withheld
  - Non-rival because one person's use of the data does not affect another's use of that same data; licensing and regulation are required for commercialization

- Space hardware

  - Excludable because someone can be prevented from using a physical product
  - Rival because one person's use of the product prevents another person's use

- Space resource extraction

  - Excludable because material once harvested can be withheld from others (assuming in-space private property rights are legally enforced)
  - Rival because one person's use of extracted material prevents another person's use of the same material

- In-space services (debris removal, satellite servicing, refueling)

  - Excludable because a service provider may withhold service
  - Rival because a service provider can only satisfy one customer at a time

- Spaceports and related ground support services

  - Excludable because a service provider may deny access to facilities
  - Rival because one person's use of a spaceport facility prevents another's use

- Provision of products or services to government customers in support of activities not suitable for commercialization (government creates a market for contracted support)[1]

  - Excludable because products and services may be withheld
  - Rival because the customer's use of a product or service inhibits other uses

Not suitable for production in markets:

- Space research – general knowledge

  - Non-excludable because knowledge is available from numerous sources around the globe for free
  - Non-rival because one person's use of data does not inhibit another's

- Space exploration

  - Non-excludable because, given the resources, anyone can proceed with space exploration (though the means to access space in order to perform exploration may be excludable)
  - Non-rival because one person exploring space does not inhibit another

- Remote sensing data collected by governments

  - Non-excludable because data is available from numerous sources around the globe
  - Non-rival because one person's use of data does not inhibit another's

While rivalry and excludability of a good or service are necessary conditions for commercialization, they are not the only factors to consider in terms of commercial potential. Additional factors include technical capability, market size, availability of capital, return on investment time, risks, degree of regulatory uncertainty, customer requirements, and other stakeholder needs. The following section contains an analysis of historical efforts, some successful some not, at commercialization in space. This historical perspective is provided to help clarify the prospect of stakeholder intrinsic value creation in the space economy.

Commercialization of Mir, the Space Shuttle, and the International Space Station

With varying success, Russia attempted commercialization of the space station Mir in several ways, including tourism, advertising, and applied research in an effort to recover operational costs. Perhaps most impactful in these efforts was Mircorp, which was formed in 1999 among RSC Energia and American entrepreneurs to facilitate commercial opportunities on Mir. Mircorp was successful in financing the first private launch and mission to space in 2000 when it launched two cosmonauts to Mir for station operation and maintenance. Commercial initiatives on Mir ceased when it was deorbited in 2001 so that Russia could focus on the International Space Station (ISS).

Professor Nikolai Anfimov noted several lessons learned from commercialization efforts involving Mir [122]. The following items were found to be necessary for successful commercialization efforts in space:

* Transparent pricing policy
* Minimal period of time from user's proposal to project implementation
* Simple and clear processes for proposal review and selection
* Confidentially and intellectual property rights

NASA's space shuttle program also had commercial aspirations. These efforts were initially aimed at delivering commercial payloads to orbit. While this did occur at first, after the Challenger disaster in 1986, new safety restrictions were levied on payloads. This and the relatively high cost of operating the space shuttle effectively ended its use as a commercial launch vehicle. Space shuttle commercialization efforts did continue, however, and starting in 1993 were based around the use of the SpaceHab module for research opportunities. The difficulty was that SpaceHab never signed any other customers beyond NASA. The lesson here was that a commercial enterprise should not rely in the long term on a single government customer and it must be realistic that a broader market will emerge.

As with Mir and the space shuttle, the ISS program also has included a continuous commercialization agenda, much of which has been successful. Building on experience with SpaceHab, the greatest commercial success on the ISS is offering use of the facility to (1) perform applied R&D and (2) test and demonstrate new space products and services. In total, research on the ISS has engaged over 5,000 scientists and engineers over the years [119]. Between 2012 and 2017, the US National Lab on the ISS hosted 190 of these investigations, 56% of which were commercial customers and 42% of which were academic customers. Only 2% of research in the lab in this time period was government-sponsored [119]. This commercial activity has included things like in-space additive manufacturing, small satellite deployment, corporate research, academic research, and payload integration and launch services.

Some commercial success was achieved with both Mir and the ISS; however, numerous challenges were encountered along the way. For example, the fact that payload customers are looking for lead times of less than eight months [123], and the fact that investors in space systems or services want a return on their investment within no more than five years [124]. These insights and others present potential opportunities to expand commercial activity in space. In this way, commercialization challenges observed over recent decades are framed in the list below as potential stakeholder intrinsic value creation opportunities [9]:

• Reduce long lead times to market related to flying experiments and products
• Reduce overall costs in order to compete better with ground-based alternatives for research and product development
• Reduce financing difficulties
• Provide necessary specialized expertise related to flying space payloads
• Reduce high launch costs
• Alleviate concerns on the frequency of guaranteed access to space
• Provide insurance services
• Provide consulting on uncertainty related to how the initial investment will be recovered

Commercialization (or not) of Remote Sensing Data

The thing about remote sensing data is that it seems like it could be commercialized. Why shouldn't it be collected and then sold to interested users? Makes sense, right? At the very least, this could cover the expense of the satellite systems if not also facilitate wider economic benefits. In particular, data related to weather, climate change, water use, and land use are all of high value to humanity [61]. It seems reasonable that valuable things to people should be able to be commercialized.

The fact is that commercialization of remote sensing data has had limited success historically, despite advocacy and policy agendas coming from the highest levels of government and industry. Numerous efforts around the globe and consistent failures over the decades at commercialization of remote sensing data have demonstrated time and again that only under certain circumstances is it practical. A trend has emerged indicating that raw, un-processed remote sensing data is difficult to commercialize, but it is possible to commercially provide value-added tools, specialized data, and products and services in government markets. Value-added tools refer to innovative tools for post-processing and applying raw data. Specialized data refers to data that is distinctive in nature or enhanced in some way compared to government-provided alternatives. Government markets refer to markets created by governments for companies to compete for support of government initiatives. The following discussion examines why these distinct boundaries have emerged relative to commercialization of remote sensing data.

The book *Open Space*, by Professor Mariel Borowitz, contains an excel-lent detailed account of historical efforts to commercialize remote sensing data [125]. *Open Space* was instrumental in researching the following dis-cussion which also outlines, but in more brevity, the history of policy and commercialization attempts related to remote sensing systems. Numerous instances are described where commercialization of remote sensing data was not feasible. Does this mean that the data in those instances do not lead to a desirable or needed benefit to society? No, it does not. Rather, what has been observed is that in certain cases, usage and hence value creation for so-ciety increases as the degree of commercialization decreases. In these cases, markets were found not to be the most efficient means to create value. The historical account that follows explains in detail commercialization chal-lenges for remote sensing.

Commercialization of Meteorological Data

Applications in concept for satellites date back to the mid-1940s, with pro-posals from science fiction author Arthur C. Clark in 1945 [126] and from a Douglas Aircraft Company report in 1946 [127]. Remote sensing data using satellites began in practice, however, with the launch of the US Navy's Van-guard 2 and NASA's TIROS 1 weather satellites in 1959 and 1960, respec-tively. These early meteorological remote sensing platforms carried cameras used for cloud cover imaging. While primitive by today's standards, the Vanguard 2 and TIROS 1 images did reinforce one fact and that is that weather is a global phenomenon crossing national borders by definition and data collection from this global perspective is required for accurate weather predictions at any given location.

It was exactly this perspective many years earlier that led to the creation of the International Meteorological Organization (IMO) in 1873. The IMO embraced the benefits to humanity of accurate weather prediction and pro-moted the notion that this is best realized if nations collaborate and openly share meteorological data free of charge. The idea is that no single nation can obtain as much useful meteorological data as the global collective and no na-tion would be better off isolated in this regard. For these compelling reasons, meteorological data has a long international history of open and free sharing.

The IMO was superseded in 1950 by the UN World Meteorological Organization (WMO) and this was followed by several decades of increasing international collaboration on weather data collection. The high cost and growing technical maturity of space-based weather prediction systems led to commercialization attempts in the 1980s. The US Congress authorized the National Ocean and Atmospheric Administration (NOAA) to begin charging data use fees to commercial users; however, further NOAA commercialization attempts met hard resistance from lawmakers. Weather data had been firmly in the realm of international sharing for a long time and the value of maintaining this stance in support of collective societal benefit carried bipartisan support.

In parallel, the Committee on Earth Observation Satellites (CEOS), formed in 1984 out of the G7 summit that year, focused on international sharing of satellite data beyond meteorology related to global change and environmental data. While CEOS initially called for open data sharing with limited restrictions even for nonmembers, this approach did not last. By the mid-1990s, CEOS formally recognized the long-standing tradition of open and free sharing of weather data but acknowledged also nations and organizations who can't do this based on the cost of their systems, effectively opening the door to increased commercialization.

Meanwhile in Europe, the European Organization for the Exploitation of Meteorological Satellites (EUMETSAT), the organization formed to operate European weather satellites, took over operation and collection of weather data in the 1990s and also pushed hard to install some cost recovery methods and sell data. EUMETSAT charged user fees for data while ESA would offer data free for research but at a cost for commercial use. At the time, this was in part a recognition of strained budgets and the reality that there would be no data at all, free or for sale, if collection costs could not be covered somehow. Eventually, it became clear that cost recovery from user fees was not going to be sufficient financial support alone. Ultimately, EUMETSAT made its data open again in 1998. Sale of value-added commercial services related to weather prediction could continue though.

This trend at the time, away from commercialization except for value-added products, also was occurring in the US. NOAA released a statement in 1991 saying it would not compete with the private sector if they offered a value-added service like tailored weather guidance for shipping, oil platforms, etc. Attempts at value-added commercialization continued around the world, and in 1995 the 12th World Meteorological Congress passed Resolution 40, which stood up a system where essential data (hurricanes, disaster warnings) would remain freely available and nonessential data would remain free only for research and education but could be commercialized otherwise [128]. The 1991 NOAA policy was later included in 2016 in NOAA's commercial space policy. The 2016 policy reinforced the criticality of space-collected weather data and that it is a public good to be provided for free from the government. The 2016 policy update also reinforced a commercial sector that uses this free data for value-added products and services.

In the case of weather data, there is rationale both against and for commercialization that depends on the customer and the nature of the service being offered. Efficient market production did not materialize for provision of basic weather data. The high value of this kind of data toward public safety and economic factors garnered strong political support against commercialization. On the other hand, there has been support for and success in commercialization of value-added products that use raw meteorological data. It is in these instances that stakeholder intrinsic value creation is possible and should be pursued. While provision of basic weather data will continue from the government, for additional value to be created, it must come via commercial means.

Commercialization of Climate Data

Another related area that emerged in the past as a priority for international remote sensing data sharing is climate change. Lisa Shafer, Deputy Director in the early 1990s at the NASA Earth Science, Modeling, Data, and Information Systems Program Office, may have described the need for climate data sharing best in a 1993 paper on NASA's remote sensing data policy:

> No individual nation can afford to develop and maintain the necessary observation and analysis capability, nor can all the scientific progress be confined to one set of researchers. Thus, the global community depends on this open access to data to support and sustain our commitment to improved understanding and monitoring of the condition of our planet.
> [129]

Like the WMO, NASA had long been a consistent proponent of open remote sensing data sharing. This originated in Earth observation programs in the 1980s, which culminated in the Mission to Planet Earth program created in 1989. In 2006, the following statement was included in NASA's updated *Earth Science Reference Handbook* [130] and remains unchanged in 2022 on NASA's website:

> NASA promotes the full and open sharing of all data with the research and applications communities, private industry, academia, and the general public. The greater the availability of the data, the more quickly and effectively the user communities can utilize the information to address basic Earth science questions and provide the basis for developing innovative practical applications to benefit the general public.

Getting to this policy point today that is shared beyond just NASA involved debate over the preceding decades.

In 1990, the WMO and others hosted the second World Climate Conference where the UN International Panel on Climate Change (IPCC) presented a report stating that humans were contributing to a planetary greenhouse effect [131]. Recommendations from the report included needs to improve and expand international collection and sharing of climate data. One outcome from this recommendation was the WMO helping to form the Global Climate Observing System (GCOS) in 1992 to focus specifically on international monitoring of climate change. Also in 1992, the UN Framework Convention on Climate Change (UNFCCC), signed initially by 154 member states at the Rio Earth Summit, required parties to collaborate and share collection and results of climate data.

Recognition of climate change as a global issue transcending national borders was growing and momentum behind increased free and open sharing of climate change data followed. To aid in this endeavor, GCOS developed the 50 Essential Climate Variables (ECVs) in 2003 to standardize specific scientific measurements for the world to use in tracking climate change [132]. Notably, half of the ECVs involve data collected by satellites. Since 2003, the list of ECVs has been expanded and now stands at 54 in total.

As insight and understanding of the challenge of climate change grew, it became evident that a dedicated equivalent to the WMO was needed entirely focused on sharing climate change data and so, resulting from the G8 summit in 2003, the Group on Earth Observation (GEO) was formed in 2005 with a purpose of advocating for and coordinating data sharing across the world, particularly concerning sustainable development and environmental management. This included remote sensing data collected in space as well as in situ data measurements. GEO created the Global Earth Observation System of Systems (GEOSS) in 2005, which persists to this day as the leading international platform for organization and facilitation of global environmental data sharing. Within GEOSS, WMO leads activity related to meteorological data and GCOS leads activity related to climate data.

At its inception, GEOSS declared nine areas of socioeconomic benefit to promote [133]:

1 Reducing loss of life and property from natural and human-induced disasters
2 Understanding environmental factors affecting human health and well-being
3 Improving management of energy resources
4 Understanding, assessing, predicting, mitigating, and adapting to climate variability and change
5 Improving water resource management through better understanding of the water cycle
6 Improving weather information, forecasting, and warning

7   Improving the management and protection of terrestrial, coastal, and
     marine ecosystems
8   Supporting sustainable agriculture and combating desertification
9   Understanding, monitoring, and conserving biodiversity

GEOSS promotes that data in these nine themes be shared openly and freely
(or at costs only to cover reproduction and distribution) and backs a position that data sharing is required in order to obtain full societal benefits
from these systems. This position is based in part on a WMO policy adopted
in 1995 on climate change data calling for a system that ensures "All data
and products are easily accessible at the lowest possible cost" [134]. Therefore, the nine GEOSS themes have limited direct opportunity for commercialization and stakeholder intrinsic value creation.

A useful way to view stakeholder intrinsic value creation in the context
of climate change data and the nine GEOSS themes is to consider instances
where additional value creation would not occur at all if not for activation of
profit-seeking enterprises. The nine GEOSS themes are most applicable to
stakeholder intrinsic value creation in the areas of value-added tools, provision of specialized data, and in support of government initiatives. The following section uses the Landsat Earth observation satellites as a case study
to help explain further why commercial opportunities in remote sensing are
limited.

Remote Sensing Commercialization Case Study: Landsat

The story of the Landsat satellites serves as a useful case study to suggest
that remote sensing data is most efficiently provided at no cost from governments. Landsat 1, originally called the Earth Resources Technology
Satellite, was announced by US President Richard Nixon in September 1969
after the first Apollo landing [135]. Landsat 1 had a TV camera and the first
multispectral camera. The plan initially was for the US Geological Survey
(USGS) to operate the Landsat system and sell data to US citizens while
NASA would provide data to the international science community for free.

By the early 1980s, momentum and congressional pressure were growing
to fully commercialize Landsat in order to realize greater efficiency, free up
federal budget for other things, and grow the US remote sensing industry.
Recall in this same era that while there *was* congressional support for Landsat commercialization, there *was no* congressional support for commercialization of weather data. In 1984, congress passed the Land Remote Sensing
Commercialization Act [136], according to which the government would operate the existing Landsat system and industry would be used to market and
sell minimally processed data. In this arrangement, industry would pay the
US government a negotiated fee based on revenue from data sales. Industry would also pay the government full market price of data that they used
themselves for value-added commercial products and services. Ultimately,

the plan was that industry would finance and operate the Landsat system itself and sell data to the government. In 1985, EOSAT was selected as the industry partner and so Landsat became commercialized. General efforts to commercialize remote sensing industries also were occurring internationally, including commercialization of the SPOT remote sensing system in France to compete with Landsat and similar efforts in Russia and India.

Despite widespread enthusiasm from government and industry, Landsat remote sensing commercialization efforts in the 1980s did not pan out. In the early 1980s, upon commercialization of Landsat data, usage plummeted and in just two years had gone from 50,000 images accessed in 1981 to only 10,000 in 1983 [137]. This included US federal agencies being charged also, at which point some declined further use of the data. This trend continued and Landsat users in academia once numbering in the thousands fell to just 450 by 1990 [138]. This was not a reflection of the value of the data though, and by the early 1990s, Landsat was recognized as important in studying climate change. USGS issued a report in 1990 noting this view and noting that high prices would limit the use and value of the system realized by society [139].

Given that the desired commercial success was not realized for Landsat initially, a tiered agreement was installed in 1992 to replace that which initially had been enacted in 1985 with EOSAT. In the new system, Landsat data would be available to US government agencies, global environmental change researchers, US government-supported researchers, and educational purposes. EOSAT still would maintain the role of data sales to commercial users. As for the satellite systems themselves, starting with Landsat 7, they would revert back to full government ownership. In 2001, after attempting the tiered approach for some years, EOSAT transferred its own Landsat assets back to the government, recognizing them as not commercially feasible anymore.

The newfound government operators, the USGS, began advocating for complete removal of fees in order to maximize societal benefit from the data. In 2008, the USGS announced at the GEO summit that year that all Landsat data going back to 1972 would be available online for free. In the first year following this announcement, one million scenes were accessed which was more than the entire preceding 38-year history of Landsat [140]. By 2012, 250,000 scenes were being accessed per month and in particular, this included many requests from researchers for the same image over many years to study environmental change [141].

Open access remote sensing data policies spread around the world. The China-Brazil Earth Resource Satellite, a collaboration initiated in 1988, made its data open to the world in 2010. In 2009, after some years of attempts to balance cost recovery efforts with the increase of Copernicus data availability to the research community, ESA adopted the "Joint Principles for a GMES Sentinel Data Policy" which includes free open sharing of all data from Sentinel remote sensing satellites and the Copernicus program. Today, the United States and Europe offer remote sensing data free to anyone for all uses [142, 143]. The Japanese Aerospace Exploration Agency announced a similar policy in 2013. After 2015, GEOSS principles were updated to reflect and capitalize on the significant shift in attitudes in its member organizations from around the world toward open sharing of environmental data [144].

Failed efforts at commercialization of remote sensing data combined with the fact that the data is of high value to society suggest that the data is best categorized as a public good and therefore most efficiently provided by government, not markets. A 2012 USGS report on the same topic corroborates this view, stating: "Landsat imagery has characteristics of a public good, meaning the socially optimal level of provision through private markets is not likely" [145]. The fact that general knowledge is non-rival, difficult to make excludable once it is released, and potentially available from numerous sources around the world also helps explain the unsuitability of remote sensing data for commercialization. The USGS report remarks on this matter as well that "Charging any positive price for a nonrival good is economically inefficient; it results in under consumption of the good and a net loss of economic benefits to society."

The USGS report mentioned above includes a survey among Landsat users investigating the nature of users and perceived value of data. One takeaway from the survey is that most of the users are in academia and this is also the group that ranks the data at the lowest *economic* value. Therefore, the maximum value to society is only realized if this group can access the data for free or at a low cost. Early stage value-added entrepreneurs are also likely priced out, according to the survey, if fees are levied.

Bruce Joffe characterizes the value of remote sensing data as "the value is in the usage, not in the data" and remarks: "Because [satellite remote sensing] data creates more value the more it is used, capturing that value will motivate local government to distribute it as widely and as inexpensively as possible" [146]. In a case for open data for Europe's Copernicus system, Sawyer and de Vries also point to the Landsat example as evidence that free data drastically increases use and therefore societal benefit as well. They argue that this effect is so dramatic that the economic benefits from free data (i.e., subsidized by the taxpayer) create more overall value for the government also than if fees were charged for cost recovery [147]. Loss from users priced out truly is a net loss benefiting nobody, or in economic terms, a deadweight loss.

Another interesting finding from the USGS survey was that among post-2008 users of Landsat data, private businesses place the highest economic value on the data. This finding confirms that commercialization of value-added tools and specialized data is feasible [145]. Finally, the USGS report also estimates that there is a worldwide direct economic value to users of Landsat data of $2.19 billion not counting value-added products. Indirect economic value is likely much greater. The $2.19 billion amount is much more than had ever been obtained through cost recovery when the data came at a fee and indicates a much larger impact on the economy compared to the cost of the system to taxpayers. Maximum value to society in this case is achieved through government collection and provision of raw data for free.

Like with Landsat, NASA has also experimented with hybrid approaches to commercialization of remote sensing data for science programs. In the Scientific Data Purchase (SDP) program, lasting from 1998 to 2002, data collection was done by private companies but NASA agreed to be a guaranteed customer. The SeaWiFS satellite, used to observe ocean color, was provided and operated by Orbital Sciences according to requirements for the system provided by NASA. NASA agreed in advance to a five-year purchase of data. Orbital Sciences could also sell data to others for commercial use but data would become open for all after five years. The outcome of NASA's approach in SDP was general success overall, but no groundbreaking revelation of cost savings. A more recent example is NASA's Commercial Smallsat Data Acquisition Program (CSDA). In CSDA, NASA sources Earth science data from commercial markets. NASA describes CSDA as not just useful in encouraging development of a commercial remote sensing market but also as a "a cost-effective means to augment and/or complement the suite of Earth observations acquired by NASA and other U.S. government agencies and those by international partners and agencies" [148].

The hybrid approach where government creates a market is one means to pursue stakeholder intrinsic value creation in areas not immediately suitable for commercialization. Ideally, in these cases at least two companies are awarded contracts and compete to provide products or services to the government.

Commercialization of Remote Sensing Data: Summary

In summary, remote sensing data is largely suited for production by governments and provided at no charge to the general public. Without the prospect for use of markets and profit-seeking, stakeholder intrinsic value creation from provision of remote sensing data is limited. There are narrow areas though where commercialization is possible: value-added products, provision of specialized data, and support of government initiatives. Some additional detail on these categories is provided below.

What kinds of value-added products are possible related to remote sensing? There is room for innovation and profit in this area through use of data mining, artificial intelligence, software development, application consulting, and business development. A prominent example of a value-added product is Google Maps. Now ubiquitous in smartphones, Google Maps is a widely known and used instance of remote sensing and GNSS data. Earth imagery in Google Maps is comprised mainly of Landsat 7 and Landsat 9 data obtained at no cost from the US government. Different components of the value-added in this product involve combination of imagery data sets from multiple sources, addition of topography based on satellite radar data, three-dimensional (3D) modeling of buildings based on photogrammetry techniques, integration of maps, integration of personal navigation services, and packaging into a user-friendly interface. Only the raw imagery data is provided by the government for free, all of these additional value-added features are necessary for the raw data to be useful. Google Maps is free for personal, research, and educational uses; however, a fee is charged for commercial use.

Concerning the prospect of stakeholder intrinsic value creation by providing specialized data, what exactly qualifies as "specialized"? This is a question that the space industry is currently in the midst of figuring out at the time of this publication in 2022; however, it typically involves enhanced spatial resolution, enhanced temporal resolution, or greater service availability compared to what is offered by governments for free. Data of this nature likely came at a price in the first place, be it through technical innovation or financial investment in a uniquely equipped system. Furthermore, it may be that a single customer is particularly demanding in needs and effectively monopolizes resources. In conditions like these or similar, a fair price is not only reasonable but necessary to develop and operate such a high-performance system. As long as the data is sufficiently "specialized" such that it garners demand, excludability can emerge. In these cases, profit-seeking and commercialization can be seen to enable value creation for humanity that would not have existed otherwise. Will Marshall, cofounder of commercial remote sensing company Planet, frames this perspective well, noting: "we started Planet because of its potential to aid humanitarian causes, and then we realized that the best way to have that impact and be sustainable was to develop a highly profitable business model" [149].

Extending access, awareness, and understanding of the value of remote sensing data to the public and to diverse types of businesses is another critical value-added need for the space industry to continue to address. That is, connecting potential end users with space services that can serve their needs, especially in cases when the potential end user is unaware of this possibility. This will require innovation and commercialization up and down the value chain involving new hardware in space, identifying new applications and markets, creating new user interface software, continued technology innovations in hardware production, innovations in project management, and more. Overall, the value chain presents a multitude of opportunities for increased stakeholder intrinsic value creation. Chapters 6 and 7 include discussion highlighting many such examples.

Support of government initiatives is another means by which to create stakeholder intrinsic value in space using remote sensing data. While remote sensing data often is most efficiently produced by the government, governments rarely have their own internal production facilities to create space systems. And in many cases, industry not only has production facilities but also valuable expertise to contribute as well. Governments can effectively create a market for companies to compete in to provide and operate remote sensing data collection systems. Profit-seeking, competition, efficiency, and innovation all exist in this arrangement but according to the discretion and resources of a single customer, the government. While a naturally occurring market may be expected to function better in these regards, government support from contracted companies can constitute stakeholder intrinsic value creation. Stakeholder intrinsic value creation in cases like this is enhanced if the government awards contracts to multiple providers.

Commercialization of Telecommunications Data

Unlike remote sensing data, telecommunications have a strong track record of commercialization. Space telecommunications was originally a government-sponsored service; however, it became the first large-scale part of the space industry to truly become commercialized. The International Telecommunications Satellite Organization (INTELSAT) was an intergovernmental organization founded in a UN agreement in 1964 among seven initial nations to provide communications and international broadcasting services. After an experimental flight in 1962, the first telecommunications satellite was launched by INTELSAT to geostationary orbit in 1965. By 1973, the organization had expanded to include 81 nations and it continued to provide global telecommunications services as an intergovernmental organization through 2001. Since 2001, INTELSAT has provided these services, but as a private company. Why was a successful government-led organization privatized in this case? And why was this successful for telecommunications data but not for remote sensing data?

Markets caught up to the government-led early days of satellite applications when INTELSAT was formed. Just as with human spaceflight, satellite technology can be said to have been ahead of its time in the early years. Early on, both mass markets and widespread understanding of the technology's applications had yet to exist. These are perfect conditions for the government to initially carry a new promising industry if some benefit or value for society can be expected as a result. By the 1990s, conditions in the satellite industry had evolved to the point that markets and technical capabilities were mature enough for the industry to stand on its own without government support. Additionally, the prospective customers and desired services were well established. While this transition did require years of industry lobbying, INTELSAT was privatized ultimately breaking the monopoly that its multinational government predecessor had enjoyed for decades.

Building on the early years of success of INTELSAT, in 1976 the UN requested that another intergovernmental organization be formed to provide satellite communications specifically for the shipping industry and to enable communication to remote corners of the world far from communication infrastructure. As a result, the International Maritime Satellite

Organization (INMARSAT) was established in 1979. Like INTELSAT, INMARSAT would provide satellite telecommunications services to its member nations. These services eventually expanded to cover aeronautical and land uses and most recently, internet service for international flights. Just as with INTELSAT, INMARSAT was privatized in the 1990s because of the growing competitiveness of the commercial satellite industry. In both cases, it was not just market pressure alone leading to privatization but also a growing reluctance of nations to openly share technical prowess in this increasingly competitive and sensitive field. In the case of INMARSAT, the original organization transitioned to a regulatory body at the time of privatization and the actual services were taken over by the UK private company Inmarsat, Ltd.

Recall that the international momentum in the satellite industry toward commercialization was occurring also for remote sensing satellites in the 1980s and 1990s. What was it about telecommunications services that was more conducive to commercialization compared to remote sensing? Satellite telecommunications data services are excludable because a provider can withhold service from users through data encryption or geographic offering. These services are non-rival because one person's use of the data does not affect another's use of that same data, therefore licensing and regulation were utilized as needed for commercialization.

Commercialization of Space Systems: Closing Remarks

This concludes the discussion in this chapter on the profitability component of the stakeholder intrinsic value criteria relative to the space industry. The following chapters include discussion on numerous and diverse types of activities in space, including descriptions of how they can create value and benefit humanity. The history of commercialization in space as well as considerations of excludability and rivalry discussed in this chapter should be kept in mind throughout the remainder of this book as different value creation opportunities are presented.

Note

1 A government-created market is not optimal in terms of efficiency and productivity compared to a naturally occurring market.

6 Sustainability in the Space Industry

Recognition is spreading that widespread market transaction externalities are resulting in an untenable level of destruction to environmental and social systems. Markets of the future must correct this trend and facilitate value creation only in ways that support the long-term prosperity of human civilization. Item 1 of the stakeholder intrinsic value criteria addresses this need through the necessity for harmony. Harmony is considered to be essential in any value creation scheme. No matter the degree of utility offered by a product or service, it is not logical to create value in ways such that the system for which it is intended to benefit is degraded as a result. Therefore, the harmony requirement may be satisfied broadly by attention to sustainability of social, environmental, and economic systems.

In the space industry, the push for greater sustainability entails for the first time a need for engineers, scientists, managers, policy-makers, and entrepreneurs to all understand the implications of their actions in the context of global impacts. This level of awareness must become ubiquitous across the industry and it must overshadow the passion many industry participants already feel toward activities in space and their particular role. Jacques Arnould points out that it is crucial to apply this perspective to space activities because "Not to do so would widen the gap between the representation of the world constructed by space-related sciences and technologies on the one hand, and the reality directly experienced by the average human on the other" [150]. If an activity in space is in conflict with the sustainability of humanity and the planet, it has no reason to occur.

In practice, space systems can support sustainability either through adhering to do no harm responsibilities or through providing direct proactive solutions. In the case of the latter, the company purpose would be centered around the particular solution being provided and formulated so that a profit is generated if the purpose is realized. As to the former, there also will be plenty of instances of stakeholder intrinsic value creation from space systems that do not constitute a direct sustainability solution. No problem with this (as long as harmony is satisfied), given that any inherently good outcome from space systems is desirable.

DOI: 10.4324/9781003268734-6

Defining Sustainability for the Space Industry

To continue this discussion, a concise understanding of what is meant by sustainability in the space industry is helpful. The 1987 Bruntland report published for the World Commission on Environment and Development defines sustainable development generically as: "development that meets the needs of the present without compromising those of the future" [151]. How does this apply to space? What does it mean specifically when it comes to value creation activities in space?

Discussion on space industry sustainability began at the UN UNISPACE III forum in 1999 where the 97 participating member states created a "blueprint for the peaceful uses of outer space in the 21st century." Among other things, the blueprint outlined use of space to help protect the environment, provide security, advance scientific knowledge, protect the space environment (i.e., mitigate orbital debris), enhance education, and promote international cooperation. In 2010, the UN Committee on the Peaceful Uses of Outer Space (COPUOS) established a working group on the "long term sustainability of space activities" to further mature the blueprint. By 2014, COPUOS had developed 33 candidate guidelines for space sustainability in four areas: (1) support of sustainable development on Earth, (2) space debris, (3) space weather, and (4) regulatory regimes and guidance. Finally, in 2019 these principles were adopted by the UN and published as the *Guidelines for the Long-term Sustainability of Outer Space Activities*.

The UN *Guidelines for the Long-term Sustainability of Outer Space Activities* [152] define sustainability in the space industry as:

> the ability to maintain the conduct of space activities indefinitely into the future in a manner that realizes the objectives of equitable access to the benefits of the exploration and use of outer space for peaceful purposes, in order to meet the needs of the present generations while preserving the outer space environment for future generations.

Some additional related selected quotes from the UN guidelines are included below:

> "Space activities are essential tools for realizing the achievement of the Sustainable Development Goals"
>
> [Guideline A.2] Promote regulations and policies that support the idea of minimizing the impacts of human activities on Earth as well as on the outer space environment. They are encouraged to plan their activities based on the Sustainable Development Goals, their main national requirements and international considerations for the sustainability of space and the Earth.

[Guideline A.4] Spacecraft and launch vehicle orbital stages that have terminated their operational phases in orbits that pass through the low Earth orbit (LEO) region should be removed from orbit in a controlled fashion. If this is not possible, they should be disposed of in orbits that avoid their long-term presence in the LEO region.

The UN is not the only organization that has promoted sustainability in the space industry. The Secure World Foundation describes sustainability in the space sector as "Ensuring that all humanity can continue to use outer space for peaceful purposes and socioeconomic benefit now and in the long term" [153]. The UN and Secure World Foundation definitions can be augmented in concept by leveraging work from the sustainability nonprofit The Natural Step. The Natural Step, not focused on space specifically, defines the "four system conditions" that are needed to "accelerate the transition to a sustainable society" [154]. The four conditions are recognized aspects of the natural world that would be stable if not for human activity. They are used to define The Four Sustainability Principles listed below:

To become a sustainable society, we must eliminate our contributions to...

1   the *systematic increase* of concentrations of substances extracted from the Earth's crust (e.g., heavy metals and fossil fuels)
2   the *systematic increase* of concentrations of substances produced by society (e.g., plastics, dioxins, PCBs and DDT)
3   the *systematic* physical degradation of nature and natural processes (e.g., overharvesting forests, destroying habitat and overfishing); and
4   conditions that *systematically* undermine people's capacity to meet their basic human needs (e.g., unsafe working conditions and not enough pay to live on).

The Four Sustainability Principles are common themes found in sustainability literature. They are particularly useful in the consideration of the space industry as each represents either a thing to avoid somehow (i.e., do no harm) or a thing that the space industry is particularly suited to support improvements on (i.e., proactive solutions).

An account of sustainability for the space industry has been described from four perspectives: the Bruntland report, the UN, the Secure World Foundation, and The Natural Step. In truth, there are multiple ways to frame sustainability in the space industry. In this book, the concept is organized as described in the box below. This perspective is founded on the Bruntland report definition and specifies areas of focus that reflect concepts found in the UN guidance, the Secure World Foundation's definition, and the Natural Step principles.

Sustainable activities in the space industry are those that meet the needs of the present without compromising the needs of the future. Sustainability in the space industry is considered in three categories:

1   The sustainability of space industry activities with respect to impacts on the social, environmental, and economic systems on Earth.
2   The sustainability of space industry activities with respect to impacts on the social, environmental, and economic systems in space.
3   Sustainability solutions for humanity provided by the space industry.

The "needs of the present" that space systems can address can be divided into categories corresponding to items 1–3 in the definition above. Items 1–3 each represent a distinctive concept involving distinctive considerations and actions. Item 1 is most familiar to existing sustainability initiatives involving impacts from all industries on Earth systems. Item 1 largely falls into the category of do no harm responsibilities for the space industry. Item 2 is conceptually the same as item 1 but in the less familiar context of outer space. Notably, the "social, environmental, and economic" systems that are alluded to may be significantly less developed if not nonexistent in many locations in space. The challenges and mitigations related to item 2 are inherently different in nature compared to item 1. Item 2 falls into the category of a do no harm responsibility, but also the potential for commercial proactive solutions exists. Item 3 is entirely framed around opportunities for providing proactive sustainability solutions for humanity using space systems. Items 1–3 are discussed at length in the following sections.

Sustainability of Space Industry Activities on Earth

Manufacturing and launching space hardware are energy- and resource-intensive activities. Even given the relatively low production volume of space hardware, highly publicized unique capabilities, and broad public support, the space industry must create value in ways that are sustainable environmentally, socially, and economically. This is a prerequisite for maximizing value creation and is reflected as such by the harmony requirement in the stakeholder intrinsic value criteria. This section is focused on the environmental impacts of the space industry on Earth. Discussion on social and economic impacts is included later in the section on sustainability solutions for humanity supported by the space industry.

Activities in outer space, despite appearances, are not severed from impacts on Earth systems. The amount of energy required to create and operate space systems is immense. It's not just the fuel needed for rockets; it's potentially thousands of people working for years on design, construction, and testing of a space system. It's energy going into everything from employees driving to work every day, to power and resources used for office equipment, to operating facilities for manufacturing. Impacts also include heavy industry construction of not just the spacecraft itself but numerous prototypes, test articles, and processing facilities. Operation of a spacecraft once in space often involves support from a team of personnel and other resources for the duration of the mission. An activity in outer space, human-tended or not, is founded entirely on an energy-intensive, Earthbound value chain that enables it. Environmental impacts on Earth from the space industry value chain frame do no harm responsibilities necessary to support harmony in the stakeholder intrinsic value criteria.

Space Hardware Production Environmental Impacts: An Overview

Any product, especially complex and highly specialized space hardware, has a life cycle full of varied environmental impacts to consider. Environmental impacts are not limited to obvious instances such as those associated with use (e.g., emissions from a launch) or eventual disposal. The true footprint of a product on the environment starts with harvest of raw materials. This is followed by material processing impacts such as use of energy, production and disposal of any ancillary industrial chemicals needed, emissions or waste involved in the extraction process, and ecosystem destruction at the extraction site. And this is only the beginning. Following raw material extraction and processing, there are many more manufacturing, use, and disposal processes involved in the overall life cycle of a product.

Consider a hypothetical spacecraft part of reasonable complexity such as a rocket cargo fairing. This hypothetical fairing is made from a composite sandwich consisting of carbon fiber-reinforced polymer facesheets adhesively bonded to an aluminum honeycomb core. Just manufacturing aluminum sheet for the core material has a complex and negative impact on the environment. Add to this consideration the (1) production of the other components in the fairing panel such as carbon fibers, polymer matrix material, and adhesive and (2) assembly and cure of the structure. All of these processes require energy and produce waste of some kind. All require specialized individual supply chains of input materials and processing chemicals that may not even be physical components of the fairing in the end.

In addition to the physical materials and industrial processing steps, there are environmental impacts associated with the facilities needed to perform the manufacturing. Ignoring the one-time cost and impacts of constructing the facility, the facility has to be maintained, powered, and operated. A far-reaching array of personnel are required as well to design and engineer the part before production can even start. Impacts related to design and engineering come from office work and travel which are not insignificant and may stretch out across years prior to the manufacturing start.

If R&D is involved, as it is for many space systems, it can be that test and prototype hardware is produced over months or years, compounding further the total environmental impact of the final flight hardware. In fact, most space hardware, especially in human-rated systems, is required by industry standards to undergo a qualification test campaign and thorough nondestructive inspection. These activities are time-consuming and involve production of dedicated ancillary hardware like test fixturing and test assemblies that also have their own environmental impacts. And this is all just to *produce* the part. Any true assessment of environmental impact must also include operation and disposal phases of the part's life cycle. Think back to Chapter 2 on circular economy principles and value management. It may become more evident with this composite fairing example how significant value recovery and hardware reuse at the end of product life may be in terms of avoiding a repeat of all of the complexity involved in production (albeit certain activities may be one-time only such as R&D and design).

The sum of all of these activities across all space systems and all space companies is what ultimately defines the impact on the planet of the space industry. Compared to other industries, space hardware is particularly energy-intensive to produce due to demanding safety and performance requirements. Understanding the environmental impact of even just one part is complicated. However, understanding the environmental impact of an entire space system is required when considering the harmony criteria in a stakeholder intrinsic value assessment. It is both unrealistic and unreasonable to think that business managers will have the technical expertise to go into the level of detail alluded to in this example to determine the precise nature of a product's environmental impact. Furthermore, it may be apparent that there is seemingly no end to how far one could go in characterizing indirect impacts from a value chain. This kind of stakeholder insight is needed though in a harmony assessment and is key in devising and implementing circular economy approaches to value creation. What can be done to understand environmental impacts in a way that is quantifiable? If stakeholder intrinsic value creation is to be adopted in the space industry, there must be a practical solution to this challenge.

Life Cycle Assessment Overview

One solution to the challenge of understanding product environmental impacts is use of a Life Cycle Assessment (LCA). The LCA methodology was developed by Giudice et al. in 2006 as a way to measure environmental impacts of a product from cradle to grave [155]. An LCA attempts to understand and quantify exactly the kinds of minute far-reaching details discussed in the composite fairing example. LCA information and procedures are described in ISO 14040 [156] and ISO 14044 [157]. These standards describe an LCA as a "compilation and evaluation of the inputs, outputs and the potential environmental impacts of a product system throughout its life cycle." The utility of an LCA is described in ISO 14040 as identifying opportunities to improve the environmental performance of products and informing decision-makers for the purpose of strategic planning, priority setting, or process design. Put differently, the utility of an LCA is to inform stakeholders about environmental impacts related to a given transaction or business decision. In doing so, this can inform on the degree of harmony with the environment in a stakeholder intrinsic value creation assessment and illuminate specific areas where improvements are desirable.

ISO 14040 states that an "LCA considers the entire life cycle of a product, from raw material extraction and acquisition, through energy and material production and manufacturing, to use and end of life treatment and final disposal." An LCA may be performed on a physical product, but also may be applied to a service, software, processed material, or even an entire mission in space. In each case, the impacts from all material and energy input streams are summed using common units to create a total score in various categories of environmental impact. For example, if a satellite thruster assembly requires 5 kg of titanium to manufacture, all of the minerals, chemicals, and energy requirements to extract, refine, machine, and assemble 5 kg of titanium are tabulated. This tabulation is repeated until all impacts from all other materials needed for the complete thruster assembly are captured.

Burden-shifting can be revealed using an LCA as well. Burden-shifting is when an environmental mitigation is undertaken that has the appearance of improvement, but in reality the "mitigation" just moves the negative impact somewhere else unseen. Burden-shifting may encompass transfer of impacts from one part of the life cycle to another, one societal generation to another, or one geographic region of the world to another. An LCA can quantify these types of design trades such that they can be weighed against one another.

Perhaps the greatest limitation of an LCA is that it is a relative tool. LCA results are always relative to the functional unit. The functional unit is defined for the product as a descriptor of its performance or of what is being studied. It is used to provide reference to input and output data as well. What this means is that a quantified impact from an LCA says nothing about whether or not that impact is acceptable to society or to a stakeholder group. An LCA can quantify impacts well and it can capture a great deal of detail and supporting data in this quantification, but it does not say if it is "ok" and it does not comment on the degree to which sustainability is supported. It is up to the interpreters of the study to make general overall conclusions.

Even with this limitation, an LCA may be the only practical means of comparing the environmental impacts of multiple value creation schemes under consideration in a stakeholder intrinsic value assessment. It also offers a means by which to iteratively design a value chain that is based on circular economy principles. A value flow map and an LCA are complementary tools that may be instrumental in a stakeholder intrinsic value assessment.

Life Cycle Assessments in the Space Industry

While the LCA concept is applied globally across many industries, the European Space Agency (ESA) leads the world in LCA expertise specifically for space systems. A literature review published in 2020 on LCAs in the space industry reveals that 87% of space LCA publications to date were based out of Europe [158]. Also, 78% of these publications are associated with ESA and most were released after 2015. Recent focus in this area is no doubt in part a result of ramping up activity and continued growth in the space economy. Additionally, EU environmental regulations play a role. Regulations that most affect the space industry applicable across all member states include the Restriction of Hazardous Substances Directive (RoHS), adopted in 2003, and Registration, Evaluation, Authorisation and Restriction of Chemicals (REACH), adopted in 2006. In each of these cases, the regulations broadly support sustainability goals across the EU and are not written exclusively for the space industry, but in practice, they affect many of the products and industrial processes needed for space hardware. One of the main tools used in reaching compliance with these regulations is use of LCAs.

LCA work in the space sector began at ESA in 2009 as part of the Ecosat project which involved an LCA to study impacts of satellite design, production, launch, and operation. Later in 2011, LCAs were performed on the Vega and Ariane 5 launchers. These studies led to an LCA performed on Ariane 6 early in the design phase, which represented the first instance where an LCA was used to help guide the design of a space vehicle [159]. Momentum continued and ESA formed the Clean Space Initiative in 2012 focusing on four areas: ecodesign, green technologies, debris mitigation, and debris remediation. This effort, and the ecodesign portion in particular, ultimately produced ESA's LCA handbook titled *Space System Life Cycle Assessment (LCA) Guidelines* which was released in 2016.

The ESA LCA handbook describes how to correctly perform an LCA in the space sector while adhering to LCA standards ISO 14040 and ISO 14044. Unique factors in the space industry to consider in an LCA include low production volumes, direct emissions into the stratosphere, testing, long development and R&D phases, specialized materials and processes for which environmental impact data is unknown, high altitude mass releases (such as orbital propulsion maneuver exhaust mixing back into the atmosphere), atomic oxygen corrosion material release, and end-of-life reentry burning and ablation emissions [160].

Part of ESA's work in LCAs for space has necessarily involved development of a Life Cycle Inventory (LCI) database that includes LCA material and energy input data on propellants, materials, spacecraft components, and manufacturing processes specific to the space industry. This particular contribution to the field from ESA is considerable, as space hardware can be highly specialized and low production volume in nature resulting in widely unavailable or unknown data related to associated environmental impacts. Also, manufacturing supply chains in the space industry can be complex, geographically diverse, and proprietary. All of these factors make collection of LCI data for space applications potentially difficult and the ESA database is an attempt to address this challenge. Finally, ESA has created a design tool, SPACE OPERA,[1] which can be used to perform an LCA and integrate this activity early in space product design. This is particularly advantageous as an LCA has the greatest ability to affect real change or direction of a product early in its design process [161].

The environmental impact categories in the space industry mostly do not differ from other industries. Common impact categories to include in a space LCA are carbon footprint (i.e., climate change), ozone depletion, human toxicity, abiotic resource depletion, and water ecotoxicity. The carbon footprint category is the most encompassing and, in some cases, may be used as the only impact category considered and treated as a generalized indication of overall environmental impact.

The following sections provide detail on the environmental impacts of the space industry. The content is informed largely by numerous space industry LCAs and other government-funded studies. This summary may help in understanding further the type of insight stakeholders can gain from use of LCAs in the space industry and how this information can be applied to deliberations related to maximization of stakeholder intrinsic value creation. Each environmental impact described may be viewed as an opportunity for increasing stakeholder intrinsic value creation of a preexisting activity if it is addressed. Mitigation in the areas described also should be considered a do no harm responsibility in support of sustainability (i.e., harmony). The nature and extent of mitigations are up to company managers and stakeholders to formulate.

Environmental Impacts from the Space Industry

The exhaust cloud during a rocket launch is a visually dominant feature of the event. At first glance to an uninformed observer, the massive exhaust plume may appear to be the primary negative impact on the environment from a launch vehicle. What is not visually apparent during a launch though are the years of complex and energy-intensive design, manufacturing, and certification work that went into the production of the rocket and its payload. These "hidden" impacts on the environment far outweigh those of emissions from the launch itself. Environmental impacts of the space industry are found in several categories: launch emissions, propellant production, hardware manufacturing, and ground services and infrastructure. Each of these categories is discussed in the following sections.

Rocket Launch Greenhouse Gas Emissions

Overall, the impacts on the atmosphere collectively from space launches are small. Regarding that huge cloud of smoke seen during a launch, a large part of it is nothing more than steam, that is, water. A massive deluge of water is poured onto the launch pad as the engines are ignited in order to suppress sound and smoke. Additionally, water is one of the exhaust components from numerous different types of rocket propulsion systems. The steam component of the giant smoke cloud is innocuous to the environment.

Regarding greenhouse gas emissions of space launches, the overall annual contribution relative to other industries is all but negligible. In 2013, total global rocket launch carbon dioxide emissions amounted to several kilotons, whereas annually aircraft emit collectively almost one million kilotons. Even the contribution from all aircraft combined is only 2–3% of total worldwide emissions from all sources [162–165]. The International Space University (ISU) published a report in 2010 titled *ecoSpace: Initiatives for Environmentally Sustainable Launch Activities*, concluding that "If the current number of space launches per year remains stable, worldwide launch activities are not expected to have a significant impact on global pollution levels" [166]. Global launch rates currently are at a level sufficiently similar to those of 2010 that the same conclusion stands. However, if significantly increased launch rates are realized in the future, it may be one day that the impacts are not so small. In this scenario, ozone destruction would be the primary concern, not greenhouse gas emissions.

Rocket Launch Ozone Layer Destruction

Destruction of the ozone layer constitutes the biggest environmental impact in the atmosphere from rocket launch emissions. The ozone layer resides in the stratosphere at approximately 20–30 km above Earth's surface and is a key component in shielding the planet from harmful ultraviolet rays and other radiation. Ozone layer destruction and mitigation are familiar issues for the world. Recovering from unsustainable and potentially ultimately disastrous levels of ozone depletion is considered one of the greatest success stories in environmental protection. Rules agreed to in the Montreal Protocol in 1987 established limits and guidelines for use of ozone-depleting substances such as chlorofluorocarbons. There are no rules in the Montreal Protocol, however, related to rocket launch emissions.

Ozone is composed of a rare molecular form of oxygen that consists of three atoms rather than the usual two. Ozone depletion occurs when trace radical molecules, such as nitrogen oxides, hydroxyl, chlorine oxides, and aluminum oxides are present to react with and crack apart ozone molecules. The overall degree of ozone depletion from a rocket launch depends heavily on the type of rocket fuel used. Cryogenic propulsion, especially the liquid hydrogen-oxygen combination (hydrolox), represents the lowest impact choice relative to ozone depletion. In the case of hydrolox, the exhaust is composed of water, oxygen, and trace amounts of nitrogen oxides. A cryogenic-fueled rocket that uses other fuel components with liquid oxygen such as kerosene (kerolox) or methane (methalox) is worse in terms of harmful emissions than using hydrogen as more carbon dioxide and soot are produced, but still largely innocuous to ozone. None of these cryogenic fuel combinations are nearly as harmful to the ozone layer as solid rocket fuel.

Solid rocket exhaust is the biggest contributor by far from rockets to ozone depletion. This occurs through deposition of radical aluminum, aluminum oxide, and chlorine molecules emitted in the exhaust [167]. Estimates have been made that a single trace radical molecule can potentially break down on the order of 10,000 ozone molecules in a matter of minutes or hours [168]. Furthermore, rocket launches are currently the only direct source of human-caused non-native compounds in the stratosphere and these compounds can accumulate lasting years [169]. A solid fuel rocket quite literally punches a hole in the ozone layer as it passes through, though this hole will naturally close and repair given enough time [168].

If limiting a propulsion system only to cryogenic fuels is not an option and solid boosters must be used to achieve design and performance requirements, system architecture may be designed to mitigate impacts on the ozone layer such that only the least harmful propulsion types, such as cryogenic, are used in flight phases through the stratosphere. In this concept, other more harmful types of fuels, such as solid fuel, are restricted for use only in lower altitudes or in outer space where ozone depletion cannot occur [169].

At recent launch rates, on the order of 100–150 orbital launches per year, the destruction of ozone from rocket exhaust is sustainable in that natural regeneration outpaces human-caused depletion. NASA, the US Air Force, and others in the past have studied this phenomenon. The results of these studies generally conclude that the net effect on the ozone layer from existing launch rates is all but negligible, something on the order of less than 0.1% of depletion per year depending on the source [162, 170–172]. More recently, The World Meteorological Organization (WMO) stated in a 2018 report on ozone depletion that "Rocket launches presently have a small effect on total stratospheric ozone depletion (much less than 0.1%)" [173]. The WMO report also recommends "periodic assessments," given the growing nature of the space industry. 0.1% of ozone depletion per year is a level that can be naturally replenished and so, for now, this is a low concern.

Other Atmospheric Impacts

Some other less-understood phenomena in the stratosphere resulting from rocket launches include radiative effects and post-combustion formation of nitrogen oxides. Injecting exhaust compounds into the stratosphere can alter radiative properties by the presence of particulates, including frozen water vapor, frozen carbon dioxide, and soot. Soot particulates may linger in the stratosphere for years [172]. When present, particulates increase solar reflection, thereby heating the stratosphere, which speeds up ozone depletion reactions and cools the Earth. The overall phenomena resulting from large deposits of particulates in the stratosphere is poorly quantified today and requires more research.

Post-combustion reactions also can affect the atmosphere. All types of rocket propulsion, even hydrolox, produce some small amounts of hydroxyl which subsequently can react with nitrogen in the air and produce small amounts of nitrogen oxide. Nitrogen oxides are known contributors to smog, acid rain, and ozone depletion.[2] One approach for ozone damage mitigation is to include afterburning suppressants, that is, additives that reduce continued combustion of fuel beyond the rocket combustion chamber. Post-combustion formation of nitrogen oxides and radiative effects, while needing more study, are thought to result in far less damage to ozone than from direct radical molecule deposits from solid rocket boosters.

Atmospheric Impacts from Launches: In Summary

Greenhouse gas emissions from rocket launches are negligible compared to total emissions from all sources. Rocket emissions do include some greenhouse gasses, but overall, there is little concern with launches contributing to climate change. If there is any aspect of rocket launch emissions to hold concern over, it is their ability to break down ozone in the stratosphere. At modern global launch rates on the order of 100–150 launches per year, ozone degradation from rocket emissions does not outpace the natural rate of repair. This is not a problem that needs to be solved today, but it is a problem that needs to be understood today so that it does not become one to solve later.

The fact is that launch rates are increasing and this should be considered a possible *eventual* limiting factor in the space economy. If launch rates should increase by a factor of 100 or more, which is exactly the goal of many well-intending ventures in the industry, there may be reason for concern related to ozone destruction. Point-to-point transportation and tourism are both areas of the space industry that could potentially see launch rates this high someday. In this scenario, mitigating factors such as fuel type, fuel type usage by altitude, afterburning suppressants, rocket efficiency, and more accurate ozone depletion modeling tools will become instrumental in maximizing sustainable access to space.

As the launch industry scales up in the future, potentially approaching levels of concern relative to ozone destruction, some means of avoiding externalization of these impacts in an equitable manner will need to be established. As many nations have aspirations to increase their activities in space, this effort will need to involve international collaboration. For now, there are two achievable actions that can be taken to promote stakeholder intrinsic value creation by avoiding a problem in the future related to ozone destruction from rocket launches:

*   Avoiding development of new products and business models that will depend on utilization of solid rocket boosters for mass-market launch rates
*   Continuing research and development related to simulation tools for the effects of rocket emissions on the ozone layer

Propellant Environmental Impacts: Launch Site, Toxicity, and Production

Environmental impacts related to rocket propulsion extend beyond emissions in the atmosphere. The most common types of propellants used in launches are hydrolox, methalox, kerolox, various hydrazine combinations, and solid fuel. Pollutants at a launch site can include hydrochloric acid, nitrogen dioxide, hydrazine, and aluminum oxide depending on the fuel type. All of these compounds are toxic; however, the distribution of these pollutants in the air and on the ground is usually limited to the immediate launch vicinity (<2 km). Beyond 8 km, impacts are found to be nonsignificant [174]. Within the launch vicinity, however, toxic propellant remnants from repeated launches can be well above the safe concentration for life [175]. In cases where there is a launch failure, potentially hundreds of tons of rocket fuel and oxidizer are deposited onto the soil and water nearby all at once. Even in successful launches, one study estimates that approximately 9% of propellant remains unused in dropped rocket stages that fall back to the surface [175]. Mitigations for environmental impacts of launches include selection of remote launch site locations, monitoring local contamination, and use of "greener" propellants.

Combustion of cryogenic fuel combinations (hydrolox, methalox, kerolox) generally has the smallest impact on the environment compared to alternatives. In certain applications though, cryogenic fuel combinations are impractical such as military vehicles or small reaction control system thrusters for in-space maneuvering. Hydrazine and numerous hydrazine derivatives are common fuels for these applications as they are more stable and longer-lasting. All fuels in the hydrazine family are highly toxic to humans and ecosystems though. To ensure safety in production, handling, and storage, there is a high cost associated with the use of hydrazine compared to other fuels. There are numerous green monopropellant alternatives to hydrazine, some of which offer higher performance and lower toxicity. As of 2022, green monopropellants have yet to catch on in a large scale in the space industry [176, 177].

Development and adoption of green fuel alternatives to hydrazine is an area deserving continued research and innovation. Typically, green propellant R&D is aimed specifically at reducing toxicity but not necessarily at improving sustainability more broadly. The greatest impact on the environment associated with rocket propulsion comes not from toxicity but as a result of the energy required for synthesis of the fuel. Part of the reason for this is that rocket propellants have high purity requirements and so the synthesis process is particularly demanding [178]. And this applies not just to toxic fuels like hydrazine. While cryogenic propulsion like hydrolox, methalox, and kerolox are green choices in terms of combustion emissions, negative environmental impacts from liquid fuel and oxidizer synthesis do exist [178]. Specifically, the biggest categories of environmental impact from cryogenic fuel production are greenhouse gas emissions and toxicity.[3] Solid rocket fuel has an order of magnitude of higher environmental impact over-all compared to cryogenic fuels. Environmental impacts associated with solid rocket fuel production include freshwater eutrophication, fossil fuel depletion, and climate change [179]. The fact is that all types of rocket propellants have negative environmental impacts associated with their synthesis, and so improvements in this area will result in increased stakeholder intrinsic value.

Opportunities for increased stakeholder intrinsic value of space systems related to mitigation of negative environmental impacts of rocket propellant include:

- Monitoring environmental impacts at launch sites
- Development of nontoxic alternatives to hydrazine
- Increasing efficiency in cryogenic fuel and oxidizer production
- Use of cryogenic propulsion systems such as hydrolox, methalox, or kerolox as much as possible

Hardware Manufacturing

As with propellant, spacecraft hardware manufacturing also has its own distinctive environmental impacts. Because spacecraft do not have long operational periods, the impacts of hardware production are high in proportion to impacts from operation. Furthermore, space systems tend to have high performance and safety requirements. This drives the use of advanced materials such as polymer composites or exotic metallic alloys for their specialized properties related to mass, strength, corrosion resistance, toughness, thermal behavior, etc. The manufacturing of advanced materials takes more energy and involves greater environmental impact than lower-performing alternatives that are more common in other industries.

Of several common material types used in spacecraft structures, production of steel has the lowest environmental impact, followed in order by aluminum, titanium, and carbon fiber-reinforced polymer composites. Production of carbon fiber composites is reported to have double the environmental impact of aluminum and ten times the impact of steel. In all cases, human toxicity can be the greatest environmental impact with fossil fuel depletion and climate change also notable contributors [179]. Table 2.1 in Chapter 2 provides additional insight on energy costs of different materials. Deliberate choice of lower-performing, less energy-intensive materials in a product design (if performance requirements allow) is one means by which to increase stakeholder intrinsic value creation.

Another promising means to increase stakeholder intrinsic value related to hardware production is adoption of additive manufacturing (AM). Environmental benefits of increased use of AM are mainly related to (1) design optimization and (2) reduced time, energy, and material input needed to produce a part. The overhead and energy required to produce an equivalent product using traditional manufacturing techniques can be much greater depending on the application. AM technology has opened up access to space hardware production to more entrepreneurs and start-ups than ever before. No longer is this aspect of the industry limited to giant aerospace corporations with huge manufacturing facilities. The challenge associated with AM is achieving consistent quality control in hardware production.

AM is mostly utilized for homogenous metallic and polymer materials and has limited applications currently for composites. Composites nonetheless are a common material choice in aerospace structures. Carbon fiber composites are energy-intensive to produce and, when used in a spacecraft, tend to have a negative effect on environmental impacts. The opposite is true in aircraft applications. Use of advanced carbon fiber-reinforced composites in a Boeing 787 fleet is predicted to result in an overall lifetime reduction of carbon dioxide of 14–15%. This prediction comes in spite of the increased fossil fuel and energy costs for the production of composite materials compared to metal. The relative carbon dioxide reduction, in this case, is due to mass savings and the associated decreased fuel use over the lifetime of the aircraft [180]. Spacecraft have a much shorter lifetime than commercial aircraft involving far fewer flights (often just one flight), so lifetime fuel efficiency savings due to reduced mass do not have the same benefit.

Additionally, it is so energetically demanding to launch to orbit, typically any structural mass savings are consumed by additional cargo capacity in order to get as much value as possible out of each launch. In theory, a lighter spacecraft would allow a heavier payload, a payload with greater capabilities and greater capacity to create value. Careful consideration by stakeholders using tools like a value flow map and an LCA can help in the assessment of true net gain from lightweighting a spacecraft at the expense of greater environmental impacts during production. Other vehicle architectural design features such as reusability, the number of stages, and the number and size of engines have a much greater influence on reducing environmental impact than use of advanced lightweight materials [181].

Of all of the options, the best way to reduce environmental impacts from hardware manufacturing, by far, is to implement as much reusability as possible in the spacecraft [181]. In some ways, this is obvious, as a spacecraft that is not reusable must be reproduced for every mission, thereby repeating the associated environmental costs each time. If reuse is not an option for some reason, designing for longevity and life extension features like servicing, maintainability, reinspection, upgrades, and reconfigurability are also ways to reduce environmental impacts.

Opportunities for increased stakeholder intrinsic value creation related to space hardware manufacturing include:

- Economic use of material with production techniques like AM
- Use of lower-performing, less energy-intensive materials
- Designing spacecraft to be reusable, serviceable, or maintainable

Ground Services and Infrastructure

The biggest source of environmental impacts from the space industry is ground services and infrastructure. These impacts eclipse all of those discussed so far. As expensive and complex as space systems are, R&D, design, and qualification work on the ground last for years and, put together, form the element of a mission with the greatest environmental impact. The launch and operation phases of a spacecraft life also often involve use of complex ground infrastructure systems like mission control and data processing. Simply put, it is the net number of labor hours in a project that can be the dominant driver of most environmental impact categories [158, 182].

Consider a hypothetical example, the first launch of a new rocket. The rocket has impacts already discussed related to hardware and propellant production. And while the launch event itself also has environmental impacts such as ozone depletion and deposition of toxic compounds in the launch vicinity, the rocket construction and launch were preceded by something on the order of hundreds or thousands of people working for years to design, certify, and build the rocket. Additionally, to support the launch and operation, there is needed ground infrastructure, including things like communication systems, mission control, propellant facilities, and data processing [159]. All of these types of ground support services have impacts mainly on climate change due to use of energy for facilities.

A released draft version of the environmental assessment report for the SpaceX Starship/Super Heavy rocket activities in Boca Chica, Texas, describes that the launch facility's natural gas power plant is expected to create emissions *two orders of magnitude* greater than the emissions from rockets at the site [183]. This is for an initial orbital launch rate of five per year and notably is for a rocket that only uses methalox propulsion which is a relatively clean fuel combination compared to some alternatives. This example is given to highlight again the disparity in environmental impacts between ground activities and the launch itself.

Of these activities, testing and R&D contribute notably to overall environmental impact. R&D can last for years. Testing can also be long in duration, require numerous duplications of hardware builds, take place in energy-intensive facilities, occur multiple times on a part, and can be demanding in terms of needed time and personnel to oversee the test and interpret results. Replacing tests with new simulation tools is one means by which to reduce the environmental impacts of this phase of a project.

Another area of high potential for reducing the overall environmental impact of a space system is to ensure efficient project management. Just like hardware and system design, project management of large space projects can be extremely challenging and complex. Optimization in this area saves time and resources on a large scale spanning years of a project. This can be achieved through things like running a lean project organization, intelligent requirements, careful contract planning early in a project, fixed-cost contracts, risk management, and stakeholder management. Opportunities discussed in this section for increased stakeholder intrinsic value related to ground services and infrastructure are summarized below:

- Efficient ground infrastructure systems
- Simulation tools to reduce the amount of required testing
- Efficient programs for R&D and testing
- Efficient project management

Is Space the Best Approach?

Planned value creation from space systems should always be placed in competition with other means to obtain similar value. An LCA is one tool that can be used to assess relative impacts of space versus other means to achieve a specific goal. Given the potential cost and complexity of a space mission and the associated environmental impacts, any alternative means by which the same value could be created should be entertained by managers and other stakeholders.

For example, consider a remote sensing mission where the goal is to collect Earth imagery data related to climate trends. Should this goal necessarily be accomplished using space assets versus aircraft? In this example, where data collection is global and periodic in nature, use of satellites is better for numerous reasons. Collection of continuous global data from aircraft would require constantly flying hundreds of aircraft all over the world. This would occur over changing weather conditions, different altitudes, and involve "stitching together" many data sets of varying quality. Use of aircraft would also involve all of the associated costs and environmental impacts of operating a fleet over a long period of time. On the other hand, satellites can easily observe global environmental phenomena all at once. In this example, the aircraft option would result in lower quality data and a much more energy-intensive process to collect it compared to a single satellite flying in orbit. The aircraft approach would result in less stakeholder intrinsic value potentially due to reduced sustainability, profitability, and value creation.

This is not to say that all assessments would turn out this way. When some need or demand from society is identified and space is considered as a possible solution, Durrieu and Nelson ask the question: "given a full accounting of environmental costs associated with space launches, are satellites necessarily the best way to sustain the flow of measurements needed to monitor the status of Earth's environment?" [174]. In other words, do satellites always offer the solution with the smallest relative environmental impact to achieve the data collection goal? Durrieu and Nelson conclude that long-term airborne infrastructure may have a lower environmental impact overall than the use of satellites only for certain limited scope remote sensing missions.

Sustainability of Space Industry Activities on Earth: Summary

The main points from this section on environmental impacts of the space industry on Earth are summarized below. Each of the points listed can be considered an opportunity for increasing stakeholder intrinsic value in the space industry if it is addressed. From a different perspective, each item also corresponds to a do no harm responsibility:

- Negative impacts on the atmosphere from rocket launches are currently low, but there may be cause for concern if a mass launch market emerges.
- Organizations involved in realization of a mass launch market should plan for an overall limit in launches or for additional technological mitigations that minimize ozone damage. This will involve international collaboration of some sort.
- When it comes to emissions of propellant types, solid propellant has the highest environmental impact and hydrolox has the lowest. Methalox and kerolox also have significantly lower impacts than solid propellant.
- Hydrazine is highly toxic and green propellant alternatives are desirable for reducing environmental impact and ground handling costs.
- The primary environmental impact from propellant derives not from combusting in the atmosphere but rather from the synthesis process.
- Use of AM is one means to minimize material use while also potentially saving time and energy on manufacturing overall.
- Production of advanced aerospace materials has a significantly higher environmental impact compared to lower-performing materials.
- Lightweighting a spacecraft structure using advanced materials may have limited benefit in terms of helping reduce overall environmental impact.
- Reuse is the most effective means by which to minimize environmental impacts from hardware manufacturing.
- Ground support can be the dominant source of environmental impacts overall for a space system. Influential areas for efficiency improvements include program management, R&D, test campaigns, operational support, and ground infrastructure.
- Space systems are not always the most efficient means to solve a given remote sensing problem.

Sustainability of Space Industry Activities in Orbit

The previous section discusses the need for sustainability relative to environmental impacts of the space industry on Earth, but unique sustainability challenges exist in orbit as well. The space industry is distinctive, in that it is the only industry that can operate physically outside of Earth's biosphere. The traditional lens on sustainability is different, in that off-planet there is no risk of damaging Earth's environment or of direct harm to humans.

Does it matter then if the natural environment in space is contaminated or degraded? Can the void of outer space be treated as a truly infinite waste sink? Well, maybe (more on this in Chapter 7), but Earth's orbit cannot be treated as an infinite waste sink and that is where humanity currently derives most of its value from space systems. An increasingly crowded orbital environment, both in terms of physical objects and in terms of utilization of radio frequencies, threatens the sustainability of space operations. Sustainability in orbit involves adopting a do no harm approach; however, there also are opportunities for space systems to create stakeholder intrinsic value directly through applied sustainability solutions.

More Spacecraft Than Ever

Orbital space today contains more spacecraft than ever before. Before examining what implications this has on sustainability, it is useful to understand why this is true and what can be expected going forward. The cost to build, launch, and operate a satellite used to range in the hundreds of millions of dollars. The satellite industry has now passed an inflection point where these costs are within the means of many more organizations than just wealthy governments. The cost of building a satellite is now as low as $7,500 using a CubeSat KitTM offered by Pumpkin, Inc., a pioneer in the small satellite revolution [184]. The reduction in cost of producing satellites has come about through continued advances in miniaturized electronics enabling an entire satellite to be no larger than a 10 cm × 10 cm × 10 cm cube. These low costs have made small satellites available for research by many new users in academia, industry, and governments.

Reduced costs of satellites are a factor in the increasing number of spacecraft in orbit, but launch cost is by far the majority of the overall cost of a satellite mission. Launch of a satellite using a rideshare service is now accessible to anyone with $1 million,[4] which is a lot for the average person but not a lot for thousands of companies and other types of organizations around the world. The reduction in cost of launches has come about through things like rocket reusability, ridesharing, small launchers, and increased market competition. The cost of launching a payload into low Earth orbit is as low as $1,500/kg using a SpaceX Falcon Heavy rocket [185]. This constitutes a price reduction per kilogram compared to using legacy rockets in the range of a factor of four and higher depending on the rocket being compared. Additionally, due to the reusability of modern rockets, the price reduction is also accompanied by a reduction in resource demand and environmental impacts. All this while increasing opportunities for value creation in space and maintaining a profitable business model. Note that this is a prime example of the circular economy principles discussed in Chapter 2 at work.

Utilizing ridesharing for small payloads is currently the cheapest way to launch mass into orbit. Another option is use of small launchers. A small launcher has a dedicated payload on the order of hundreds or a few thousand kilograms in mass. While the total cost for a single small launch is an order of magnitude less than the total cost of a heavy-lift rocket, the price per kilogram tends to be higher. However, as small launch providers will point out, price per kilogram is not everything. Flexibility in scheduling, location, and specific customer needs all are more possible with a small launch service compared to ridesharing on a heavy-lift rocket. Small launch services are an evolving and competitive market where, at the time of publication of this book in 2022, it remains to be seen what fraction of total orbital launches is desired for smaller rockets. Whatever this market share ends up being, small satellites will continue to offer value creation opportunities through greater diversity in options for affordable access to space.

While the annual number of orbital launches has historically been relatively stable, the number of new objects placed into orbit has grown at an ever-increasing rate. A single SpaceX Falcon 9 launch now can deploy dozens of small satellites. The upcoming SpaceX Starship will be able to deploy hundreds of small satellites in a single launch. In 2015, the total number of operational satellites was approximately 1,400. In 2019, this number increased to 2,400 with remote sensing satellites as the main driver. In 2020 alone, due to multi-payload rockets, there were over 1,000 individual spacecraft launched, the vast majority of which were commercial in nature. This is more than double the number in 2019 and up to an order of magnitude greater than years past [186]. Several companies now have started to build out small satellite constellations consisting of tens of thousands of spacecraft. Even if these numbers are realized, compared to the *total* number of human-made objects in space, actual functioning spacecraft would still be a small percentage.

More spacecraft in orbit have resulted in an increase in value creation from space and this will continue for the foreseeable future. Along with this benefit have come heightened concerns about Earth's orbit becoming more and more crowded. A natural question arises when considering the prospect of the ever-increasing numbers of objects being launched into orbit: is this dramatic increase in value creation occurring in a way that is sustainable or is it a final burst of productivity in the near term that will lead to low Earth orbit being rendered no longer useful for future generations? Continued growth of value creation in space through use of small satellites and other means must occur in ways that do not sacrifice this capability for the future.

Space Debris: The Problem

Currently, there are over 27,000 objects in orbit being tracked by the US Space Surveillance Network (SSN) [187]. Of this total number of objects tracked, 22% are spacecraft (operational and defunct), 12% are spent rocket upper stages, 10% are mission-related objects, and 56% are fragments. And 27,000 is just the number of objects that can be tracked by radar, which means objects less than approximately 10 cm in size are not counted [188].

The vast majority of objects in orbit fall into this undetectable range. They consist of everything from micrometeoroids, to flecks of paint, to bits of metal. There are an estimated several hundred thousand objects sized at 1 cm–10 cm and over 100 million objects sized at 1 mm–1 cm [189]. Overall, there are thought to be 500,000 objects in orbit capable of destroying a spacecraft if a direct hit were to occur [190].

Where did these millions of untrackable objects come from? There have been several satellites destroyed in orbit whose fragments contribute to most of the untrackable debris. In 2007, China destroyed the defunct Fengyun-1c satellite in an anti-satellite missile test creating 3,000 new pieces of trackable debris and an estimated 150,000+ new pieces of untrackable debris. In 2009, an unintentional satellite collision occurred between the Iridium 33 and Cosmos-2251 satellites creating 2,000 new pieces of trackable debris and countless additional untrackable pieces [153]. In 2021, Russia destroyed their Cosmos-1408 satellite in an anti-satellite missile test generating 1,500 new trackable pieces of debris [191]. The United States and India both have also conducted an anti-satellite missile test in low Earth orbit. There have been numerous other debris-producing collisions and explosions dating back to the 1960s. In all cases, debris may take years or decades to fall out of orbit back to Earth. The tiny untrackable debris pieces are the most dangerous. They are traveling ten times the speed of a bullet at orbital velocities of around 27,300 km/h (17,000 mph), so even impact in the right location of a spacecraft from a piece of debris on the order of millimeters in size could be catastrophic.

All of this is to point out the challenge that the space industry is faced with regarding space debris and the sustainability of space systems in orbit. The main concern with space debris, for now, is the onset of a rapid increase in the number of objects through a chain reaction of collisions generating ever more fragments and increasing the chances of another collision each time one occurs. At a certain point, the process is irreversible and orbital space is so cluttered with debris that it is rendered useless or at best highly risky to place any new object in. This is the theory anyway. NASA researcher Donald Kessler described this phenomenon in a 1978 paper and it became known as the Kessler syndrome [192]. Kessler proposes that this process is already underway in a 2012 paper [193]. Kessler reaffirms this position in a 2021 article, postulating that if all launches ceased today, collisions in orbit would continue as would the rise in number of orbital debris objects [194].

What are the actual odds of a collision? The ESA *Space Debris Mitigation Handbook* listed in 1999 that the average time between collisions between a spacecraft and a piece of debris can be as low as 1.5 days for debris objects less than 1 mm in size and beyond 100 years for debris objects 1 cm in size or greater [195]. What this means is that spacecraft must be designed for micrometeoroid impacts as this is expected to occur often. Larger impacts are unlikely but become more probable with time in space and the size of a spacecraft. These odds date back to the late 1990s, so as the amount of debris has increased over the years since then, the odds can be expected to have increased also.

If dangerous debris objects continue to increase in number, significant use of orbital space may eventually be lost. For instance, in May 2021, the International Space Station (ISS) robotic arm was struck by an untrackable piece of space debris creating a hole in the structure [196]. The arm remains functional, but one can imagine more critical locations on the ISS that could have been hit instead. If events like this increase in frequency, stakeholder intrinsic value creation in orbit will become much more challenging, if not impossible. In *Green Swans* [197], sustainability pioneer John Elkington identified space debris as one of humanity's most "wicked problems," where a wicked problem is one that is critical to solve but where a true solution is seemingly impossible. Space debris is listed by Elkington in this category of problems for humanity alongside climate change, obesity, drug resistance diseases, and plastic waste. The loss of value creation in low Earth orbit would constitute an enormous setback for humanity. As this book continues, consider the negative implications if all of the value creation opportunities in space that are discussed turned out to be no longer possible. While a complete solution to the space debris problem is elusive, there are mitigations that can be implemented.

Space Debris: Mitigations

While increasing amounts of space debris threaten the space industry's prospect of perpetual stakeholder intrinsic value creation, this challenge also poses an opportunity. Some companies may choose to define their purpose and business entirely around providing proactive solutions to the space debris challenge. This may involve providing solutions to governments and/ or commercial space system operators. Proactive commercial solutions to space debris challenges stand to create stakeholder intrinsic value by improving sustainability, thereby improving the prospect of continuous value creation in space. Any activity in space, no matter the purpose, must at least passively mitigate the problem of space debris through do no harm measures in order to support harmony.

Avoidance, protection, removal, and prevention are all strategies by which to mitigate the negative repercussions of space debris [9]. The Inter-Agency Space Debris Coordination Committee (IADC) developed space debris mitigation guidelines in 2002 where each of these strategies is addressed. The IADC *Space Debris Mitigation Guidelines* were adopted by the UN-COPUOS in 2007 and now are available for voluntary use [198]. Complying with the IADC guidelines is a means to meet do no harm responsibilities in support of harmony in a stakeholder intrinsic value assessment.

In terms of prevention, one of the major principles of in-orbit sustainability that the IADC guidelines recommend is planned disposal of decommissioned spacecraft. Once a spacecraft or other large piece of debris is removed from orbit, it no longer has the capacity to become involved in a collision incident and produce thousands more undetectable pieces of debris. If a spacecraft is left unattended as clutter at the end of its service life, this represents a cost externality where all other space system operators (and beneficiaries of space systems on Earth) bear the burden.

Active spacecraft disposal involves two options: either maneuver to a "graveyard" orbit out of harm's way or intentionally deorbit and burn up in the atmosphere. How does deorbiting work exactly? All orbits decay, but the duration of this process depends on the altitude. At 600 km, an object's orbit will decay in a few years or months due to atmospheric drag. At 650 km or higher, this process takes longer. Objects in geostationary orbit at 35,000 km will remain there for millions of years. Deorbiting most satellites requires a deliberate end-of-life propulsive maneuver to a different orbit that has a much faster decay rate. An alternative to using a propulsive maneuver is unfurling a tether that slightly increases atmospheric drag and thereby speeds up orbital decay. Spacecraft disposal is not always the only choice. Satellite servicing spacecraft may be used to extend the useful life of existing satellites, thereby eliminating the need to launch and introduce a new replacement spacecraft in orbit [199].

What about older, long abandoned debris where deorbiting is an afterthought? If avoiding some runaway debris-generating process is the goal, then it makes sense to remove as much mass as possible from orbit and focus first on the biggest nonoperational items as they stand to produce the greatest amount of new smaller debris if a collision were to occur. An attractive place to start is spent upper stages as they represent 50% of the mass in orbit and offer no obvious value after their use [200]. Active removal of spent upper stages to either decaying or junkyard orbits using a "space tug" is one step that can be taken and even commercialized in the context of stakeholder intrinsic value creation. While long-term feasibility has yet to be demonstrated, multiple companies are currently building hardware and business models to do exactly this.

Unfortunately, when it comes to small undetectable debris, there are no known means to remove the millions of pieces already in orbit. And while these small pieces are the most dangerous category of debris, all that can be done in terms of mitigation currently is protecting spacecraft with debris shields and preventing the problem from getting worse. The best way to prevent the problem from getting worse is taking measures to reduce the likelihood of an unintentional collision from occurring.

Other Space Debris Mitigation Approaches

Garrett Hardin famously published an article in 1968 on the issue of the tragedy of the commons [201]. Repeated and exhaustive use of orbital space by individual parties such that it becomes unusable one day for all due to excessive debris would truly be a tragedy of the commons. Hardin claimed in his book that the only ways to avoid this kind of outcome are installing management policies or privatization. As discussed in Chapter 2, heavy-handed regulations are not a preferable solution. Unwanted regulation will be subverted and undermined. New corrective regulations should be limited for use in cases either with general support or as a last resort. Privatization may work in some cases but generally is not possible for provision of a common resource. The only means in which it can become possible is if the government installs and enforces new forms of private property that can be bought and sold. In the case of orbital debris, this would entail some sort of international agreement to commoditize orbital slots and create the equivalent of a real estate market in low Earth orbit. While functional in theory, this appears unlikely to occur.

Elinor Ostrom published another influential work in 1990 on management of common resources titled Governing the Commons [202]. Ostrom promotes "collective choice" decision-making when it comes to common resources, emphasizing that all stakeholders should participate in developing and implementing policies. This approach builds ownership of those policies by the users and others involved and it helps the creation of policies that are most appropriate for the details of the situation. Ostrom's perspective is one that is highly compatible with stakeholder intrinsic value creation. The IADC Space Debris Mitigation Guidelines may serve as the basis for a universal industry approach to managing orbital sustainability that is in line with Ostrom's views.

Another view on managing common resources is the use of incentives. Molly Macauley studied incentive-based methods rather than regulation for managing space debris. One idea is that for each new item placed into orbit, the hardware operator gives a deposit at launch and gets it back when the craft is deorbited [203]. Another idea is a cap-and-trade system similar to that used for carbon emissions in some places [204]. Professor Moriba Jah introduced the concept of a space traffic footprint that would be used to assign bounties to certain objects in orbit targeted for removal. This type of system could introduce security concerns among nations, and so to be successful would necessitate international collaboration and agreement [194]. Incentive-based mitigations for space debris are best suited to function with companies and likely less effective with state-owned and state-operated space systems. For this reason, some have said incentive-based solutions are only useful in a space industry that is dominated by commercial activity [190].

A big part of space debris management and risk mitigation is Space Situational Awareness (SSA). SSA essentially consists of tracking individual space debris objects continuously in order to predict and avoid collisions. In the US military, space debris is tracked in the SSN. With certain friendly nations, the US military shares SSN data except for classified assets. If a potential collision is detected, the US military will warn the satellite operators regardless of what nations are involved. There is no standing data-sharing agreement with Russia; however, Russia also has its own SSA capability. The primary international collaboration related to SSA data-sharing is the IADC where NASA, ESA, and Roscosmos are three of 13 total members.

Many organizations advocate that SSA data should be collected jointly by all space actors, not just the United States and Russia [188]. This would increase access to the data but also increase ownership and a sense of responsibility to those participating. In other words, this would enable a shift from the paradigm where most operators are simply informed if a collision is imminent to one where all participants are monitoring and collaborating on mitigation in unison. Enhanced SSA services may be an opportunity for stakeholder intrinsic value creation.

One effort related to orbital sustainability, soon to debut at the time of this book's publication, is the Space Sustainability Rating (SSR) [205]. The SSR concept was formed by the World Economic Forum's Global Future Council on Space Technologies and later assigned to a consortium of multiple organizations for development. The SSR is a voluntary rating that a mission can seek where its sustainability performance will be scored in terms of compliance with international space debris mitigation guidelines. Scores will be publicly available, but technical details of the mission will remain confidential. This voluntary program may be used as a factor influencing assessment of stakeholder intrinsic value creation just as LCA studies can be. The SSR is analogous to the LEED certification program for building efficiency in the construction industry. Also voluntary, LEED certifications have had the effect of promoting increased efficiency simply by providing a common rating system to use and advertise compliance with.

Radio frequency Allocation

In addition to debris, the other major element of in-space sustainability is radio frequency allocation. The UN *Guidelines for the Long-term Sustainability of Outer Space Activities* describes radio frequencies as a "limited natural resource" that must be used "rationally, efficiently and economically" [152]. The electromagnetic spectrum, like physical orbital space, is a common resource that must be shared by all for radio transmission of data. In 1963, the International Telecommunications Union (ITU) was tasked by the UN to begin management of geostationary orbit satellite radio transmissions. The ITU takes requests for radio frequency utilization on a first come, first serve basis. Today, the ITU regulates radio frequency usage and orbital slots, and while the organization has no real means of enforcement, so far it has been successful in managing these resources.

Regarding stakeholder intrinsic value creation, is responsible radio frequency use simply a do no harm consideration? Yes, in many cases, though opportunities exist to create additional value by providing new technical solutions to ease demand on radio frequency usage. For example, line-of-sight laser communications that do not interfere with general radio frequency use. Another opportunity for increased stakeholder intrinsic value creation is improving equitable access to radio frequency bands for nations that cannot afford to develop, operate, and directly benefit from their own space systems.

Sustainability of Space Industry Activities in Orbit: Summary

Attention to debris mitigation measures and responsible radio frequency use will boost stakeholder intrinsic value of a spacecraft/mission by supporting the harmony requirement. A spacecraft/mission that neglects do no harm responsibilities in these areas is unsustainable and therefore questionable as to whether or not value is really being created overall. Unlike international adherence to ITU orbital slot and radio frequency assignments, there is no such understanding dictating end-of-life spacecraft disposal or debris mitigation. The IADC *Space Debris Mitigation Guidelines* remain voluntary and hence are applied inconsistently. If greater progress toward both removal and prevention of space debris does not occur, value creation in space will decline in future years and humanity will be worse off for it. This challenge represents broadly an enormous opportunity for stakeholder intrinsic value creation.

Strategies for space debris mitigation and responsible radio frequency use are summarized below:

- Preventing the introduction of new debris
- Shielding spacecraft from small untrackable objects
- Maneuvering a spacecraft either to a graveyard orbit or to a rapidly decaying orbit at the end of its useful life
- Use of a "space tug" to actively seek out and remove from orbit large inert objects like nonoperational satellites and spent rocket stages
- Adoption of the IADC *Space Debris Mitigation Guidelines* as standard practice
- SSA systems to inform proactive execution of spacecraft maneuvers needed to avoid collisions with trackable objects
- Incentives related to space policy, licensing, cap and trade, and debris removal bounties
- Incentives related to use of the publicly available SSR scores
- Adherence to all ITU orbit and frequency assignments
- Line-of-sight data transfer technologies that do not interfere with radio frequency use

Sustainability Solutions for Humanity Supported by the Space Industry

Despite appearances, this book is not a promotion of the space industry. It is a promotion of the long-term prosperity of humanity. Commercial space systems can be configured not to conflict with this end and even go so far as to offer direct contributions to it. This involves being cognizant during formulation of company purpose and strategy of the distinction between what *can* be done in space versus what *should* be done in space. In other words, it's not enough for a space system to be just exciting and compelling to space enthusiasts. Nor is it enough for one to simply be expected to make money. It must create real value for society and it must do so without sacrificing the well-being of future generations. Chapter 4 suggested that it is preferable that the space industry does good things, not bad things, and among the good things that are possible, there is a focus on those which are most important. From this perspective, one of the most important uses of space systems may well be commercial sustainability solutions.

Thomas Diegelman frames a similar perspective, saying: "The quest for sustainable space commerce, then, is the search for space based commodities and activities that might similarly make life better for the entire human community..." [206]. Referring back to Chapter 2, the merchants trading across Europe and Asia and the formation of companies were driven by the same motivation, just in a different context. Making life better for humanity is what commerce did then and it is what it has done for centuries ever since. Use of the stakeholder intrinsic value criteria is a means to continue and help hone this approach in the space industry.

Diegelman suggests interrogating a space commerce activity as follows:

- What problem on Earth is being addressed?
- Which nations would be involved as leaders or beneficiaries?
- How much will Earth (and humanity) benefit?
- Are there ethical or cultural concerns? Sustainability concerns?

The intent of Diegelman's themes can be restated to be more in-line with the stakeholder intrinsic value criteria. The list below may be useful in a stakeholder intrinsic value assessment:

For a given product or service in the space industry...

- Which of the goodness virtues in the stakeholder intrinsic value criteria[5] does it support the most and are they supported in a way that is profitable?
- How could it be modified to enhance or broaden its satisfaction of the goodness virtues?
- How does the overall level of stakeholder intrinsic value compare to other potential similar goods or services that could be pursued instead?
- Are there any stakeholders objecting strongly and what is the stakeholder consensus regarding harmony?

These questions about how space can help humanity trace back decades. In the 1970s, Harvard scientist Michael McElroy became the first to propose the use of NASA space assets for studying Earth and for promoting humanity's well-being directly [207]. The Soviet Union became interested in this concept as well. In 1978, the Soviet Union formed Biosphere, an Earth observation program among communist countries of the era. Biosphere was utilized for domestic purposes like urban planning and resource management. Several years later, in 1985, NASA Office of Space Science and Applications administrator Burton Edelson published an article in *Science* titled "Mission to Planet Earth" [208]. This was the era when the ozone hole was a big issue in the public view. Climate change also came onto the radar for the US government in the 1980s, including testimony by NASA scientist James Hansen to congress in 1988 where he stated with "99% confidence" that a global greenhouse-effect-driven change was underway. Edelson's *Science* article in effect capitalized on growing awareness of planetary environmental problems to act as a catalyst in the US to spur progress in studying Earth from space. In 1986, NASA proposed the formation of the Earth Observing System (EOS) program to facilitate increased remote sensing of Earth (see Chapter 5).

A lot has occurred since the 1980s in the area of Earth observation from space. Today, environmental monitoring and study of humanity from space is an all but essential feature of society and the global economy. Humanity simply cannot manage civilization and resources without capabilities in space to support things like sustainability goals, climate change mitigation, natural disaster management, economic development, education, telecommunications, and much more. There is continued commercial opportunity to apply these capabilities in the areas of greatest need.

UN Sustainable Development Goals: Introduction

Perhaps the most universal attempt to articulate the need for a more sustainable civilization is captured in the 17 Sustainable Development Goals (SDG) as part of the UN 2030 Agenda. The 17 SDGs serve as a convenient context to frame a discussion on opportunities for sustainability solutions, as they are designed to envelop the topic entirely.

The UN and 193 member states adopted the 17 SDGs in 2015 at the UN Sustainable Development Summit. The UN Sustainability Goals replaced the similar Millennium Development Goals that had been adopted in 2000. While years of awareness and discussion across the world had occurred on sustainability topics prior to 2015, in some ways 2015 may be seen as a symbolic turning point when sustainability truly shifted into the mainstream. Many also consider the 17 SDGs to be an improvement on the Millennium Development Goals, in that they are broader in terms of number of issues covered and their content is more specific in nature. It is by design that the SDGs are comprised of quantifiable and measurable targets in order to bring increased accountability for governments via reporting and data requirements.

The SDGs represent the greatest needs of humanity. They represent specific calls for value creation in instances so lacking a solution from society, government, industry, from anyone, so lacking that the UN has included them in this list. Profit-seeking has been applied globally for hundreds of years as the best means to meet critical basic needs for humanity, many of which are similar to those expressed by the SDGs. Unmet needs, so great that they are articulated as unfulfilled SDGs, are tremendous stakeholder intrinsic value creation opportunities.

It may seem to some that many of the activities described in this section are the responsibilities of governments or charities rather than profit-seeking organizations. It is true that many of the challenges expressed by SDGs can and should be addressed by governments, charities, and nonprofits. Furthermore, in numerous instances, supporting an SDG is not conducive to a commercial approach in the first place, due to reasons discussed in Chapter 5. However, the fact that an SDG exists at all is precisely because insufficient value is currently being created in that area by existing means. If there is a choice between no additional value created and additional value created for a profit where it is possible, there should be no objection to the latter. If there is a desire to help and empower more people, this must occur through any means available. Knowing that for-profit value creation occurs in an efficient, innovative, and win-win manner makes it all the more attractive of an option. Additionally, by enabling commercial means to address SDG challenges, the solution space is made available to those beyond just wealthy governments. The commercial space industry is one means, of several, to help people that would otherwise go unattended relative to needs expressed by the SDGs.

SDGs and Stakeholder Intrinsic Value

The following sections describe ways in which the space industry can create stakeholder intrinsic value in support of each SDG. In general, for all of the SDGs, the space industry can either make a direct contribution to the SDG or has more of a do no harm responsibility. In this context, questions on profitability arise for each SDG. Is profitability possible? Is it appropriate? The answers vary, but across most SDGs there exist opportunities for stakeholder intrinsic value creation, at least in support of government customers if not more broadly in a commercial market.

Historically, space systems have been exclusively used by governments and large companies. At this day in age, many of the activities described in this section could be utilized directly by a farmer, a city, a small business, a public utility, or an individual, though generally continued development in accessibility and user tools is required to reach more and smaller customers. This effort involves packaging tools that take satellite system capabilities like remote sensing or Global Navigation and Satellite Systems (GNSS) into user software focused on specific needs. Progress in this area can be seen as a generic stakeholder intrinsic value creation opportunity across all SDGs.

Another generic opportunity for space to create stakeholder intrinsic value in the context of the SDGs is through global satellite-provided internet. Morgan Stanley estimates that 50–70% of space industry growth through 2040 will be related to satellite-provided broadband [1]. At the time of publication of this book in 2022, deployments of satellite internet constellations are underway by several commercial providers. The potential positive impact of providing broadband internet access to the whole world, including to remote and poor communities, cannot be overstated. The internet has already revolutionized economies in developed countries. It has enabled an entirely new generation of entrepreneurs, services, and innovation. This is no secret to the world, but in some rural areas or poor households, the internet may as well be as inaccessible as going to the Moon. If the entire world is granted access to broadband internet, the possibilities for economic growth are endless. Economic opportunities lead naturally to things like education, safety, healthcare, equality, and greater food security. And best of all, this is an enabling process where local participants need not rely on charity but are placed permanently in control of their own fortunes.

Global internet can itself be considered to have stakeholder intrinsic value per criteria 2b given that it can have "Instrumental value that is based on an innate property where the instrumental value is a means to enable an external bearer of the criteria in item 1." Regarding the goodness virtues (pleasure, knowledge, justice, beauty, and benevolence), any one of them can be supported, broadly speaking, via internet-enabled activities. The same can be said for harmony and profitability. In this regard, satellite-provided internet represents a generic platform for stakeholder intrinsic value creation. Creating value using satellite-provided internet is discussed in the upcoming section on SDG 9: Industry, Innovation, and Infrastructure, though global internet should be kept in mind as a means to address many, if not all, of the SDGs in some way.

The upcoming sections on each SDG mostly avoid citing specific historic examples of space system applications. The discussion here is focused more generically on the opportunities for stakeholder intrinsic value creation relative to the SDGs. For additional detail on specific projects and the history of space systems supporting the SDGs, the reader is referred to the resources listed below:

- United Nations [209]: United Nations, "European Global Navigation Satellite System and Copernicus: Supporting the Sustainable Development Goals," Vienna, Austria, 2018.
- European Space Agency [210]: European Space Agency, "ESA Activities Supporting Sustainable Development," 2016.
- Maxar [211]: Maxar, "Satellite data's role in supporting sustainable development goals: Empowering organizations with Earth observation, geospatial information and big data," 2019.

- NASA [212]: NASA, "Sustainable Development Goals," 26 June 2020. [Online]. Available: https://earthdata.nasa.gov/learn/backgrounders/ sdg. [Accessed 12 April 2021].
- ISS [119]: International Space Station Program Science Forum, "International Space Station Benefits for Humanity (3rd. edition)," 2019.

SDG 1: No Poverty

Poverty has long been among the greatest inhibitors of human prosperity going back thousands of years. It can be seen as an embodiment of an antithesis to the stakeholder intrinsic value virtues used to define goodness. Economic development and especially capitalism have proven historically to be an effective means to reduce poverty on a large scale. Progress in this regard is still occurring in real time, as from 1990 to 2015 the number of people in extreme poverty dropped from 1.9 billion to 836 million [209]. This trend can continue and space can help.

Many of the contributions from space systems to other SDGs will indirectly help alleviate poverty. Contributions such as remote education (SDG 4), remote banking (SDG 8), telemedicine (SDG 3), precision agriculture (SDG 2), and satellite-provided internet (SDG 9) all have overlapping and positive effects on poverty reduction. Details on space activities that address other SDGs but also indirectly address SDG 1 are discussed in the following sections.

One direct contribution from space systems to address SDG 1 is use of remote sensing to help map poverty and monitor progress toward its reduction. One way to do this is by tracking housing types and human migrations. For example, the type of housing, be it tents, apartment buildings, or single-family homes, in a city neighborhood can be observed from space and correlated to the poverty level. Other indicators like car ownership, car movements, green space, and building density can be used as indicators of poverty as well. Trends across years or decades can support other data sources to indicate societal progress or lack thereof in locations of interest. The best opportunities for stakeholder intrinsic value creation related to SDG 1 may be supporting government efforts through efficient collection of data and/or value-added processing tools.

SDG 2: Zero Hunger

The modern agricultural industry is highly productive and able to generate, in theory, more food than the world needs. However, this is only possible due to heavy use of fertilizer and pesticides which comes at the cost of soil nutritional depletion, soil loss, loss of species diversity, a danger to nearby residents of chemical exposure, heavy fresh water use, and a large energy-intensive distribution network. These practices deplete the means of food production over time and so current high crop yields are not sustainable in the long term. In nations with industrialized food production, the short-term benefits of having plenty of food cannot by definition last forever. A stakeholder intrinsic value approach is one that recognizes the need for sustainable agriculture practices and helps make commercial food production more efficient, more available, and able to carry on indefinitely.

Precision agriculture was one of the earliest applications of remote sensing satellite data for life on Earth. It involves monitoring and study of agricultural land in order to proactively determine the exact needs for crop performance. In this way, use of water, pesticides, fertilizer, and machinery is tailored based on factors like location, weather, disease, and demand. The demonstrated results of using space systems for precision agriculture can be on the order of an increase in crop yields by 10% while simultaneously reducing input costs like fuel, water, and fertilizer by up to 20% [209, 213].

Enhanced agricultural efficiency is obtained by monitoring several metrics in agricultural fields. Remote sensing data can be gathered to measure biomass quantity/growth, soil moisture content, soil erosion, air humidity, air pollution, weather, and total leaf area. All of this data can be collected across either large regions or across a single field enabling farmers the ability to tailor with fine precision the water, fertilizer, and pesticide needs for different parts of their land. Farmers also can determine ideal plant dates with more insight and improve risk management. This insight can be combined with automated machinery such as tractors and sprinklers that utilize GNSS capabilities for guidance. In the case of livestock, GNSS services may enable herd tracking and use of virtual fences.

Remote sensing data can also be used to provide warning and insight for problems such as drought or insect infestations that could cause shortages or crop disease. In the case of fish farms, remote sensing data can track pollution emitted or pollution that threatens the farm. Authorities use this kind of information in order to plan for regional food distribution. In the most severe cases, agricultural remote sensing data can be used to provide warning of famine. The Famine Early Warning System Network, originally founded by the US Agency for International Development (USAID) in 1985, offers this service using, in part, remote sensing data.

There is opportunity to extend precision agriculture techniques to more customers around the world. Not just governments or large agricultural operations but local farms, community gardens, landscaping companies, even individuals. This opportunity involves use of existing open-source software tools as well as pursuing advances in marketing, data processing, data collection, customer training, consulting, new value-added software tools, and widespread awareness and expertise in the field. There is an expansive value chain in precision agriculture with many opportunities to pursue stakeholder intrinsic value creation.

SDG 3: Good Health and Well-Being

Improving the health and well-being of humanity involves confronting challenges such as insufficient healthcare coverage, stemming the spread of disease, mitigating health impacts from climate change and increased urbanization, and keeping up with treatments for mutating and drug-resistant bacteria. The space industry can create value in several ways in these areas and the advent of telemedicine via global satellite-provided internet is a big part of this. Telemedicine refers to use of healthcare services remotely through a data link. Plenty of communities around the globe do not have access to healthcare services either due to a remote location, undeveloped healthcare infrastructure, or poverty. Telemedicine services can range from awareness and education, to physician consultation, to medical research, to robotic surgery. And this is not just beneficial for developing nations. Plenty of communities exist throughout the developed world that are not near an advanced medical center. There are opportunities for stakeholder intrinsic value creation related to supporting the infrastructure and workforce needed for telemedicine services.

Another use of space systems to advance good health and well-being is tracking and management of disease. Satellite data related to environmental conditions like temperature, humidity, weather, and even human movements can help correlate and develop epidemiological models to help stem the spread of diseases. For example, currently 50% of the world population is at risk of getting Malaria [6]. Factors like greenness, temperature, proximity to water, and humidity correlate with mosquito presence, which is the means by which Malaria and other diseases spread in warm climates. These factors combined with data on size, proximity, and poverty level of nearby populations can be measured and used to either understand disease vectors or to plan mitigations like mosquito net distribution, vaccinations, or targeted mosquito fogging.

This type of prevention also may involve geographically mapping remote areas in order to determine access, population distribution, and to properly quantify overall risks and mitigation needs. Similarly, remote sensing data may be used simply to monitor air quality and develop spatial and temporal correlations with respiratory health across a nation or city. One means by which stakeholder intrinsic value creation can occur related to tracking and mitigating disease is by providing the expertise and the services described here to authorities or health organizations.

Another application of space systems supporting SDG 3 combines GNSS and remote sensing capabilities to promote healthy outdoor recreation. This can involve aiding search and rescue for those carrying tracking devices while performing higher-risk activities like backcountry skiing or backpacking. Or it can involve navigation and mapping for more common activities like hiking, jogging, biking, or sightseeing. These are good examples of stakeholder intrinsic value creation opportunities that support the pleasure virtue, but not necessarily at the cost of harmony as improving human health through outdoor recreation contribute to social sustainability. These opportunities are also good examples of stakeholder intrinsic value creation that occurs downstream of the space system provider in the form of a value-added product. The product in these cases creates a new form of value made possible by a preexisting space service, GNSS, that is available to all at no cost.

SDG 4: Quality Education

Quality education is listed as an SDG because the availability and quality of educational resources have historically been inconsistent across wealth, cultural, and geographical demographics. Specifically, inconsistencies lie in areas like availability of infrastructure, access to pre-K programs, and graduation rates. A lack of quality education options limits the chances of prosperity for many across the globe.

A means by which the space industry can create stakeholder intrinsic value relative to SDG 4 is through the support of remote education opportunities. Remote education can occur through use of global satellite-provided internet services. Many communities are not located near colleges or universities, and whether they exist in developing or developed nations, they stand to benefit from access to online classes and training opportunities. In communities such as these, the space industry is able to emphasize the availability of Science, Technology, Engineering, and Mathematics (STEM) education across genders and cultures in ways that are more equitable than local current conditions may be. The prevalence of remote learning has been spreading already, though further enabling it via satellite-provided internet services will increase the market and increase the potential for stakeholder intrinsic value creation overall.

SDG 4 also happens to be a challenge that the space industry has a direct interest in. The space industry relies on a highly educated workforce and therefore has always had a strong link with education ranging from elementary to graduate students. Industry support of science and math education programs through scholarships, internships, events, grants, donations, and volunteer activities has a direct benefit to the companies themselves. Simultaneously, this support also has a significant benefit to society and local communities. A true win-win all around. And to strengthen this position, the space industry has an outsized presence in the media relative to its size. This is due to the fact that activities in space resonate with and excite people across the world. This offers the industry a powerful means to engage and promote education, to offer a path for people that are interested in participating, to serve as a way to teach young and old about science and the universe outside of classrooms, and to promote equality in these things. Stakeholder intrinsic value creation in a given space company should necessarily do no harm to the education system if not include proactive support to STEM initiatives.

SDG 5: Gender Equality

The need for greater gender equality reflects numerous instances around the world of disproportionate discrimination or mistreatment of women and girls. This includes things like forced childhood marriage, unequal pay for the same job performed, underrepresentation in government and corporate leadership, and access to healthcare, especially concerning reproductive care.

The space industry has the responsibility to regard genders equally in terms of respect, earning potential, opportunities, and access. This responsibility is not unique to the space industry; however, there may be an opportunity for disproportionate progress, given that STEM fields have historically been dominated by male participants. Given the far reach of space through remote connectivity and through international partnerships in the industry, gender equality values may be spread more easily than in other industries. Concerning use of global internet services for remote education and remote economic development, these represent direct opportunities to promote and enable gender equality. The same can be said relative to engaging in new equitable international partnerships (see section on SDG 17).

Gender equality should be a key factor in any stakeholder intrinsic value assessment. It may not in itself be a direct means to create stakeholder intrinsic value but it is important enough to make or break a stakeholder consensus on harmony. A company or an activity occurring in space that degrades gender equality is not socially sustainable and therefore not in support of harmony.

SDG 6: Clean Water and Sanitation

Today, the UN estimates that water scarcity affects 40% of people on Earth, and that this number is expected to rise as climate change continues to intensify in the coming years. Worldwide, water usage can be broken down as 70% for agriculture, 20% for industry, and only 10% for domestic use [214]. In the United States, water use for industry is much higher at 46% [215]. Improved efficiency in industrial and agricultural uses offers the greatest potential impact. Additionally, water treatment and sanitation for domestic use across much of the world are lacking and natural bodies of water are used as waste sinks for sewage, pesticides, fertilizers, and industrial byproducts. How can space help?

Regional or national management of freshwater resources is something that the space industry can assist with through use of remote sensing systems. Collection of water management data from space is ideal as large regions can be covered where natural water systems cross jurisdictional borders. Relevant data collected for water management include surface water quality (based on coloration and presence of algae or cyanobacteria scum), soil moisture, evapotranspiration, snowpack water equivalent, surface water level, pollution sources, and algae blooms. It simply would not be feasible to install and maintain a ground network of sensors to produce an equivalent data collection apparatus across an entire nation's natural water supply system involving lakes, rivers, reservoirs, aquifers, snowpack, and rainfall. That said, a limited ground sensor system (e.g., flow meters in water mains) can complement well a remote sensing data collection system.

These types of remote sensing data can be employed to manage water distribution and usage. They also can be used to predict shortages in advance. For example, measurement of snowpack water potential is a direct indication as to the level of water to be available later in the year (as well as an indication as to the level of flooding to expect). Remote sensing data can even be collected on underground water resources through monitoring of subsistence on land as aquifers are consumed [216]. This type of measurement combined with ground-collected data from wells can be critical to avoid temporary or even permeant aquifer depletion.

Toward improved sustainability of the agriculture industry, remote sensing data can be used to understand effects on water supplies from farming activities. Global food production relies on nitrogen fertilizers. When nitrates run into and build up in water eutrophication occurs. Eutrophication involves prolific growth of algae and other marine plants that change the qualities of the water like oxygen and pH level, which can impact fisheries and fresh water safety. Monitoring from space can detect eutrophication and also detect the sources of contamination (when and where). This same approach can be applied to other potential sources of contamination such as sewage, industrial waste, or power plant cooling effluent.

Water management using remote sensing data consists of a far-reaching value chain with many opportunities for stakeholder intrinsic value creation involving marketing, data processing, data collection, customer training, consulting, and new value-added software tools. Governments and businesses interested in measuring facility impacts are likely the primary customers.

SDG 7: Affordable and Clean Energy

Increased use of clean energy and the associated reduction in greenhouse gas emissions will be the single most effective means to reverse climate change. A shift to clean energy will reduce the environmental impact not just of obvious energy uses like driving a car or turning on the lights, but also, and more importantly, will reduce the impact of "hidden" energy uses like manufacturing household products and building construction materials. There are numerous ways in which space systems can support the shift toward affordable clean energy for humanity.

Remote sensing systems can collect data on sunlight, wind, and cloud cover. This data can be used to predict solar and wind activity for the purpose of power plant planning and management. Radiative properties of different regions can be measured in order to best place new solar facilities. Wind patterns can be mapped and understood before planning a new wind farm or network of wind farms. Daily and weekly weather forecasts can be used to manage energy production from numerous sources if one is predicted to temporarily underperform due to meteorological conditions. Beyond remote sensing, GNSS systems can be used for electrical grid and generation system management. For example, many data collection points can exist throughout a power system and this data can be collected by satellites and used in a time-synchronized management system. Services related to using space systems to assist with power generation planning and management are opportunities for stakeholder intrinsic value creation.

There also is opportunity for power generation in space. One means, yet to be implemented, is creating a large-scale solar power plant in space and beaming energy to designated reception points on Earth. Sounds like science fiction, but the concept is sound. An in-space solar plant would have much higher efficiency and generation capacity compared to solar facilities on Earth that are partially shielded from the Sun by the atmosphere. To date, no such facility has been created in space. It remains yet to be seen if the associated cost and complexity of such a system can be reduced to the extent that this approach for clean energy production becomes competitive with other alternatives.

Another concept for use of space resources for power production is mining helium-3 for use as fuel in nuclear fusion reactors. Compared to other power sources, nuclear fusion is emission-free and produces far less waste than existing nuclear fission technology. Helium-3 happens to be extremely rare on Earth and also an extremely efficient fuel for use in a fusion reactor. On the Moon, helium-3 is not rare at all. Accumulating slowly over billions of years, about 100 kg of helium-3 exists in a 2 km^2 area of the lunar surface down to a depth of 3 m. This is enough to supply electricity for one million people for an entire year. In total, the Moon may have enough helium-3 to provide humanity's energy needs for thousands of years [217].

Former astronaut Harrison Schmitt writes at length on this topic in *Return to the Moon* [218]. Schmitt's assessment concludes that the economics are favorable for helium-3 mining, processing, and return to Earth based on coal power energy rates of the 2010–2020 time frame. At the 2015 market rate for helium-3 of $14.5 billion per ton,[6] one may see how this could be feasible [219]. Some have proposed that mining helium-3 from the Moon for use in fusion reactors will be the first off-planet resource mining economy.[7] Technology to extract and refine helium-3 from the Moon does not exist today, but could be developed given some time and a motivated financier. Lack of a functional helium-3 fusion power plant is the most obvious constraint to this scheme overall. Until such technology exists, helium-3 fuel will be of little use for clean energy production.

Stakeholder intrinsic value creation can occur from space systems in support of SDG 7 in several areas. Most realistically, and using existing capabilities, space systems can be employed to help planning and management of clean power generation on Earth. Further out, and requiring overcoming technological and financial challenges, space systems may be used more directly in clean power generation through in-space solar or helium-3 mining. Finally, even if a space company is engaged in value creation in some other area unrelated to power generation, SDG 7 remains a do no harm consideration in a stakeholder intrinsic value assessment. If energy use associated with value creation is unsustainable and degrades the environment, harmony and the other virtues in the stakeholder intrinsic value criteria are negatively affected.

SDG 8: Decent Work and Economic Growth

Economic growth has been the enabler for billions of people throughout history to rise out of poverty. Economic growth means more jobs, better jobs, and a better quality of life. A lesson that has come out of this process is that growth must occur in ways that are sustainable, and if it does not, the benefits are short-lived. Nevertheless, economic growth transcends many of the SDGs because if it occurs in a given location, other problems related to poverty, education, healthcare, equality, and more may simply go away or become reduced. This section highlights that the space industry generally has a positive impact on economic and social sustainability.

A strong space industry is considered around the world to be one hallmark of an advanced and productive economy. While there are elements of national pride and prestige involved with this view, it is founded on several facts related to real societal benefits. The space industry is synonymous with high wages and high levels of education. The advanced and technical nature of the industry necessitates a far-reaching value chain as well as robust social support conditions for the workforce. If a space industry can become established in a nation, it becomes part of a positive feedback loop involving industry jobs, good wages, supply chain jobs, an education pipeline, indirect jobs in the local economy, international partnerships, and a path to retirement for those involved. All of this occurs while also pushing the frontier of scientific research and technology, thereby feeding back into its own momentum and the competitive advantage of the organizations and people involved. Also, the space industry tends to attract a young, skilled demographic with permanent employment contracts [220] which is desirable for economic stability.

The prospect of the economic benefits described above is a strong motivation for government-supported research and commercial incentives. NASA finds that in 2019 with a budget of $21.5 billion the total impact on the economy of this investment by the government was $64.3 billion and 312,000 jobs [221]. ESA, with a 2020 budget of €6.68 billion, supports roughly 50,000 jobs directly and estimates that €1 spent by the government on space stimulates up to €4 of activity in the overall European economy [222]. Also, the job counts cited here do not capture indirect jobs created. For example, in Europe and the United States, it is estimated that for every space-related job, 2–3 additional jobs elsewhere are created as a result (teachers, healthcare workers, retail, etc.) [222, 223]. The trend from numerous studies is clear: the spin-off economic benefits from the space industry are considerable.

Jobs in the space industry may also be more shielded from global trends toward increasing use of industrial automation and artificial intelligence. This is due to the fact that space industry jobs are inherently closer to the limits of science and technology and therefore require more innovation, hands-on engagement, and creativity. As other types of jobs are lost to automation, it is the expanding and cutting-edge industries like space that will offer new jobs to replace them. This is a highly relevant attribute of the space industry, as a transition to sustainability overall cannot result in a net loss of jobs or economic well-being if the transition is to be truly successful.

Generally, support of broad economic growth in the ways described here is best viewed as an attractive outcome of the space industry rather than a direct source of stakeholder intrinsic value. An area related to SDG 8 that does involve a direct opportunity for stakeholder intrinsic value creation is facilitating access to space systems for developing nations. Satellite-provided internet and GNSS services support small businesses by improving access to the financial system, microloans, business development resources, consulting, regulatory compliance assistance, and navigation and tracking services. Access to these capabilities opens doors for entrepreneurs to markets, customers, and business partnerships, resulting in lasting self-sufficient economic development. Realizing economic benefits enabled by satellite-provided internet is among the most impactful uses of space systems.

SDG 9: Industry, Innovation, and Infrastructure

Industrialization is an embodiment of economic growth. As long as this process occurs sustainably, it will continue to drive a positive transformation away from poverty in struggling societies around the world. Industrialization involves manufacturing, innovation, R&D, and national infrastructure for things like transportation, energy, internet, and sanitation. SDG 9 is aimed at advancing these things in the developing world and improving them in developed countries.

As of 2021, 37% of the world population still does not have internet access [224]. Because of this large disparity, one of the most influential sources of value that space can offer is global satellite-provided internet. This service is transformational, in that it represents a platform that can be applied to help with virtually all of the SDGs in some way. While some of these applications are known and expected such as telemedicine, access to banking, and remote education, it will be up to industry and the next generation of entrepreneurs to continue to listen, innovate, and act on new ways to create value for people using the internet. This service will provide the opportunity for people to create value for themselves and their communities.

The expanded utilization of satellite-provided internet will occur primarily in the developing world as a new "bottom-up" economy. The developing world represents an enormous, currently untapped market in this area where needs are also the greatest. And while government and nonprofit organizations currently attempt to address these needs, there is more to be done. Provision of the internet from space is a tremendous opportunity for stakeholder intrinsic value creation. If realized, this will constitute a net increase in value creation across the world and serve as a foundation for countless new stakeholder intrinsic value creation enterprises. All of the value creation to come from satellite-provided internet will not have occurred otherwise if not for a commercial approach.

In the developed world, increased demand for internet connectivity will continue as well and be related to advances in the internet of things, autonomous vehicles, and artificial intelligence. Furthermore, adoption of sustainable circular economy principles by both developed and developing economies can be aided by increased internet availability. This will open access to rental markets and the sharing economy through peer-to-peer exchanges. Efforts to manage and recover product value may also be aided.

Space systems can offer more in support of SDG 9 beyond satellite-provided internet. Many people are familiar with the now ubiquitous use of GNSS services for private automobile navigation. Air traffic control and trains are also managed through GNSS services in order to increase throughput and safety. Other transportation applications include management of public transit, waste containers, shipping, seaport traffic, delivery truck fleets, and infrastructure mapping. The shipping industry, subject to International Maritime Organization regulations on emissions, benefits also by using GNSS combined with weather information to allow ships to plot more efficient courses, thereby saving fuel [39]. Similarly, observations of sea currents and wind from Doppler scatterometry measurements can help track and predict sea ice, which may become increasingly relevant as Arctic ice melting opens up new shipping routes.

Infrastructure maintenance can be aided by remote sensing and GNSS systems as well. Land settlement can be tracked using LIDAR or synthetic aperture radar sensors to monitor movement of water dams, mining waste dams, pipelines, soil retention features, bridge foundations, and the ground near construction sites. While this type of monitoring from space can occur in urban settings, it is in some ways even more advantageous for applications in remote areas lacking infrastructure or a constant human presence. Remote sensing services may also be useful for land surveying related to new construction projects in any location. Land surveying capabilities can be used widely in the real estate industry by numerous types of customers, including buyers, sellers, insurance agencies, property managers, builders, inspectors, and investors. Monitoring and surveying services such as those described here are all potential sources for stakeholder intrinsic value creation. There are numerous areas related to SDG 9 where direct sustainability solutions are possible through stakeholder intrinsic value creation. Of all the SDGs, SDG 9 is among those where this is most true.

SDG 10: Reduced Inequalities

Inequality is an obstacle impeding access to a decent life for many people. Unequal treatment and opportunities can exist as a result of numerous factors, including gender, age, citizenship status, income level, race, religion, and culture. Additionally, on a national level, historical data shows a positive correlation between the degree of equality and economic growth [225]. Inside the space industry, there has been a concerted effort to avoid these kinds of problems since the beginning. The 1967 UN Outer Space Treaty states:

> Outer space, including the moon and other celestial bodies, shall be free
> for exploration and use by all States without discrimination of any kind,
> on a basis of equality and in accordance with international law, and
> there shall be free access to all areas of celestial bodies.

By the foundational principles adopted by most nations on Earth, space is framed in terms promoting equality. This applies to things like exploration, radio frequency use, orbital slot use, mineral extraction, and scientific discovery.

Contributions from space systems toward reduced inequalities overlap with numerous other SDGs, but in particular may occur as the result of stakeholder intrinsic value creation associated with SDG 3 (good health and well-being), SDG 4 (quality education), SDG 8 (decent work and economic growth), and SDG 9 (industry, innovation, and infrastructure). Contributions from space in these areas revolve around global satellite-provided internet. Telemedicine services support SDG 3 directly, and in doing so reduce inequality. As discussed in the section on SDG 4, remote education and training is one important enabler for poor people in developing countries to enter the economy. It's also an enabler for anyone in developed countries who doesn't have access to education for any reason, including limitations related to geographic location, finances, or discrimination. Regarding SDG 8 (decent work and economic growth), universal access to the economy or, better yet, access to a new virtual economy that will exist after the entire globe becomes connected on the internet will have a positive impact on SDG 10. Health, education, and economic engagement are all key in reducing inequality and space systems can contribute through opportunities made possible by satellite-provided internet.

Another area where space systems can help reduce inequality is disaster mitigation and management. Poor communities are often the most vulnerable to natural disasters like hurricanes, floods, earthquakes, and fires. Use of satellite data leading up to and in the aftermath of a natural disaster can save lives by helping people either prepare up-front or cope afterwards. Some examples include predicting storm surge levels, observing landmass movement leading up to an earthquake, wildfire tracking, and gauging population locations and densities in order to properly scale response resources. The type of indiscriminate and transparent insight that remote sensing offers can be important during the aftermath of a disaster because, with typical ground infrastructure and access in chaos, satellite imagery may offer the only visibility on what is happening.

How does stakeholder intrinsic value apply in the context of disaster response? And should disaster response services be provided by government or for-profit companies? From an economic perspective, emergency response can be regarded as a natural monopoly, non-rival, and excludable. One could choose to exclude the response service from a given need, but once a disaster is mitigated this affects everyone. Certain natural monopolies can be made to function in markets, but others such as police or firefighters are typically left to governments. On the surface, it would seem that emergency situations where lives are at stake transcend desires for production efficiency and profitability. The government has no need to make a profit and therefore is completely uninhibited in this regard to respond in an emergency in any way possible with all haste. What is less immediately obvious is that the government may do exactly this by hiring companies to execute.

Commercial disaster response services have proven advantageous in the past. In cases where authorities have taken this approach, the results have been response and recovery overall that is cheaper, faster, and more adept than could have been achieved using only preexisting government resources [226, 227]. This is not surprising as there are companies now that specialize in this role. The types of services provided can be wide-ranging, including planning, medical, rescue, accounting, transportation, construction, supplies, and use of space systems. As natural disaster occurrences increase due to climate change, executing government-led preparation, response, and remediation efforts stands to be a high-value service that the commercial space industry can provide through stakeholder intrinsic value creation.

Stakeholder intrinsic value creation can occur in this context not just with disaster response services but also in the development and production of systems used by governments in disasters. A high-profile example of this is the International Charter Space and Major Disasters which was initiated in 1999. In this nonbinding agreement, space agencies around the world agree to provide immediate satellite data to assist emergency response organizations responding to a natural disaster. This is a case where government is providing value, but the tools used to do so were provided by commercial means prior to the actual emergency.

SDG 10 is an area that can benefit from the space industry and an area that should be considered as a do no harm responsibility in stakeholders' assessments with regards to harmony and social sustainability. Opportunities exist for stakeholder intrinsic value creation related to support of government-led disaster response activities.

SDG 11: Sustainable Cities and Communities

As of 2020, 56% of people in the world live in cities and this percentage continues to grow [228]. The design of cities will need to evolve in order to manage increased populations and the accompanying demands placed on resources, transportation, housing, and more. Cities are economic drivers and it is in humanity's interest to make them as livable, sustainable, healthy, and productive as possible. Challenges associated with this endeavor include ageing infrastructure, lack of funds for basic services, congestion, housing shortages, and exposure to natural disasters.

Both remote sensing and GNSS data have uses in urban sustainability such as traffic management, street light maintenance, air quality monitoring, security of sites of heritage or of other interest, management of large events, housing density analysis, mapping, tracking human migration, tracking poverty, building thermal efficiency measurements, and urban planning. Applications such as traffic management and street light maintenance may have in situ data collection alternatives; however, the advantage of using remote sensing data is that the satellite can quite literally be everywhere at once monitoring the entire system all the while avoiding installation and constant maintenance of a ground-based sensor network. Saving money and resources on an extensive ground sensor network is a universal advantage to using space systems for infrastructure monitoring [229].

GNSS uses in cities can be diverse and range from waste bin collection tracking, to prioritizing public buses in traffic light intersections, to providing satellite-based, real-time tracking and management for emergency vehicles [229]. GNSS-managed transit systems are particularly valuable in small- or medium-sized cities that do not warrant dedicated right-of-ways for transit. In these cases, the transit system is superimposed on public streets driving a heightened need for efficient management. In larger cities, metro rail systems now also use GNSS to manage train movements, increasing both throughput and safety.

Use of remote sensing data for urban forestry management can improve the health of a city's trees and parks. The effects of more robust urban forest management are enhanced aesthetic appeal as well as functional advantages of urban trees like building energy efficiency and cleaner air. To this end, remote sensing data can be collected to measure leaf area and chlorophyll content to quantify and track vegetation density and growth. These measurements can be correlated with other variables such as water availability, pollution, and sunlight access in order to plan urban forests and make adjustments as needed over time.

Numerous opportunities exist for space systems to create stakeholder intrinsic value through addressing urban challenges. Most of the customers are likely to be local municipalities. Due to the inherent complexity of cities and the diversity of needs, SDG 11 is an area prime for creativity, novel solutions, and stakeholder intrinsic value creation from space systems beyond what is described here or known today.

SDG 12: Responsible Consumption and Production

Part of the impetus for this book is based around the fact that modern societies do not consume resources and energy in a way that is sustainable. The result of this manifests as climate change and mass species extinction, among other things. Space can support responsible consumption and production most effectively by striving for an efficient industry on Earth that embodies circular economy principles as much as possible. This is an area where space does not necessarily have a direct means for stakeholder intrinsic value creation. Rather, the space industry has a do no harm responsibility to devise and implement value creation practices that minimize resource use and waste, thereby supporting the harmony requirement in the stakeholder intrinsic value criterion.

SDG 13: Climate Action

Climate change is one of the greatest threats facing humanity. A change in climate negatively affects fresh water availability (SDG 6) and food production (SDG 2), which, in turn, impacts health and well-being (SDG 3). These impacts affect poverty (SDG 1), decent work and economic growth (SDG 8), and inequality (SDG 10). Conversely, a stabilization or reversal of climate change has a positive impact in all of these categories. The overlap and interconnectedness of climate change across other SDGs make contributions from space systems to SDG 13, particularly high value.

The 54 Essential Climate Variables (ECV) are defined by the UN Global Climate Observing System (GCOS) [230]. The ECVs were developed as metrics that are measurable and have a high significance relative to climate change and environmental policies. Remote sensing systems are able to collect data corresponding to dozens of the 54 ECVs, including measurements related to sea ice thickness, glacier size and thickness, pollution plume source and distribution, clouds, wind speed, rainfall, sea state, ocean surface temperature and salinity, ocean color, sea level rise, greenhouse gases, aerosols, ozone, humidity, and wildfires. There really is no other practical way besides satellites to measure these environmental parameters across the entire globe in a way that is spatially and temporally consistent.

Monitoring ECVs helps in tracking progress on specific targets, collecting data to inform and validate climate models, enforcing environmental regulations, and providing transparent accountability of progress or lack thereof. On the issue of enforcement, an advantage of using remote sensing systems is that there is complete accountability. Any country in the world can observe the extent to which another country is living up to an environmental commitment. Remote sensing systems used to collect climate data are of high value to the world and are essential in measuring and monitoring progress related to climate changes.

A challenge that the world will face in the coming decades as a result of climate change is mass migration away from the now thriving coastal communities due to sea level rise. In the past 100 years, global sea level has already risen 20 cm [231]. Continued rise, which is expected to accelerate annually for the foreseeable future, will impact millions of people. Anticipating the location and scale of climate change, migration can be achieved in part using remote sensing data that tracks sea level rise due to melting icecaps and glaciers as well as thermal expansion of the oceans. Land elevation data can help predict when and where conditions may become untenable and also where resources, urban or natural, exist for the displaced population. There is opportunity for stakeholder intrinsic value creation related to working with governments to plan for and manage these migrations, thereby minimizing hardship and disruptions to the world economy.

Generally, stakeholder intrinsic value creation opportunities related to SDG 13 are limited to supporting government initiatives (see Chapter 5); however, there is a notable exception. Monitoring emissions and contributions to climate change can occur at a targeted level. Private space companies now offer services to companies that are interested in managing and improving emission performance of a specific facility. This service can include monitoring local emissions as well as emissions from a specific but geographically distributed supply chain. Industries that can benefit in this way include power generation, oil and gas, steel, aluminum, concrete, and manufacturing. In particular, targeted observation of the "first mile" portion of a supply chain related to raw material extraction and processing at mines, forests, farms, mills, refineries, and more may inform improvements in a product's impact directed from far up the supply chain [39].

Climate impacts rank high in considerations related to harmony in the stakeholder intrinsic value criteria and so SDG 13 can be viewed as a do no harm responsibility. The best means for stakeholder intrinsic value creation within SDG 13 is supporting government and nonprofit efforts related to collection and processing climate data. Other opportunities for stakeholder intrinsic value creation exist related to services for companies interested in proactively monitoring their own impacts on the environment.

SDG 14: Life Below Water

The oceans are a planetary engine for life on Earth. Natural life-giving elements of the environment like air, precipitation, food, and carbon absorption are enabled by the oceans. Professor Danielle Wood remarks on this perspective that "a full chain in investigation starts with ocean temperature which influences rainfall, which influences soil moisture, which supports vigorous crops which leads to food security" [232]. Oceans are a deeply integrated component of humanity's well-being. Additionally, approximately 40% of the human population lives in coastal communities and therefore directly relies on the ocean economically in some way. The World Wildlife Fund estimates that three billion people rely on wild caught and farmed seafood as their primary source of protein [233]. Coastal and marine resources like transportation, tourism, and trade all add up to a $28 trillion piece of the world economy by one UN estimate [209]. It is in the interest of everyone on Earth that the oceans remain healthy and functional.

Remote sensing data can be used to monitor and map coastal areas tracking pollution sources and water quality. The health and quality of water can be ascertained by water color which gives an indication of the types of animal and plant life present. Factors like sea grass, coral reefs, water temperature, pH, salinity, and plankton all can be measured from orbit by satellites and give an indication of ocean health and serve as an indicator of biodiversity. Shipping activity in ports that can impact SDG 14 such as pollution plumes, oil spills, and ballast water release is also monitored by remote sensing systems.

Provision of much of this type of data is not conducive to commercialization, and so SDG 14 mainly represents a do no harm responsibility relative to stakeholder intrinsic value creation. Opportunities for stakeholder intrinsic value in the context of SDG 14 are mostly limited to support of government activities; however, some opportunities may also exist to provide services to companies interested in proactively monitoring their own impacts on the environment.

SDG 15: Life on Land

Sadly, the planet is in the midst of a mass extinction event. Species are going extinct now at a rate not seen since the end of the dinosaurs 65 million years ago. The current extinction event is caused by human activity in the form of habitat destruction, pollution, overhunting/fishing, clear-cutting, and introduction of invasive species. One estimate predicts 50% of existing species will be gone by 2100 [234]. The planetary life support system consists of geological, atmospheric, oceanic, and biological components. It is what yields things like clean water, breathable air, and food (recall discussion in Chapter 4 on ecosystem services). If 50% of the biological diversity is removed from the system, what are the implications to these life support functions that everyone takes for granted? The planetary biological system is so big and complicated that the answer is difficult to predict, but the stakes could not be higher.

Mitigations to help curb the mass extinction that is underway include conservation, restoration, and designing human activity to act in symbiosis with nature. Sustainable development to these ends in support of life on land involves considerations of forests, wildlife, animal habitats, biodiversity, and ecosystem health. A common way in which space systems can help support sustainable development is through forest management. Remote sensing data can be collected on local environmental features like rainfall, soil moisture, and pollution to understand stresses or changes in a forest. Additionally, remote sensing data can be used to track attributes of the forest itself such as canopy height and tree health by measuring leaf cover and biomass. These types of insights can assist with accounting for impacts or lack thereof from nearby human activity.

Remote sensing of forests can also support law enforcement. Simply having eyes on a forest can act as a passive form of enforcement and mitigate clandestine illegal logging that goes against public national commitments toward SDGs. This type of enforcement can help predict and avoid devastating desertification processes from taking place and prevent contributions to carbon dioxide emissions related to loss of forests [235].

It is intuitive that these same capabilities can also be used to track and manage wildfires. Unfortunately, wildfires are expected to become an increasingly common effect of climate change. Having a constant observation presence from space to manage firefighting efforts and public safety will be priceless as fires become larger and greater in number. As noted for SDG 10, opportunities for natural disaster mitigation and response exist for space services in support of government-led efforts. In the case of wildfires, this includes real-time emergency response as well as provision of monitoring systems in advance of a disaster.

In addition to monitoring and preserving vegetation, space systems can be used to preserve wildlife. Monitoring public land, national parks, and other conservation areas can help enforce poaching laws. GNSS and remote sensing systems can also be applied to tracking wildlife movement. This type of insight can help scientists understand ecosystem and habitat boundaries and thereby inform general land management strategies balancing agriculture, wildlife, and human infrastructure.

Ecosystem accounting is an applied methodology to manage life on land that uses the concepts discussed in this section. It involves taking a finite plot of land and quantifying elements of the ecosystem such as biomass of different plant types, canopy height, water features, and any other metrics of interest. Much of this data collection can occur from space. These measurements can be used to understand biodiversity, carbon storage, and other natural features and thereby enable managed human development on a plot of land that minimizes environmental impacts. Ecosystem accounting is an opportunity for direct stakeholder intrinsic value creation for customers interested in proactive support of SDG 15.

As with SDGs 13 and 14, SDG 15 is best viewed as a do no harm consideration in a stakeholder intrinsic value assessment. Direct opportunities for stakeholder intrinsic value creation are most likely to emerge as supporting roles for government or nonprofit efforts. Exceptions to this may be providing value-added services such as ecosystem accounting to customers interested in proactively mitigating their own impacts on the environment.

SDG 16: Peace, Justice, and Strong Institutions

Stable, conflict-free, and peaceful societies are universal goals. Problems like homicide, political instability, human trafficking, unequipped justice systems, corruption, and human rights violations are challenges present to varying degrees in all nations. Peace is a goal just like economic development or climate change mitigation where, if attained, numerous other problems tend to go away. Many of the applications of space systems in support of other SDGs indirectly help secure peace through maintaining a stable supply of basic needs and reducing inequality. In *Post-2030 Agenda and Role of Space*, Anne-Sophie Martin frames SDG 16 in this context as "there cannot be sustainable development without peace, and there can be no lasting peace without sustainable development" [236].

Law enforcement assistance is possible using remote sensing data for border monitoring, port security, wartime refugee assistance, and monitoring routes used for human trafficking [209]. Additionally, remote sensing data can be used to track and discover evidence of human rights violations such as destruction of homes and villages, mass graves, fires, and explosions. Another peace and security concern for the whole world is monitoring the use of nuclear material. Remote sensing and GNSS data can both be used to monitor nuclear fuel processing and to detect unauthorized activities related to mining uranium oxide, power station operations, and nuclear waste storage. Stakeholder intrinsic value creation is possible in all these areas. Governments have a lead role when it comes to justice and maintaining peace; however, their monitoring and observation tools by which to achieve this can be provided through commercial means.

Commercially provided remote sensing and GNSS data can also be used as evidence in international courts [236]. Instances of using satellite-generated data as court evidence began in the 1980s and included settling border disputes and documentation of illegal presence of military forces. Now, GNSS services can be used to supply court evidence related to tracking people via ankle monitors, vehicles involved in illegal activity, and ships performing clandestine activities like overfishing or illegal cargo transfer. A powerful feature of using remote sensing and GNSS data as evidence is that it is becoming increasingly available and democratized. Gone are the days when this type of data is available only to wealthy governments. Greater access to transparent data to be used as court evidence drives more account-ability. It also lends credibility to use of data from space systems as impar-tial evidence if the data is publicly available from multiple sources.

Providing the tools and services for law enforcement is one means for the space industry to create stakeholder intrinsic value relative to SDG 16. At the same time, any stakeholder assessment should include consideration as to whether or not a product or service is in support of or contrary to the goal of peace. Peace is central to achieving long-term sustainability and making progress in other SDGs, and so is an important do no harm component of harmony in the stakeholder intrinsic value criteria.

SDG 17: Partnerships

> We are entering a new space age, and I hope this will help to create a new unity. Space exploration has already been a great unifier—we seem able to cooperate between nations in space in a way we can only envy on Earth.
>
> —Stephen Hawking [237]

By definition, to operate a global economy in space, nations must cooperate and work together. Because space is an international commons and because some of the distinctive capabilities offered by space systems are global in na-ture, value creation in space goes hand in hand with international partner-ships. International cooperation in space activities started in earnest with over 100 countries signing the 1967 UN Outer Space Treaty. The principal themes of the treaty support international collaboration, stating that the exploration and use of outer space shall be for peaceful purposes for the benefit of all humankind. Other details include things like barring national appropriation of land or resources, banning weapons in space, assigning states the responsibility of monitoring activities in space whether public or commercial, assigning liability to states, and declaring that states should avoid harmful contamination of space and celestial bodies.

Following the signing of the Outer Space Treaty, space has continued ever since to motivate and unify interest among people across political bor-ders, across cultures, across genders, and across generations. For example, consider the seemingly unlikely but highly productive and long-term col-laboration between Russia and the United States on the ISS. Or consider NASA's next generation human spaceflight programs. In the Gateway lunar space station and the Orion crew exploration vehicle programs, the group of international partners providing major hardware components includes the United States, the EU, Canada, and Japan.

The modern era of human space exploration also has produced a new international space policy agreement, the Artemis Accords. The Artemis Accords, initially among ten countries, is growing in number of signatories and describes rules of cooperation to adhere to in outer space for those involved with NASA's Artemis program and/or involved with the space economy in general. The NASA website for the agreement states: "The Artemis Accords will describe a shared vision for principles, grounded in the Outer Space Treaty of 1967, to create a safe and transparent environment which facilitates exploration, science, and commercial activities for all of humanity to enjoy" [238]. The agreement addresses topics like orbital debris mitigation,[8] public sharing of scientific data, promotion of the "sustainable and beneficial use of space for all humankind," a commitment to emergency assistance, adherence to the UN *Guidelines for the Long-term Sustainability of Outer Space Activities* [152], and resource extraction[9] all the while promoting international cooperation and commercial approaches. There is strong alignment with much of the content in the Artemis Accords and the stakeholder intrinsic value criteria and so adherence with the Artemis Accords can be seen generally as supportive of stakeholder intrinsic value creation.

Creating value in space happens to captivate and excite people around the world. This is a unifying feature of the industry that is convenient when forming international partnerships and agreements. In these cases, support of SDG 17 is a welcome benefit, but likely not the core driver for value creation or profit. The space industry primarily has a do no harm responsibility relative to SDG 17 to consider in a stakeholder intrinsic value assessment. That said, stakeholder intrinsic value creation in space may be enhanced in cases involving productive international partnerships.

Notes

1 An alternative to SPACE OPERA now available also is the open-source Strathclyde Space Systems Database (SSSD). Like SPACE OPERA, SSSD is a software tool for performing LCAs specifically in the space sector and it also adheres to the ESA LCA handbook [161].
2 Nitrogen oxide is also a byproduct of any solid object entering the atmosphere and becoming superheated such as asteroids or reentering spacecraft; however, it is estimated that the effect in 2020 on the stratosphere of human-made debris reentering the atmosphere is negligible [270].
3 For reference, a single space shuttle launch required 113 tons of liquid hydrogen. Using the coal-reliant energy of decades past, this amount of liquid hydrogen would require 1,400 kwh of power to produce, which equates to approximately 700 tons of carbon dioxide in the atmosphere for one launch [267] (compared to a single international aircraft flight which emits on the order of one ton of carbon dioxide).
4 $1 million is approximately the cost of a rideshare launch on a SpaceX Falcon 9 rocket in 2021 [269].
5 Harmony, pleasure, knowledge, justice, beauty, and benevolence.
6 Helium-3 can currently be produced on Earth in small amounts at great expense for applications in research and in instruments used for scans of shipping containers to detect nuclear material.
7 Thomas Diegelman observes that salt was the first globally traded commodity and responsible for standing up and motivating global trade networks that

formed the first global economy [206]. He points out that so far, there is no analogous "salt" for deep space, but helium-3 may be a candidate in the future.

8 Notably, specific reference to the IADC *Space Debris Mitigation Guidelines* [198] is not included.

9 The content on resource extraction is perhaps the most controversial. The Artemis Accords reaffirm the prohibition by the Outer Space Treaty of national appropriation of space resources or of any nation staking claim to a planetary body. At the same time, the Artemis Accords also declare that resource extraction activities do not constitute national appropriation and this can occur for the benefit of humankind. The intent of the content on resource extraction is thought to help enable commercial activity in this area.

7   The Business of Human Space Exploration

Human spaceflight and deep space exploration are pinnacles of the space industry in terms of technical challenge and historical achievement. Human spaceflight and deep space exploration also are among the least mature segments of the industry in terms of commercialization. Stakeholder intrinsic value creation, which necessitates profitability, has been suggested in this book as the best means for creating value in space. Do stakeholder intrinsic value creation goals apply when it comes to human spaceflight and deep space exploration? Are challenges related to commercialization reconcilable in this context? This chapter will explore the answers to these questions. The virtues in the stakeholder intrinsic value criteria, "pleasure, knowledge, justice, beauty, and benevolence," can be supported in various ways by human spaceflight and exploration. Satisfying the harmony and profitability requirements is less straightforward.

Why Should Humans Go to Space?

To understand if stakeholder intrinsic value creation is possible in human space exploration, it is helpful to first examine the rationale behind sending humans to space in the first place. There are numerous views on the best justification for human spaceflight that are described in this section. Opposition to sending humans to space often characterizes it as a frivolous activity where the considerable required resources would be better spent directly solving problems on Earth. This view tends to be an oversimplification.

Historically, human spaceflight occurred for political motivations described, in part, by John F. Kennedy in his Apollo-era speech at Rice University in 1962:

> For space science, like nuclear science and all technology, has no conscience of its own. Whether it will become a force for good or ill depends on man, and only if the United States occupies a position of pre-eminence can we help decide whether this new ocean will be a sea of peace or a new terrifying theater of war.

DOI: 10.4324/9781003268734-7

Political influence and national prestige were the original motivations for human space exploration.

Since the 1960s, many have considered the same issue and devised alternative motivations for humans to go to space. Planetary scientist William K. Hartmann said on the matter in a 1992 *Smithsonian* article: "space exploration ought to do something for our civilization" and "the [space] program would be a blend of data gathering and exploration, research and adventure, robotic and human activity" [239]. Hartmann casts a wide net but offers an important foundational position, in that *space exploration should do something for humanity.*

Paul Weiland suggests "greed, fear, and curiosity" as reasons for humans going to space [240]. Weiland's suggestions can be seen as building on Hartmann's view in a way by providing practical ties to motivations rooted in human nature. For example, greed may drive exploration related to extraction of space resources for profit. Or fear of an Earthly cataclysm may drive formation of human colonies on Mars. Curiosity has already and will continue to drive scientific investigations across the solar system. Curiosity can be seen as a need just as other human needs. Some needs are admittedly more immediate and critical like food and water, but satisfying curiosity is a need found in the natural human disposition nonetheless. So long as people are curious, there will always be demand for space exploration.

Hartmann's and Weiland's views described here are fairly broad. How about something more specific? One of the most common justifications offered for deep space exploration is to better ensure the long-term survival of humanity [113, 121]. In this argument, supporters point out that a cataclysmic species-killing event on Earth is all but guaranteed in the long term. Whether it is an asteroid, nuclear war, global pandemic, or another ice age, eventually something globally devastating like this is sure to occur. Therefore, the *only* scenario in which humanity survives is one where it becomes a multiplanetary species. Furthermore, there is an argument for urgency, given that it is unknown for how long current technological, economic, and political conditions will exist that are enabling the space industry to flourish [241]. This view is not unreasonable, given the potential negative outcomes of climate change and other unsustainable behavior that will increasingly strain human civilization in the coming years.

Tony Milligan is one such proponent of both urgency and the duty for space exploration in order to promote the survival of humanity. Milligan rationalizes this position by claiming:

> (1) all other things being equal, it is better if humanity (or some offshoot of the latter) continues to exist rather than ceasing to exist; and (2) some currently existing humans may well have at least some moral obligation to assist in attempting to bring this about.
>
> [113]

Milligan also asserts, in-line with the theme of this book, that human settlement in space "may best be done (and perhaps it may only be done) by promoting the kind of incentives that will encourage the private sector to invest heavily in space" [242]. Milligan balances his view however by recognizing that it may interfere with a need for preservation of nature and could exist in parallel with a code of ethics "...in order to allay fears about the potential misuse of resources once private property becomes entrenched" [113].

While clear in his recommendation, Milligan allows for some flexibility noting that the duty to settle space does not imply "at any means necessary" or at "whatever expense" [242]. Milligan's perspective overlaps with the concept of stakeholder intrinsic value, in that (1) profitability is emphasized as the best means for value creation and (2) there are multiple and often conflicting elements to consider regarding the legitimacy or value of something. From this nuanced vantage point, the case is made by Milligan for human space settlement in order to help preserve longevity of the human species.

Another rationale suggested for space exploration is to increase scientific knowledge of the universe [13]. Within this view, however, many suggest that there is still little justification for sending humans and space exploration is more appropriate for robots. Use of robots is cheaper, less risky, and they can endure longer and harsher conditions than any astronaut could. These are all good reasons why robots should continue *most* space exploration. Practically speaking, what humans bring to the table are opinions, experience, and real-time decision-making. Robots are excellent at obtaining vast amounts of data in extreme environments. They are not excellent at spotting features that are surprising, interesting, unexpected, or troubling for some reason. Nor are they as good at modifying a scientific study in real time based on intuition or experience.

Some examples highlighting the value of humans in data collection are useful. In 1978, the Soviet Union began the Biosphere program. Biosphere pooled resources from communist countries around the globe such as Hungary, Vietnam, East Germany, and Cuba in order to collect satellite imagery for domestic planning and environmental monitoring. Data collection involved use of satellites and also cosmonauts on the Salyut 6 space station to take photos. By placing humans in orbit to collect data, the result was something different in nature than that from the satellites alone. In cases where a human is in orbit, like Salyut 6 or today on the International Space Station (ISS), they actively seek out the most interesting and relevant features to collect and present data on. Satellites collect imagery on everything indiscriminately missing chances to focus resources on that which is most interesting to humanity. Perhaps the most famous example of this is the "Earthrise" photo taken during the Apollo 8 mission by NASA astronaut, William Anders, on Christmas Eve in 1968 while orbiting the Moon. This photo, seen in Figure 7.1, helped to inspire the environmental movement in the 1970s which had far-reaching positive impacts on Earth that resonate to this day.

Some have proposed that a human presence in space exploration and the unique perspective that comes with it will enable reflection on applying

Figure 7.1 "Earthrise" photo taken by NASA astronaut William Anders while orbiting the Moon in 1968.

what is found to the sustainability challenges on Earth. Charles Cockell shares this view, saying: "To really understand your own country it is good to visit others; it helps to develop a perspective on your own culture and origins. So travelling to new planets can help us understand home" [243]. There has been a tremendous amount of insight gained already about Earth since humans entered space in the 1950s. For example, Mars has been found to have no ozone or magnetic field and the planet appears to be in later stages of an apparent historic global change in climate and topography. On Venus a runaway greenhouse effect has been observed, similar to but more severe than that which is occurring on Earth. More broadly, no signs of life have yet been found in the solar system which helps to reinforce how rare and important the conditions of Earth's biosphere are [243]. Insights like these from Mars, Venus, the Moon, and more will continue with further robotic exploration but stand to be enhanced and have a greater impact on humanity if human explorers are involved.

In justifying human space exploration, there is another motivation that is less pragmatic but no less powerful than species survival and scientific knowledge. Exploration is simply part of human nature. It's not for everyone as there is a great diversity in spirit when it comes to adventure seeking, pushing boundaries, and taking risks, but since the beginning of time, an enabling feature of humanity's survival has been the inclination to explore, expand, and adapt to new challenging conditions. And even though this inclination only manifests in a small number of people, the benefits can resonate across generations if an individual makes a significant breakthrough and establishes a foothold for others to follow. This concept applies to any type of frontier physical, intellectual, artistic, or spiritual. It certainly applies to frontiers in space exploration.

Jacques Arnould ponders: "...what would have happened to our species if, since its birth, it had not stayed true to its natural curiosity and penchant for exploration?" [244]. Similarly, Robert Zubrin says: "The human desire to explore is thus one of our primary adaptations. We have a fundamental need to see what is on the other side of the hill, because our ancestors did, and we are alive because they did" [245]. On the one hand, this particular justification for human space exploration does not appear to be very pragmatic or of great obvious utility, however, since when have humans been pragmatic about satisfying basic instinctual inclinations? Especially in cases where the means to do so exist and there is no harmful impact on others?

Refraining from space exploration would entail extinguishing the flame of curiosity embedded in human nature. This would be a collective expression of restraint that is largely unrealistic if nothing else. It would take proactive, long-term, and multigenerational resistance to suppress the inevitability of continued interest in space exploration. Look no further than recent history as suggested by Pittman et al.: "All evidence indicates that we will explore space forever. After more than fifty years in space, interest has not waned, and the number and diversity of people and organizations that want to do things in space continues to increase" [246]. Pittman's view is supported by data from a General Social Services survey on this topic. The survey indicates that from 2008 to 2014, 67% of Americans were either very or moderately interested in space exploration [13, 247]. This result is not surprising as it is generally known that there is some amount of public interest in space rooted in both curiosity and a natural inclination to explore. The fact is that demand for human space exploration exists and it has staying power.

The inclination for exploration and challenging frontiers can have broad positive effects. One consequence of forging a path into unknown territory is that it is no longer a frontier and a door is potentially opened for others to follow. A process can begin of opportunity-seeking and economic expansion made possible in part by that first daring explorer. This process has happened countless times in the past in the realms of geography, science, art, philosophy, and religion. Migration into space today is no different in concept.

So what? Well, now that the technology exists, those interested need not be caged by the limits of the biosphere on Earth. The natural environment does not stop at the boundary of the atmosphere just like it didn't stop at the edges of the African continent for early humans millennia ago. Years later, as soon as wind-powered ships offered the means, people used them to expand boundaries yet again and to pursue new opportunities in other newly accessible locations. The same can be said relative to the advent of wagons, cars, airplanes, and submarines. Human space exploration is a continuation of natural behavior that has occurred for thousands of years.

As noted, what can follow exploration once a door is opened are others seeking new opportunities. Any notions of living, having a job, building a home, seeking adventure can occur anywhere in the natural environment that is accessible and relatively safe. Why shouldn't someone do these things on the Moon or on Mars or at the bottom of the ocean for that matter if the means exist, they have the desire, and it does not cause undue harm to others? Of all seven billion people on Earth, there are plenty that are willing to follow in the footsteps of the first explorers on an adventure like this in space, just as there were in the past for frontiers on Earth. And in scenarios like this, one day the adventurous frontier is not so adventurous anymore and there are just "normal" people living their lives. The long-term view of space exploration may be seen as simply an expansion of civilization no different than that which has occurred for thousands of years.

In conclusion, the most common motivations offered by advocates for human space exploration are listed below:

* Political influence and national prestige
* Ensuring long-term survival of humanity
* Creation of new knowledge
* Human nature and the inclination for curiosity and exploration
* Natural expansion of civilization

How do the activities listed above relate to commercialization and stakeholder intrinsic value creation? There are several areas related to human spaceflight and a deep space economy around which a commercial market either is already forming or has potential to form in the near future. These are discussed in the following sections and include tourism, resource harvesting, deep space cargo services, and deep space telecommunications. These activities can be driven by any of the motivations listed above; however, ultimately they all potentially feed into the expansion of civilization category.

Space Tourism

The stepping-stone to stakeholder intrinsic value creation opportunities related to human spaceflight lies in space tourism. Technical advances and dropping costs are making this area the new dominant driver of human spaceflight. A value chain is forming in support of this growing area that includes launch vehicles, training facilities, in-space food production, communication and data infrastructure, orbital habitat facilities, marketing, insurance, manufacturing, and in-space recreational activities. This new value chain will result in spacecraft that are more affordable and safer than ever. All of this can be considered as a stepping-stone because, while financially compelled to meet tourism demands, the same systems once operational can be applied to support any of the other justifications discussed for human spaceflight in the previous section. It's up to the next generation of entrepreneurs to figure out new value creation schemes that leverage the first-ever affordable human spaceflight platforms.

Space tourism has actually been around for a while; it is only the affordability aspect that is new. Toyohiro Akiyama became the first space tourist in 1990 when Russia hosted him on Mir. From 2001 to 2009, Russia also sent several tourists to the ISS for approximately $20 million each. What is significant and changing compared to instances of space tourism in the past is the formation of a *mass* space tourism market. The cost to go to space today, in 2022, is as low as $450,000 [248]. Who can afford this? As of 2020, there were almost two million people in the world with a net worth of $10 million and almost 40 million people with a net worth of at least $1 million [249]. These groups of people represent the existing and near-future space tourist markets, respectively. As tourism capabilities increase, the services and opportunities for the higher-end experience will evolve as well, which will, in turn, flow new innovations and accessibility downstream to others across the space industry. In 2021, several companies at long last and with great fanfare debuted commercial spaceflight vehicles that are available now to paying customers. Also, in 2020 NASA announced, in an agency-first, that ISS access for paying customers in US modules would be permitted and partially accommodated by a planned commercial habitat module to be added to the station [250].

In one sense, simply serving as a destination, an end point for the trip, is an important role that the ISS has had in creation of the space tourism industry. The ISS will not exist forever as a tourism destination though, and while an exact retirement date is not known, many expect it to be somewhere in the 2030 timeframe. Commercial space stations may be the next major development in human spaceflight and space tourism. NASA and others are pushing for commercial space stations to takeover and expand the role that the ISS currently has. As of late 2021, NASA is cost-sharing development of three commercial space stations hoping to repeat the hand-off to industry process that was done successfully in the commercial crew and cargo programs. Commercial space stations will not only be central to the space tourism industry, they will also offer facilities for numerous additional activities, including fundamental research, applied research, and in-space manufacturing.

Both orbital and suborbital launches offer commercial potential related to tourism. Regarding suborbital launches in particular, they are a cheaper choice than an orbital launch or use of an orbital facility if the relatively short window of microgravity (a matter of minutes) is all that is needed. Suborbital human spaceflight applications include recreation, R&D, and point-to-point global transportation [251]. If sustainability considerations are minded by the companies involved, space tourism (orbital and suborbital) may be a source of stakeholder intrinsic value creation in the areas of pleasure, knowledge, and enabling other bearers of stakeholder intrinsic value. Space tourism stands as the most immediately promising area for commercializing human spaceflight.

Space Resources

Extracting space resources for profit is a potential area of stakeholder intrinsic value creation for the future. Harvesting space resources has been suggested as a means to address two different needs: (1) growing demand on Earth and (2) utilization in space. Regarding growing demand on Earth, as population and wealth increase globally, there will be more and more conflict and competition for Earth's resources. And it is a fact that, in the case of many minerals, space has enough resources to support the needs of at least several thousand times the population on Earth [252]. Asteroids in particular are considered the greatest off-world potential source of resources in the solar system, including numerous substances of use to humans such as water, platinum, nickel, cobalt, iron, aluminum, titanium, and rare Earth elements [253].

Annette Toivonen goes so far as to say on this point in *Sustainable Space Tourism* that "Opening access to the unlimited resources in space could therefore facilitate world peace and security" [254]. Any access to resources or a single resource may serve to alleviate pressure on the supply on Earth as well as to alleviate environmental impacts associated with its extraction and processing. Similarly, Robert Jacobson says in *Space is Open for Business*: "Most people live with the assumption that we're constrained by Earth and its materials" and goes on to point out that "the only way to have continuous growth is to incorporate space as part of Earth's economic influence and activity" [15]. The suggestion is that continuing economic growth around the world and spreading the associated benefits in ways that are equitable and sustainable will, in part, rely on new sources of natural resources.

There are theoretical environmental benefits to space resource extraction also. Space offers the only instance where burden shifting (see Life Cycle Assessment (LCA) section in Chapter 6) can occur beyond the biosphere. If raw materials were harvested in space, this would remove the burden on Earth's environment associated with mining and processing. Amazon and Blue Origin founder Jeff Bezos is outspoken on advocating for the migration of heavy industry into outer space [255]. This migration would not necessarily mean that heavy industries would pollute less, it just would mean that the waste sink moves off-planet and the environmental burden is shifted to the expanse of space. Notably, as Bezos points out, a large part of this burden shift would be due to relocating off-planet energy production for high demand manufacturing operations.

There are several potential backfire scenarios that have been identified related to space resource harvesting. One challenge will be harvesting and utilizing resources in a way that is equitable. Toivonen points out that "no one has yet coherently explained how these resources will possibly benefit the whole of humankind rather than a handful of rich companies and countries" [254]. The fear is that the availability of more resources will likely not meet the needs of the poor but rather increase consumption rates overall and exacerbate inequality by benefiting the super-wealthy that do the extraction [256].

Another potential backfire of space resource extraction for use on Earth is that by unlocking an infinite supply of resources, mass consumption and mass production on Earth would follow [243]. The same risk exists relative to a scenario where an unlimited, cheap, clean energy source becomes available someday. In either case, the risk is that the surge in supply results in a surge in use and waste overshadowing any benefit given by efficiency or reduced production impacts. A third backfire scenario with commercial space resource extraction is that a flood of space resources into the marketplace would introduce such an oversupply that the price would plummet and render space harvesting no longer economical. A self-defeating activity in this scenario.

The reality is that mining resources in space for use on Earth has risks from numerous perspectives and it will only occur if it is capable of driving commercial success. Space resource extraction, if realized, may ultimately serve to empower humanity by providing security and independence from the limitations of Earth; however, it is not clear yet if this is actually needed. Upon further assessment, it may become obvious that despite great societal challenges, it is easier and more economical to simply make do with what is available on Earth. If a compelling need does emerge for space resource harvesting for use on Earth, this activity could occur through stakeholder intrinsic value creation.

On the other hand, a stronger case already exists for space resource harvesting for utilization *in space*. Currently, everything needed in space is built on and launched from Earth. Escaping Earth's gravity is costly and energy-intensive. Resources in space can be harvested to produce propellant, life support consumables (i.e., water and oxygen), or raw materials for in-space manufacturing. On the Moon, the regolith itself can be used as an additive manufacturing construction material when fused together by a high-energy beam. Additionally, useful compounds are found in lunar regolith and can be extracted such as oxygen, silicon, aluminum, and iron. On Mars, the carbon dioxide-rich atmosphere can be used to create oxygen or methane rocket fuel if reacted with water, which is also found on Mars [257]. Any opportunity to avoid launching mass from Earth that is related to needs in space offers potential for increased launch efficiency, reduced environmental impacts on Earth, greater mission capabilities, and greater self-sufficiency of a human presence in space. All means to increase stakeholder intrinsic value.

In addition to saving processing and launch expenditures to send hardware to space from Earth, utilization of resources in space may have a compounding effect that enables even more activity in space. Some go so far as to say that continued long-term expansion into deeper space *depends* on strategic use of the early and easiest to access space resources. James Schwartz remarks:

> The incredibly vast array of resources available at higher Δv budgets (the rest of the NEO population; the Main Belt asteroids; the planets and their satellites; Kiuper belt objects; etc.) will become permanently inaccessible to us if we do not reserve enough of our early spoils for the expansion of spaceflight capabilities [13].

Expected to be first on the list of space resources harvested and processed off-planet is water. The uses for water in space are numerous and include drinking, breathable air, hygiene, radiation shielding, and splitting it into its hydrogen and oxygen components to refuel cryogenic rockets. The Moon has 600 million tons of frozen water at one pole, it is three days away, and it is orders of magnitude easier to launch off of the Moon compared to the Earth. Overall environmental benefit on Earth may be realized from harvesting and using water in space as long as the mass of water harvested exceeds the mass of the spacecraft and equipment launched to do the harvesting [258]. Given that human activity in cis-lunar space (CLS) is expected to increase over the next decade, harvesting water in space stands as a potential near-term stakeholder intrinsic value creation opportunity.

Two high-profile prospective space resource companies folded in 2020. This indicates that at least for the time being, space resource harvesting lacks a substantial market and therefore is not a feasible commercial venture. In addition to unclear markets, another impediment to continued development of space resource extraction is relatively immature regulations. Recall from Chapter 2 the important role that private property rights play in a commercial endeavor. No company is likely to expend the considerable resources needed for harvesting materials in space if they are not confident that those materials will legally belong to them afterwards to sell and profit from.

To help with this legal challenge, the US government approved the US Commercial Space Launch Competitiveness Act of 2015, which states:

> A United States citizen engaged in commercial recovery of an asteroid resource or a space resource under this chapter shall be entitled to any asteroid resource or space resource obtained, including to possess, own,

transport, use, and sell the asteroid resource or space resource obtained in accordance with applicable law, including the international obligations of the United States.

Luxemburg passed similar legislation in 2016 followed by the UAE in 2019 and Japan in 2021. More are sure to follow, though some consider these early national legal frameworks for resource extraction to be controversial as the Outer Space Treaty does prohibit appropriation of celestial bodies. The 2015 US legislation effectively codifies an interpretation of this element of the treaty. According to the legislation, a private actor may extract and appropriate resources such as water or minerals from a celestial body, but may not appropriate the body itself as the Outer Space Treaty directs. To complicate this matter further, the 1979 Moon Treaty, of which there are only 16 signatories,[1] explicitly bans the appropriation of resources in space.

Commercial space resource extraction activity will depend in part on increasing the maturity of regulations through both national laws and international agreements in the future. This is needed in order to minimize the perceived risk to entrepreneurs and investors by providing confidence that resources extracted will be honored as private property that can be sold and profited from. Without this legal assurance, it will be more difficult to attract investments necessary to form and operate a resource extraction company. Stakeholder intrinsic value creation is possible if the progress in increasing legal certainty continues up to the international level and market demand emerges. If a commercial space harvesting industry does not emerge, resource extraction may still occur, but only in limited volumes for bespoke government-led activities.

Deep Space Cargo and Telecommunications Services

A real example of a deep space commercial market that is forming currently is lunar cargo delivery services. Formation of this market was instigated by NASA's Commercial Lunar Payload Services (CLPS) initiative which was kicked off in 2018. As NASA's Commercial Orbital Transportation Services program spurred a commercial cargo delivery market for low Earth orbit (LEO), CLPS intends to do the same but with the Moon as the destination. Cargo delivery services to the surface of the Moon may end up being the first deep space commercial market. The program involves NASA cost-sharing development of spacecraft with numerous companies and also acting as a guaranteed first customer. Future customers for these companies could include other governments or actors within the space tourism industry.

Another area of deep space commerce already in initial stages of formation is industry-provided telecommunications services for landers, orbiters, space stations, and settlements on the Moon and Mars [259]. Like with lunar cargo delivery, government will play the initial role of guaranteed customer and assist with technology development. After a telecommunications system is established in deep space by governments, entrepreneurs will be able to innovate around and expand the system, perhaps ultimately taking it over. Recall that this is the process that occurred in the past with Earth orbit telecommunications systems. Both lunar cargo delivery services and deep space telecommunications stand as stakeholder intrinsic value creation opportunities.

Commercial Human Space Exploration?

Commercial human spaceflight has come about just in recent years. NASA now relies on companies in the American commercial space industry competing with each other to deliver reliable, safe, and cost-effective crew and cargo to LEO. These commercial platforms are beginning already to attract additional customers beyond the US government, thereby expanding the space economy even more. Furthermore, space tourism is now opening human spaceflight to the general public. Does all of this mean that human space *exploration* is on track to becoming commercialized? Not exactly.

Outer space and the act of deep space exploration may be seen as a public good, non-excludable and non-rival. Given the size and nature of outer space, one person cannot be excluded from exploring.[2] In terms of rivalry, one person undertaking exploration in no way prevents another from also performing space exploration somewhere else. In practice though, *access* to space is excludable and rival due to financial, regulatory, and technological needs [260]. There simply are limited resources and opportunities to undertake space exploration and a limited number of organizations that can provide the necessary infrastructure and expertise. For example, a company can choose to exclude those who cannot afford the established ticket price in a spacecraft launch. Occupation of a specific rocket and spaceship does prevent another from using that particular system.

The oceans on Earth present a useful analogy. In the high seas in international territory, one cannot be excluded from exploring and one person exploring does not prevent another from also exploring. However, in practice one needs to activate commercial means such as a boat and a crew for access. While the act of exploration in space (and in the oceans) is non-excludable and non-rival, the fact that there is and will continue to be a demand for human access to space indicates that commercialization of access and the equipment needed for exploration is possible.

In short, space exploration cannot be commercialized because it is a public good, but the means to access space can be. This partially illustrates why the technical ability has existed since the 1960s, but commercial human spaceflight has only arisen recently once the prospect of space tourism become profitable and relatively safe. Tourism has acted as the means by which profit can be obtained through providing human spaceflight systems that incidentally also could be used for exploration. Human exploration of deep space will have to continue in a nonprofit-seeking auspice at the behest of either governments or motivated wealthy individuals. Stakeholder intrinsic value creation does not apply to human space exploration directly.

Stakeholder Intrinsic Value Criteria in Deep Space

Are the tenets of stakeholder intrinsic value such as harmony and the other goodness virtues applicable or as important when considering value creation at a deep space locale? Some examples of stakeholder intrinsic value creation opportunities in a deep space economy have been mentioned already in this chapter. Further examination of this topic is necessary though to better understand the role of harmony and goodness in a value assessment in this context.

Pittman et al. have identified six factors that are thought to be necessary to make a continuous human space presence a reality [246]. Pittman's six factors represent the minimal infrastructure capabilities that are required. All six factors may be seen as components of a commercial market enabling access to space and are potential stakeholder intrinsic value creation opportunities.

1   Frequent, reliable, and cheap access to LEO for people and a wide range of cargo sizes
2   Vehicles capable of moving payloads and passengers beyond LEO to orbits around other planetary bodies
3   In-space resource extraction and processing systems to provide materials needed to support operations in CLS
4   Resource depots in LEO and out in CLS to support asteroid and Mars missions
5   Reliable high bandwidth communication and navigation
6   Landers capable of landing people and equipment upon bodies with significant gravitational fields.

How do Pittman's six factors fit into the narrative of stakeholder intrinsic value creation? Item 2 in the stakeholder intrinsic value criteria holds that properties of harmony and goodness of a product or activity are due to innate features or due to instrumental value enabling an external bearer of harmony and goodness. The activities listed by Pittman may fall into either category, but likely are mostly enablers of some other form of inherent goodness such as knowledge or pleasure. If this is true, then the need for harmony and attention to sustainability becomes the primary focus of a stakeholder intrinsic value assessment. The list of virtues defining goodness are realized not directly by Pittman's factors but by the ends that they enable.

Pittman's six factors offer some specific examples, but what about a broader view of stakeholder intrinsic value creation relative to the various justifications for human spaceflight that were previously discussed? Below is an assessment of each in terms of its inherent goodness according to the stakeholder intrinsic value criteria. In all cases, harmony applies as a consideration but not always as the primary goal. The other goodness virtues are listed only if they correspond to a direct goal of the activity (i.e., not listed if they may occur as an eventual indirect result).

*   Political influence and national prestige – Supports the virtues of harmony, pleasure, justice, and benevolence.
*   Off-world colonies to ensure the long-term survival of humanity – Supports the virtues of harmony, pleasure, knowledge, and benevolence. Harmony may be a challenge if the environmental impacts on Earth are high or excessive resource demands compete with other pressing needs.
*   Creation of new knowledge – Supports the virtues of harmony, knowledge, justice, beauty, and benevolence.
*   Satisfy human curiosity – Supports the virtues of harmony, pleasure, knowledge, and benevolence.
*   Expanding the economy and civilization into space – Supports the virtues of harmony, pleasure, knowledge, justice, beauty, and benevolence. Harmony may be a challenge if the environmental impacts on Earth are high or excessive resource demands compete with other pressing needs.

Stakeholder intrinsic value creation is possible in deep space both in terms of profitability and in terms of doing things that are inherently good. The question of harmony, however, has expanded in scope relative to the previous discussions. Do environmental impacts and sustainability matter in locations beyond Earth's environment? Beyond areas that are regularly travelled or utilized today by humans? Should the need for harmony apply in the same way in deep space as it does on Earth? The following section examines these questions.

Harmony of the Space Economy in Deep Space

The stakeholder intrinsic value criteria call for harmony, which has been interpreted as a need for sustainability so far in this book. The intent of this criteria is that space products and activities must be harmonious with environmental and social systems in order to be inherently good. On Earth, this naturally calls for sustainability. How about settings in deep space?

Space systems for use in a deep space economy will have impacts on Earth because they are produced on Earth using Earth's resources. The earlier discussions therefore on environmental impacts from the space industry and its do no harm responsibilities apply equally to deep space hardware. Beyond production though, there is admittedly not the same sense of urgency related to sustainability of space environments at locations far from Earth. At the very least, this concept is more abstract than sustainability on Earth. It is not necessarily obvious that environmental impacts completely removed from Earth's biosphere should be a concern ever. Discussion on this point is warranted nonetheless for two reasons: (1) harmony plays a central role in the stakeholder intrinsic value criteria and (2) this discussion is largely about future applications of the criteria in an industry that is just beginning to form.

In *Icarus' Second Chance*, Jacques Arnould offers three options for exploitation of deep space and regard for the environment: (1) treat it as a complete sanctuary not to be disturbed, (2) controlled exploitation, and (3) first come, first served exploitation [261]. Option 1, complete sanctuary, Arnould points out is wholly unrealistic as "once a use with high economic value or a strategic use arises, the pressure for its practical implementation will be irresistible." Elvis and Milligan also observe that "We have no good reason to believe that such an off-world economy would behave in a radically different way from terrestrial economies and the latter (as we know) grow exponentially" [262]. Complete sanctuary effectively is off the table, given what is known about human nature and how industries and exploitation of resources on Earth has occurred in the past.

That leaves Options 2 and 3, controlled exploitation and first come, first served, respectively. Controlled exploitation is akin to stakeholder intrinsic value where some activities are more permissible than others depending on their degree of harmony and goodness. However, does the harmony requirement apply to activities that occur well beyond the physical limits of the natural and industrial systems on Earth? Or is there license to either be more "flexible" in this area or to completely ignore tenets of environmental sustainability if one is operating physically outside of Earth and its vicinity?

Addressing climate change and the sustainability of humanity is as important as anything humans have ever done in the past. The notion that significant accomplishments and awareness in the area of sustainability are disregarded simply because one is off-planet does not seem appropriate. At the same time, a compelling pragmatic argument to support the need for deep space environmental sustainability is elusive. A need for social sustainability in deep space is a bit more evident (provided there is a human presence eventually) but still feels quite different than social needs on Earth. Return though to the previous thought, does it seem right to *completely* disregard in any location the collective awareness and behavior obtained at great cost that was necessary to preserve humanity?

Danielle Wood remarks on the matter:

> We don't need to wait until we have created problems that are almost impossible to solve, as we have done on Earth. Instead, we can put in place new guidelines, policies, and cultural norms that will establish our future space societies on foundations that support economic equality, gender equality, sustainable consumption, and sustainable communities.
>
> [263]

Similarly, the Secure World Foundation states in *Space Sustainability: A Practical Guide*: "Addressing the need for space sustainability now means we can prevent negative trends from becoming norms, and ensure that outer space can be used by all countries, not just technologically sophisticated ones."

Sustainability off-planet at least stands to help prevent familiar problems on Earth from arising someday in space through institutionalizing non-sustainable behavior from the start. In other words, environmentally and socially sustainable behavior should be a permanent feature of humanity, no matter the location. There is at least some amount of compelling logic associated with this statement. To disregard monumental and hard-earned perspectives on sustainability that are only just beginning to crystalize as cooperation among nations across the world is troubling even in the context of deep space. The following sections discuss how to practically approach this topic in several specific scenarios.

Space Environments with Instrumental Value

The relevance of deep space environmental sustainability may be less ambiguous in cases where there actually is an immediate and pragmatic consideration. The most pragmatic need today for sustainability in deep space is on and around the Moon. There actually are realistic plans to increase cis-lunar human activities in the near term. Sustainability of lunar resources and lunar orbit may well be the first instance where deep space sustainability becomes a practical consideration. Contamination activities including landing, liftoff, extra-vehicular activities, dust raising, atmospheric contamination, vibration, radio contamination, waste from nuclear power sources, and site destruction may impact natural resources and affect planned activities [264]. Lunar resources, such as water, may have high instrumental value to humans as long as they are not contaminated. Lunar water also may have high scientific value serving as an ancient chemical record of early periods of the Earth and Moon formation.

Concerning lunar orbital debris, the Moon has no atmosphere so the option of deorbiting space junk and letting it burn up does not exist. Maybe a crowded lunar orbit problem is a long way off, but LEO debris was a long way off once also. Had the problem been effectively solved before it ever existed, there would not be a seemingly intractable dilemma of how to continue to use LEO safely and sustainably today. It also is not a stretch to imagine a debris problem forming at Lagrange points. These locations potentially offer high instrumental value to humanity as places to locate habitats, depots for fuel and other supplies, and scientific instruments. Therefore, stakeholder intrinsic value creation at lunar resource sites, useful orbits, and Lagrange points should consider environmental sustainability in support of the harmony requirement.

Space Environments with the Potential for Life

CLS, lunar resources, and Lagrange points are about as immediate and pragmatic as it gets when considering potential deep space environmental priorities relative to humanity's needs. Another of humanity's needs is continued pursuit of new knowledge and understanding about the universe and origins of life. A great source of information in this area may come from space environments that have the potential to contain microbial life. The suggestion from many is to avoid destruction and contamination of these locations in order to preserve maximum scientific value. So, exactly what level of environmental protection should be afforded to these locations?

Referring back to discussion in Chapter 3 on intrinsic value, the fundamental question that G.E. Moore would have asked regarding environmental preservation in space is: would microbial life be better off existing or not existing? On the surface, with no other information, it would seem that the answer from most people would be that microbial life is better off existing if for nothing else the potential scientific value to humanity. This position may be weakened though if the microbial life in question turns out to be harmful or obstructive to some greater, more important realization of value. It also is helpful to remember for context that the vast majority of people have little to no regard for preserving microbial life here on Earth in their day-to-day routines.

Therefore, some reasonable approach to deep space exploration and exploitation that allows in some way for respect of potential life in space is useful in a stakeholder intrinsic value assessment. Charles Cockell proposes three guidelines in this area that are both considerate and pragmatic [265]:

1   We have a duty to preserve individual microbes except when doing so puts constraints on human activities that are considered to be a part of daily life
2   We have a duty to protect ecosystems and communities of microbial life
3   We have a general duty to show respect toward microscopic organisms in our activities

Stakeholder intrinsic value assessments related to deep space exploration and potentially encountering microbial life can consider Cockell's guidelines. Such assessments may find grounding also in the fact that, compared to microbial life on Earth, the main differentiating factor with encountering such life in space is the significant scientific value.

Compared to Cockell's suggestions, more specificity on environmental protection in space can be found in the UN Committee of Space Research (COSPAR) *Planetary Protection Policy* (PPP). Though recent updates to the PPP occurred in 2017 and 2021, it was first outlined in 1964 and served as the basis of Article IX in the Outer Space Treaty. While Cockell's suggestions offer some perspective on high-level guidelines, the PPP goes a level deeper and provides protection guidelines pertaining to different mission types and different types of destinations. It also contains rules related to spacecraft sterilization during manufacturing and rules to protect Earth from reverse contamination. The COSPAR PPP has now served as the basis for NASA's agency-level planetary protection requirements *NPR 8715.24 Planetary Protection Provisions for Robotic Extraterrestrial Missions. NPR 8715.24* goes yet another level deeper in specificity structuring the COSPAR PPP guidance as actionable requirements for a space program.

Cockell's guidelines, the COSPAR PPP, and *NPR 8715.24* may all be used in a stakeholder intrinsic value assessment to determine degrees of harmony related to interaction with space environments that could host life. Until the 2021 update, the COSPAR PPP did not levy any environmental protection for locations in space that are unlikely to host life. In the 2021 update, the PPP was modified to include protection for permanently shadowed regions (PSRs) on the lunar surface. PSRs are thought to be locations containing water and potential scientific value.

Space Environments Devoid of Life and Instrumental Value

What about deep space environments that pose neither obvious instrumental value to humans nor conditions likely to host microbial life? Should the harmony requirement in stakeholder intrinsic value apply to impacting environments in space that are both lifeless and unconnected to the well-being of humans and Earth? Does destruction of these environments make humanity less sustainable? Perhaps not, but the criteria in stakeholder intrinsic value is harmony, not sustainability. The sustainability of humanity is just one manifestation of harmony. Harmony with nature and other systems is included in the criteria as a component of inherent goodness and goodness is not a function of location. Harmony does apply in the context of lifeless non-instrumentally valuable locations, but not in the same way nor for the same reasons as in cases on Earth where environmental and social sustainability are at stake.

Tony Milligan poses an interesting thought experiment in *Nobody Owns the Moon* [113]. What if everyone had the power to decide if the Moon should or should not exist from now on? Furthermore, assume that there would be no negative effects on the planet if it were to not exist (i.e., ocean tides would continue). Milligan presupposes that the vast majority of people would prefer that the Moon did exist. Why? Most people will never go there. Most people spend very little time thinking about the Moon. Still, there is an undeniable reverence for natural monuments and formations that drives a preference, given the choice, for preservation. This doesn't mean that this preference cannot be overwhelmed by other motivations like resource extraction or economic development, but all things equal, there generally needs to be some outside motivation for the destruction of a natural formation. Note, Milligan points out that this mental exercise is useful but not conclusive as it is based on intuition which is subject to error. Also, the Moon is not comparable perhaps to a nondescript asteroid in terms of commanding reverence.

Father of modern environmental ethics Holmes Rolston III considered the same question as to what level of environmental protection is reasonable, if any, to lifeless environments in space. Rolston suggests several rule of thumb guidelines based on the idea that some nonliving things are "recognizably different from their backgrounds and surroundings. They may have striking particularity, symmetry, harmony, grace, spatio-temporal unity and continuity, historical identity, story, even though they are also diffuse, partial, broken" [266]. Such places, according to Rolston, are "loci of value so far as they are products of natural formative processes." They are remarkable and memorable. They also may have no instrumental value whatsoever to human life or life on Earth, yet still they appear to have value according to how one would value other similarly remarkable and distinctive natural formations on Earth. For example, societies today collectively consider to be remarkable things like the Grand Canyon, the arches in Arches National Park, the Rock of Gibraltar in Europe, the El Capitan face in Yosemite National Park, a gem or fossil in a natural history museum, the list could go on. These are things that have garnered interest in preservation even though much of what they are physically is just lifeless rock.

Rolston's guidelines suggest that one should:

> respect any natural place spontaneously worthy of a proper name... respect exotic extremes in natural projects...respect places of historical value...respect places of active and potential creativity [i.e., places that are dynamic and natural creativity is still occurring]...respect places of aesthetic value...respect places of transformative value [i.e., places that radically transform perspective].
>
> [266]

Rolston's suggestions on respect and value for nonliving things in space are not unlike the approach for conservation on Earth, and while less than scientific, they offer a perspective that most people can relate to. A commonsense view that places that are remarkable or memorable deserve preservation. Simple and intuitive. Rolston's guidelines may be useful in consideration of harmony in a stakeholder intrinsic value assessment that concerns impacts on a lifeless environment in space.

Does following Rolston's guidelines rule out resource extraction in space? Mining and resource extraction off-world may be considered similar to how it is considered on Earth. If some level of environmental destruction can be justified in the name of resource extraction on Earth, which is teeming with life and cultural history, surely there can be no great objection to performing the same activity in unseen locations in space that are devoid of both. There can be an innate preference in people for preservation of nature; however, it is potentially reasonable for this preference to become overwhelmed by value creation goals as long as preservation is given due consideration by stakeholders.

Space Environments Devoid of Everything

A final category in which to consider impacts on deep space environments after those with instrumental value, potential for microbial life, or other source of reverence is simply empty space. The void of space far from useful orbits, transitways, Lagrange points, resources, and sources of scientific value. One cannot help but to consider the notion that perhaps the interstellar vacuum of space *is* an acceptable landfill and effectively the ultimate exception to the need for consideration of preserving the environment and managing waste. If civilization is going to produce waste (and maybe there is motivation and means to avoid this even using circular economy principles in space), there really is no better waste sink than the void of space away from planets and useful orbits. In a stakeholder intrinsic value assessment, deposition of waste or debris into the voids of space may not conflict with harmony.

Deep Space Sustainability: In Conclusion

This section started off essentially questioning the harmony requirement in stakeholder intrinsic value when it comes to activities in deep space. Is it applicable in this context? If so, is it more flexible or to be interpreted differently than with activities on Earth? The answers to these questions are yes and yes. It is applicable first of all because this is the mentality humanity must have collectively to survive going forward. Second, harmony is an element of goodness and the space industry should only do things that are good. It is not helpful to carve out exceptions and allow pockets of ignorance and bad practice to take hold. Furthermore, certain locations in deep space are associated with instrumental value such as natural resources, scientific data, or useful orbits. Disrupting instances of instrumental value like these stands to reduce potential for value creation from the space industry overall. The interpretation of harmony may become more flexible concerning lifeless and unremarkable natural features. This flexibility is especially appropriate at locations in space that do not possess physical objects, utility for spacecraft, or risk negatively impacting really anything at all.

Notes

1 Moon Treaty signatories do not include Russia, China, or the United States.
2 Additionally, the non-excludability of space exploration is enshrined in the Outer Space Treaty.

8 Maximum Value Creation in Space

Some Answers

This chapter considers all of the stakeholder intrinsic value creation opportunities that have been discussed in this book. A preliminary assessment of goodness, types of markets, and do no harm responsibilities for each is provided. This exercise offers the beginning of an answer to the question posed initially: What *should* be done in space? Recall, this question was posed with the presumption that there is a goal to maximize value creation and this can be achieved through commercial efforts focused on things most important to humanity.

While the first steps may be similar, the assessment presented here is not intended to represent the procedure for a stakeholder intrinsic value assessment in practice. For one, all items in this review are assumed either to be profitable directly or not impede profitability. A detailed financial evaluation would normally be part of any stakeholder intrinsic value assessment. Also, the goodness virtue compliance that is described is subject to correction on a case-by-case basis. Finally, there was not a stakeholder group involved in this review nor were tools such as a Life Cycle Assessment (LCA) or value flow map utilized. All this review is intended to offer is preliminary insight as to which activities appear to hold the most promise as areas to maximize value creation in space.

Table 8.1 lists all opportunities for stakeholder intrinsic value creation in the space industry that have been mentioned in this book. Recall from Chapter 4 that bearers of stakeholder intrinsic value can be diverse and include physical objects, information, algorithms, activities, services, actions, tasks, decisions, choices, and states of affairs. Items listed in Table 8.1 vary across numerous different types of bearers, and so the means to reflect upon each item and consider the goodness virtues, types of markets, and do no harm responsibilities are not the same in all cases. To help process all of the listed stakeholder intrinsic value opportunities, four categories are defined below that reflect the nature of markets and do no harm responsibilities for each item:

- Category I: Stakeholder intrinsic value creation opportunities that consist of direct solutions for sustainability challenges. Items in Category

DOI: 10.4324/9781003268734-8

I describe activities where a space company can provide a specialized product or service that helps address one of the UN Sustainable Development Goals. Bearers in Category I are mostly limited to products and services.

- Category II: Stakeholder intrinsic value creation opportunities that are not direct solutions for sustainability challenges, but consist of value creation for humanity nonetheless according to harmony, goodness, and profitability criteria. Bearers in Category II are mostly limited to products and services.
- Category III: Stakeholder intrinsic value creation opportunities that are based around providing products or services in government markets. Bearers in Category III are mostly limited to products and services.
- Category IV: Descriptors of areas to ensure or increase stakeholder intrinsic value through meeting a do no harm responsibility. These items are viewed as considerations in a stakeholder intrinsic value assessment, but not necessarily the core source of value and profit for a company. Bearers in Category IV are diverse including concepts, actions, activities, states of affairs, products, and decisions.

Note that a single item in Table 8.1 may fall into more than one category. For example, stakeholder intrinsic value creation in a given instance could occur in both private markets and government markets. If an item in the list is associated with multiple categories, this may be interpreted as a case with heightened potential for overall value creation. A single item also may support multiple goodness virtues. While all items in the list can support harmony, the other five goodness virtues are marked somewhat conservatively. For example, pleasure is marked only if it is meant to occur directly as the intent of the activity. Tourism, for example. Pleasure can result ultimately from any useful activity, but the intent in this particular grading exercise is to be more selective and only identify activities where this is the primary purpose. A similar view is taken when marking the knowledge and beauty virtues. Justice is marked only in cases pertaining to law enforcement, the justice system, and security. One could argue that justice also applies in cases involving environmental and social justice; however, these forms of justice are not included in this screening. Benevolence is flagged only in cases where the item listed could be said to be truly motivated from a place of caring and compassion for others.

Of 99 total items in the list of stakeholder intrinsic value creation opportunities in Table 8.1, 38% fall into Category I, 37% fall into Category II, 21% fall into Category III, and 41% fall into Category IV. 31% of all items fall into two or more categories. Regarding goodness, 25% of the list only corresponds to one virtue (harmony). This group is most associated with do no harm responsibilities. The other 75% of the list is associated with multiple goodness virtues.

Table 8.1 Assessment of stakeholder intrinsic value creation opportunities.

Stakeholder Intrinsic Value Creation Opportunity	Category				Goodness Virtues					
	I	II	III	IV	Harmony	Pleasure	Knowledge	Justice	Beauty	Benevolence
Additive manufacturing	✓			✓	✓					
Afterburning suppressants to avoid ozone destruction	✓			✓	✓					✓
Artificial Intelligence (AI), data mining, and blockchain to enhance existing space systems		✓				✓	✓	✓	✓	✓
Assessment of alternatives to using space systems		✓		✓	✓	✓	✓			
Automobile navigation services				✓	✓					
Avoid use of solid propellant				✓	✓					
Business models that avoid ozone destruction				✓	✓					
Collecting and processing climate data (ECV)	✓			✓	✓		✓			✓
Consider harmony for environmental destruction in deep space				✓	✓					✓
Consulting on use of space systems		✓			✓	✓	✓	✓	✓	
Creating new scientific knowledge			✓		✓		✓	✓	✓	
Data mining tools for remote sensing data	✓	✓	✓		✓		✓			
Data transfer technology that doesn't further crowd radio frequencies	✓	✓			✓		✓			
Deep space cargo and telecommunications		✓		✓	✓		✓			
Design systems to be reusable, serviceable, and maintainable				✓	✓					
Disaster mitigation and response services	✓			✓	✓	✓				✓
Downcycling material in parts that cannot be reused or recycled	✓	✓	✓	✓	✓			✓	✓	
Economic development services based on satellite-provided internet	✓				✓	✓		✓	✓	✓
Economic use of material in hardware design	✓			✓	✓					✓

Stakeholder Intrinsic Value Creation Opportunity	Category				Goodness Virtues					
	I	II	III	IV	Harmony	Pleasure	Knowledge	Justice	Beauty	Benevolence
Ecosystem accounting services/tools	✓		✓		✓	✓	✓		✓	
Efficient program management and operational support				✓	✓	✓	✓			
Efficient research and development (R&D) and test campaigns		✓		✓	✓		✓			
Evidence for international courts	✓					✓	✓	✓	✓	✓
Expanding the economy and civilization into space			✓		✓	✓	✓	✓	✓	✓
Exploration (human and robotic)			✓		✓	✓				
Full spacecraft recycling services	✓		✓		✓					
GNSS system					✓		✓			
Greater capacity of existing systems		✓			✓		✓	✓		
Green production of cryogenic fuels				✓	✓			✓		
Harvesting and processing space resources		✓			✓		✓			
Inter-Agency Space Debris Coordination Committee (IADC) Space Debris Mitigation Guidelines				✓	✓	✓	✓			✓
In-space manufacturing		✓			✓	✓	✓			
Infrastructure monitoring and maintenance	✓			✓	✓		✓	✓	✓	✓
International Telecommunications Union (ITU) orbital slot and radiofrequency assignments					✓		✓			
Land surveying services	✓	✓		✓	✓	✓	✓	✓		✓
Launch services		✓		✓	✓		✓	✓		
Launch site environmental monitoring	✓	✓			✓		✓	✓		
Law enforcement assistance	✓	✓		✓			✓	✓		
Making space systems available to developing nations			✓	✓	✓		✓	✓	✓	✓
Managing transportation systems	✓	✓			✓		✓	✓		
Navigation for the shipping industry	✓	✓			✓		✓	✓		
Navigation for tourism and outdoor recreation	✓	✓			✓	✓	✓			

(Continued)

Stakeholder Intrinsic Value Creation Opportunity	Category				Goodness Virtues					
	I	II	III	IV	Harmony	Pleasure	Knowledge	Justice	Beauty	Benevolence
Nontoxic alternatives to hydrazine				✓	✓					✓
Off-world colonies		✓			✓	✓	✓			✓
Orbital debris mitigation			✓	✓	✓		✓			
Outer Space Treaty			✓	✓	✓					✓
Perform active spacecraft disposal from orbit at end of life				✓	✓					
Planning mass migration from coastal areas	✓	✓			✓					
Political influence, national prestige			✓		✓	✓	✓	✓		✓
Power generation in space (helium-3, solar power)	✓				✓	✓				✓
Power value chain with renewable energy				✓	✓	✓			✓	
Precision agriculture services	✓				✓					
Prevent introduction of any new orbital debris	✓			✓	✓					
Proactive orbital debris removal	✓			✓	✓			✓		
Product life cycle value management				✓	✓		✓			✓
Productive international partnerships				✓	✓	✓	✓	✓		✓
Promoting equality				✓	✓	✓	✓	✓	✓	✓
Propulsion systems and mission profiles that avoid ozone destruction					✓		✓	✓		
Provide ozone depletion simulation tools	✓				✓		✓			
Provide Space Situational Awareness (SSA) data and SSA value-added tools	✓				✓		✓	✓		
Providing access to and around space		✓			✓	✓	✓	✓	✓	
Providing products or services in support of government initiatives	✓	✓			✓		✓	✓		
Provision of crew and cargo to low Earth orbit					✓	✓	✓	✓	✓	✓
Provision of space systems	✓	✓			✓	✓	✓	✓	✓	
Real estate industry services	✓	✓			✓	✓	✓			

Stakeholder Intrinsic Value Creation Opportunity	Category				Goodness Virtues					
	I	II	III	IV	Harmony	Pleasure	Knowledge	Justice	Beauty	Benevolence
Remote banking	✓				✓		✓			✓
Remote education services	✓				✓	✓	✓	✓		✓
Renewable energy and building efficiency for ground infrastructure				✓	✓					
Satellite servicing	✓				✓					
Satellite-provided internet	✓	✓			✓		✓	✓	✓	✓
Satellites to manage water resources			✓		✓		✓			
Satellites to help climate, life on land, and life below water				✓	✓		✓		✓	
Satellites to help poverty, disease, food insecurity, and human rights	✓				✓	✓	✓	✓	✓	✓
Satisfy human curiosity	✓				✓	✓	✓			
Service business models				✓	✓		✓			
Simulation tools to reduce testing needed					✓		✓			
Solar and wind power planning			✓		✓	✓	✓		✓	✓
Space applications consulting	✓		✓		✓		✓		✓	✓
Space LCA services	✓		✓		✓		✓		✓	✓
Space Sustainability Rating	✓	✓			✓		✓	✓		
Space tourism				✓	✓	✓	✓		✓	
Specialized remote sensing data	✓	✓			✓		✓			✓
Supporting the education community	✓	✓			✓		✓	✓	✓	✓
System time synchronization services	✓			✓	✓		✓			
Targeted environmental impact monitoring services	✓				✓	✓				
Telecommunications services					✓	✓	✓	✓	✓	✓
Telemedicine services	✓				✓		✓			

(Continued)

Stakeholder Intrinsic Value Creation Opportunity	Category				Goodness Virtues					
	I	II	III	IV	Harmony	Pleasure	Knowledge	Justice	Beauty	Benevolence
UN Guidelines for the Long-Term Sustainability of Outer Space Activities				✓	✓					✓
Urban development planning tools	✓				✓				✓	✓
Use of cryogenic propulsion as much as possible			✓	✓	✓		✓			
Use of less energy-intensive materials			✓	✓	✓					
Use of recycled raw materials			✓	✓	✓					
Use of repurposed parts and components			✓	✓	✓					
Value chain innovations		✓	✓		✓	✓	✓	✓		✓
Value-added software tools		✓			✓	✓	✓	✓	✓	✓
Value-added weather forecast tools		✓			✓	✓	✓		✓	
Weather prediction services			✓	✓	✓	✓	✓			✓
Zero-waste production				✓	✓					

Further insight is provided by filtering the list into three groups: (1) items corresponding to two or more categories, (2) items corresponding to four or more goodness virtues, and (3) items corresponding to two or more categories *and* four or more goodness virtues. The items in this third group would be those that involve diverse markets and diverse sources of goodness. The results of this sorting are shown below and give some indication of what the most important value creation activities in the space industry are. In other words, which *should* be done as priorities. A shortcoming present in this sorting scheme is that no weighting is placed on the filtered attributes.

Group 1: Items corresponding to two or more categories:

- Additive manufacturing
- Afterburning suppressants to avoid ozone destruction
- Collecting and processing climate data (Essential Climate Variables [ECVs])
- Data mining tools for remote sensing data
- Downcycling material in parts that cannot be reused or recycled
- Ecosystem accounting services/tools
- Full spacecraft recycling services
- Land surveying services
- Launch services
- Law enforcement assistance
- Making space systems available to developing nations
- Managing transportation systems
- Navigation for the shipping industry
- Navigation for tourism and outdoor recreation
- Off-world colonies
- Planning mass migration from coastal areas
- Providing access to and around space
- Providing products or services in support of government initiatives
- Provision of space systems
- Remote banking
- Satellite-provided internet
- Solar and wind power planning
- Space applications consulting
- Space LCA services
- Specialized remote sensing data
- Supporting the education community
- System time synchronization services
- Use of cryogenic propulsion as much as possible
- Use of less energy-intensive materials
- Use of recycled raw materials
- Use of repurposed parts and components
- Value chain innovations

Group 2: Items corresponding to four or more goodness virtues:

- Artificial Intelligence, data mining, and blockchain to enhance existing space systems
- Consulting on use of space systems
- Creating new scientific knowledge
- Data mining tools for remote sensing data
- Disaster mitigation and response services
- Economic development services based on satellite-provided internet
- Ecosystem accounting services/tools
- Evidence for international courts
- Expanding the economy and civilization into space
- Exploration (human and robotic)
- Global Navigation and Satellite Systems (GNSS)
- Greater capacity of existing systems
- Launch services
- Law enforcement assistance
- Making space systems available to developing nations
- Off-world colonies
- Political influence, national prestige
- Precision agriculture services
- Productive international partnerships
- Promoting equality
- Providing access to and around space
- Provision of space systems
- Remote education services
- Satellite-provided internet
- Satellites to help poverty, disease, food insecurity, and human rights
- Satisfy human curiosity
- Space applications consulting
- Targeted environmental impact monitoring services
- Telecommunications services
- Telemedicine services
- Urban development planning tools
- Value chain innovations
- Value-added software tools
- Weather prediction services

Group 3: Items corresponding to two or more categories *and* four or more goodness virtues:

- Data mining tools for remote sensing data
- Ecosystem accounting services/tools
- Launch services
- Law enforcement assistance
- Making space systems available to developing nations

- Off-world colonies
- Providing access to and around space
- Provision of space systems
- Satellite-provided internet
- Space applications consulting
- Value chain innovations

The items listed in Group 3 stand as an interim suggestion for activities that are the most important for the commercial space industry to undertake. A more rigorous assessment methodology involving stakeholders and other tools may reveal different conclusions. Nonetheless, Group 3 list stands as a preliminary view of areas that hold promise in maximizing value creation in space.

9 Conclusions

There are two notable historic transformations currently underway in the world. The space industry is transforming from a government-led industry to one that is becoming dominated by commercial activity. The result is a rapidly growing industry that is creating more value from space for more people than ever before. At the same time, the need for sustainability is driving a global transformation of how capitalism is implemented in all areas of the economy. Businesses are changing management practices to reduce cost externalization and adopt a more purpose-driven stakeholder approach to value creation. This metamorphosis of capitalism is required for human prosperity to continue and increase in the future, and so the newly forming commercial space industry must grow according to practices that align with this trend.

For the entrepreneurs, managers, investors, and innovators in the space industry, how best can one go about aligning commercial space industry growth with the new sustainable implementation of capitalism? The perspective that this book takes is that it can be achieved by striving to maximize value creation. This is a loaded concept the details of which are the primary theme of the book. Maximum value creation occurs when profit-seeking and markets are used to efficiently create good things for humanity. It occurs according to the results of an assessment of the defining features of a company's identity such as their products, services, activities, strategy, purpose, impacts, and decisions. Maximum value creation occurs when the needs of all stakeholders are considered and sustainability of a value creation scheme is placed as a prerequisite. And finally, maximum value creation occurs when thought goes into what an organization *should* focus its resources on, that is, what activities and purpose are most important for it to pursue.

Maximum value creation is the preferable outcome of the space industry. The reason for any industry to exist is to meet demands from society and benefit humanity in doing so. This is creating value. Advocating for anything less, or worse yet, permissive policies that allow for a net loss in value through cumulative damage to social and environmental systems, is illogical. Stakeholder intrinsic value is presented in this book as

DOI: 10.4324/9781003268734-9

a practical tool for industry leaders to use in order to maximize value creation in their organizations.

Achieving Maximum Value Creation in the Space Industry: A Recap

The formulation of stakeholder intrinsic value is presented throughout the first half of the book. This begins with capitalism. A core premise in the concept of stakeholder intrinsic value is that value creation occurs by means of profit-seeking and markets. The rationale is that capitalism has proven to be the most effective and equitable system in history to meet humanity's wants and needs. Attractive aspects of using capitalism for value creation include efficiency, innovation, a direct reflection of society's needs, the ability for self-sustaining/lasting value production, win-win outcomes of market transactions, opportunities for billions of people to participate voluntarily, long-term prosperity, stability, and a system that resonates strongly with human nature. Using capitalism is a natural approach to derive as much benefit from space systems as possible.

The first half of Chapter 2 outlines exactly what capitalism is, how it works, and how it has evolved over the centuries. This perspective is necessary to truly appreciate why benefits listed above exist and why capitalism should be utilized for value creation in space. The history of capitalism as presented follows merchant trade caravans, multigenerational firms, and publicly traded companies allowing one to appreciate better what exactly companies are and why they are so effective as value creation tools for society. Examination of the concept of private property and the industrialization process offers basic insights as to how capitalism can best function and benefit people. Finally, a review of the shareholder primacy ideology leads to discussion on certain characteristics of the modern implementation of capitalism that must be improved. Specifically, these areas are cost externalization and hyper-efficiency of meeting the needs of shareholders and investors at the expense of critical social and environmental systems.

The second half of Chapter 2 provides a view of the future of capitalism. A shift away from the shareholder primacy ideology toward a version of capitalism that is sustainable and does not result in the destruction of environmental and social systems. Practical means to achieve this are use of stakeholder management and implementing circular economy principles. In the space industry, this means adopting practices like product value management, product value recovery, service business models, recycling, and reuse. These things can be achieved through deliberate design of value chains and products based on insight from stakeholders and use of tools such as a value flow map and/or a Life Cycle Assessment (LCA).

Having established that a sustainable version of capitalism should be used, Chapter 3 then moves the discussion to value theory. The whole book is about maximizing value creation in space so some time is spent articulating this concept. Upon reflecting on historical discourse related to value theory, two concepts of value emerge: exchange value and "true value." What also emerges is that both of these concepts of value are relevant for different reasons and neither can be discounted. Of the two, the concept of true value is most nebulous. Intrinsic value is a form of value long discussed in the field of philosophy and resembles closely what is characterized in this book as true value. After an examination of intrinsic value, elements of the concept are extracted for use in characterizing value creation goals for the space industry.

Using the discussion on the history of value theory, Chapter 4 then assembles a pragmatic unified value theory for use in the space industry, stakeholder intrinsic value. The definition for stakeholder intrinsic value is shown below, repeated from Chapter 4. The definition is intended to be a succinct and pragmatic set of criteria that space industry leaders can use in assessing the merits and methods of a value creation scheme. Efforts were made to root the concepts within stakeholder intrinsic value rigorously in historical discourse in the fields of philosophy, economics, sustainability, and value theory but produce guidance such that users need not be experts in, or even interested in, these areas from an academic perspective.

SOMETHING HAS STAKEHOLDER INTRINSIC VALUE IF:

1   It is inherently good by way of embodying harmony plus option-
    ally one or more of the following virtues: pleasure, knowledge,
    justice, beauty, and benevolence
2   Item 1 is true as a result of one or both of the following:
    a   Innate properties that are unaffected by external influence
    b   Instrumental value that is based on an innate property where
        the instrumental value is a means to enable an external bearer
        of the criteria in item 1
3   It is profitable in a free market
4   Conclusions on items 1 through 3 are determined collectively by a
    company and all of its stakeholders

The stakeholder intrinsic value criteria require that the activities that a company pursues are inherently good. Goodness is extracted from historical discourse on economics and philosophy as a core component of value. The premise behind this feature of stakeholder intrinsic value is simple: it is desirable that the commercial space industry do good things. Goodness can be a subjective concept, so to be practical it is defined explicitly in the stakeholder intrinsic value criteria. Goodness is attained through the virtues of harmony, pleasure, knowledge, justice, beauty, and/or benevolence. A commercial space company should steer products, decisions, and value creation activities in ways that maximize realization of these virtues.

Among these virtues, harmony is declared in Chapter 4 as a prerequisite. The other virtues (pleasure, knowledge, beauty, justice, and benevolence) are considered optional, in that they merely serve to enhance goodness even more as long as harmony is satisfied. If something were destructive toward its surroundings or toward things it interacts with, this would be a form of inflicting harm, destruction, malfeasance, ignorance, wastefulness, or inefficiency. These are not desirable qualities, and so harmony is necessary to avoid them and realize goodness. Sustainability is framed largely in this book as a means by which to achieve harmony. The extent to which the full list of goodness virtues is embodied contributes to an indication of the total degree of stakeholder intrinsic value.

Profitability is paired with harmony and goodness in the stakeholder intrinsic value criteria. Profitability is recognized as essential for any company to exist. Any intent toward goodness and harmony in a company is irrelevant if that company cannot be profitable. Profitability represents a different kind of value, exchange value, that does not directly benefit humanity but rather serves as an enabler to activate efficient value creation methods.

In a given stakeholder intrinsic value creation assessment, degrees of goodness, harmony, and profitability should be captured so that they can be compared to other assessments. There are expected to be inconsistent sources of information and conflicting perspectives on priorities in this process. Stakeholder intrinsic value approaches these challenges through the practice of stakeholder management where numerous perspectives and sources of information are required. The outcome of a stakeholder intrinsic value assessment should reveal degrees of compliance with the criteria and give an indication of overall value creation. A company can seek to maximize value creation by performing multiple assessments of different strategies and decisions and selecting to pursue only those which rate highest.

Some questions that may assist in a stakeholder intrinsic value assessment are listed below (repeated from Chapter 6):

For a given product or service in the space industry...

- Which of the goodness virtues in the stakeholder intrinsic value criteria does it support the most and are they supported in a way that is profitable?
- How could it be modified to enhance or broaden its satisfaction of the goodness virtues?
- How does the overall level of stakeholder intrinsic value compare to other potential similar goods or services that could be pursued instead?
- Are there any stakeholders objecting strongly and what is the stakeholder consensus regarding harmony?

After defining stakeholder intrinsic value in Chapter 4, the remainder of the book covers use of the concept in the space industry. This starts in Chapter 5 with applying classical commercialization criteria in the context of space systems. Specifically, excludability and rivalry are assessed relative to activities in space. The role of the government in providing value where commercialization is not possible is also carefully considered using several historical examples. Overall, Chapter 5 provides an understanding of how to identify commercialization opportunities and clarifies that in some cases it is desirable and economically efficient for the government to create value.

Chapter 6 covers sustainability in the space industry. This topic is discussed both in the context of value creation opportunities and responsibilities relevant in supporting the harmony requirement. A convenient means to articulate the greatest opportunities for value creation in general is the list of 17 UN Sustainable Development Goals (SDGs). The SDGs describe needs of humanity that are the greatest in terms of criticality and in terms of being insufficiently met. Chapter 6 discusses the space industry's unique value proposition relative to the SDGs. Through seeking commercial solutions, the space industry can have positive contributions to humanity in areas like poverty, education, equality, security, environmental health, and economic development. The running assertion throughout Chapter 6 is that in any case where possible, a commercial approach should be taken to create value in response to an SDG as this will result in more value creation than would otherwise occur.

Chapter 6 also describes numerous do no harm responsibilities. These are related to both environmental and social impacts from the space industry. Neglecting mitigations related to a do no harm responsibility would have the effect of exacerbating sustainability challenges that the world already faces. Minding these responsibilities is inherent in meeting the harmony requirement in the stakeholder intrinsic value criteria. Therefore, improving performance relative to a do no harm responsibility is one way to increase stakeholder intrinsic value creation.

Chapter 7 turns the focus to human spaceflight and deep space exploration. This chapter covers more opportunities for stakeholder intrinsic value creation in space beyond direct sustainability solutions. While certain opportunities related to human spaceflight and exploration do exist for stakeholder intrinsic value creation, they are somewhat limited to supporting government markets. This limitation may fade over time as the space economy grows. The applicability of the harmony requirement in deep space is also examined. Because impacting a deep space environment is fundamentally different in nature than affecting the Earth's environment, it is less obvious why and how the harmony requirement applies. The conclusion in Chapter 7 is that harmony is part of the definition of goodness and the space industry should do good things independent of location. This does mean different things though in practice in deep space. A stakeholder intrinsic value assessment should consider attributes of a deep space environment such as potential to host life, uniqueness, and utility to humans. These factors will guide an assessment of harmony.

Finally, Chapter 8 includes a cursory review of all of the stakeholder intrinsic value creation opportunities that are mentioned throughout the book. For each item, customer diversity, goodness virtue compliance, and do no harm responsibilities are considered. Upon filtering the results, a short list is derived identifying activities in space that are most compliant with the stakeholder intrinsic value criteria. While this review has the appearance of the beginning of a value creation assessment, it is crude in nature and is intended to serve only as a preliminary review of value creation in space. For a single line item, additional assessment steps not described in Chapter 8 would be use of stakeholders, detailed financial evaluations, use of a value flow map, use of an LCA, and a trade study considering numerous strategies. Nevertheless, the short list of activities from Chapter 8 that is most compliant with stakeholder intrinsic value criteria (Group 3) offers some insight related to a major question of this book: what *should* be done in space?

- Data mining tools for remote sensing data
- Ecosystem accounting services/tools
- Launch services
- Law enforcement assistance
- Making space systems available to developing nations
- Off-world colonies
- Providing access to and around space
- Provision of space systems
- Satellite-provided internet
- Space applications consulting
- Value chain innovations

Closing Remarks

The preferable outcome of increasing activity in space is that the space industry does good things, not bad things, and among the good things that are possible, there is a focus on those which are most important. This will result in maximum value creation from space and it necessarily involves embracing the global trend toward a sustainable economy. Stakeholder intrinsic value is presented to facilitate this outcome in the space industry of the future. The proposition of this book is that space industry professionals should use the stakeholder intrinsic value criteria to undertake an assessment of any and all value creation schemes in their organizations and enact only the strategies that rate highest.

Bibliography

[1] M. Stanley, "Space: Invetsing in the Final Frontier," 24 July 2020. [Online]. Available: https://www.morganstanley.com/ideas/investing-in-space. [Accessed 2 May 2021].

[2] M. Sheetz, "Bank of America Expects the Space Industry to Triple to a $1.4 Trillion Market Within a Decade," *CNBC*, 4 October 2020.

[3] Space Foundation, "The Space Report 2021 Q2," 2021.

[4] M. Sheetz, "Investment in Space Companies Put at Record $8.9 Billion in 2020 Despite Covid," *CNBC*, 25 January 2021.

[5] Space Foundation, "Space Investment Quarterly: Q3 2021," 2021.

[6] National Academies of Sciences, Engineering, and Medicine, *Thriving on Our Changing Planet: A Decadal Strategy for Earth Observation from Space*, Washington, DC: National Academies Press, 2018.

[7] IEEE Spectrum, "Remembering Sputnik: Sir Arthur C. Clarke," *IEEE Spectrum*, 1 October 2007.

[8] W. S. Bainbridge, *The Spaceflight Revolution: A Sociological Study*, New York, NY: Wiley, 1976.

[9] S. Tkatchova, *Emerging Space Markets*, Berlin, Germany: Microcosm Press and Springer, 2018.

[10] H. W. Jones, "The Recent Large Reduction in Space Launch Cost," in *48th International Conference on Environmental Systems*, Albuquerque, NM, 2018.

[11] M. Sheetz, "NASA's Deal to Fly Astronauts with Boeing Is Turning Out to Be Much More Expensive than SpaceX," *CNBC*, 19 November 2019.

[12] J. Kelvey, "Inspiration 4: How Much Does a Ticket to Space Cost?," *Inverse*, 15 September 2021.

[13] J. S. Schwartz, *The Value of Science in Space Exploration*, New York, NY: Oxford University Press, 2020.

[14] K. Raworth, *Doughnut Economics*, White River Junction, VT: Chelsea Green Publishing, 2017.

[15] R. C. Jacobson, *Space Is Open for Business: The Industry That Can Transform Humanity*, Los Angeles, CA, 2020.

[16] Global Footprint Network, "National Footprint Accounts 2016 Are Out! Carbon Makes Up 60% of World's Ecological Footprint," 8 March 2016. [Online]. Available: https://www.footprintnetwork.org/2016/03/08/national-footprint-accounts-2016-carbon-makes-60-worlds-ecological-footprint/. [Accessed 13 April 2021].

[17] V. Masson-Delmotte, P. Zhai, A. Pirani, S. L. Connors, C. Péan, S. Berger, N. Caud, Y. Chen, L. Goldfarb, M. I. Gomis, M. Huang, K. Leitzell, E. Lonnoy, J. Matthews, T. K. Maycock, T. Waterfield, O. Yelekçi, R. Yu and B. Z. (eds.), "IPCC, 2021: Summary for Policymakers," in: *Climate Change 2021: The Physical Science Basis. Contribution of Working Group I to the Sixth Assessment Report of the Intergovernmental Panel on Climate Change*, Cambridge, UK: Cambridge University Press, 2021.

[18] R. Hugonnet, R. McNabb, E. Berthier, B. Menounos, C. Nuth, L. Girod, D. Farinotti, M. Huss, I. Dussaillant, F. Brun and A. Kääb, "Accelerated Global Glacier Mass Loss in the Early Twenty-First Century," *Nature,* vol. 592, pp. 726–731, 2021.

[19] A. Tooze, "Why Central Banks Need to Step Up on Global Warming," *Foreign Policy,* 20 July 2019.

[20] J. Lazo, M. Lawson, P. Larsen and D. Waldman, "U.S. Economic Sensitivity to Weather Variability," *Bulletin of the American Meteorological Society,* vol. 92, no. 6, pp. 709–720, 2011.

[21] M. A. Borg, J. Xiang, O. Anikeeva, D. Pisaniello, A. Hansen, K. Zander, K. Dear, M. R. Sim and P. Bi, "Occupational Heat Stress and Economic Burden: A Review of Global Evidence," *Environmental Research,* vol. 195, pp. 1–14, 2021.

[22] United Nations Environment Programme, *"Emissions Gap Report 2021: The Heat Is On – A World of Climate Promises Not Yet Delivered – Executive Summary,"* United Nations, Nairobi, Kenya, 2021.

[23] P. Lacy and J. Rutqvist, *Waste to Wealth: The Circular Economy Advantage*, New York, NY: Palgrave Macmillan, 2015.

[24] D. H. Meadows, D. L. Meadows, J. Randers and W. W. B. III, *The Limits to Growth: A Report for the Club of Rome's Project on the Predicament of Mankind*, New York, NY: Universe Books, 1972.

[25] B. Ewing, D. Moore, S. Goldfinger, A. Oursler, A. Reed and M. Wackernagel, *The Ecological Footprint Atlas 2010*, Oakland, CA: Global Footprint Network, 2010.

[26] P. Gilding, *The Great Disruption: Why the Climate Crisis Will Bring on the End of Shopping and the Birth of a New World*, New York, NY: Bloomsbury Press, 2011.

[27] A. Smith, *The Wealth of Nations*, London, UK: W. Strahan and T. Cadell, 1776.

[28] M. Friedman, "The Social Responsibility of Business Is to Increase Its Profits," *New York Times Magazine,* pp. 122–126, 13 September 1970.

[29] L. Stout, *The Shareholder Value Myth: How Putting Shareholders First Harms Investors, Corporations, and the Public*, Oakland, CA: Berrett-Koehler Publishers Inc., 2012.

[30] L. Strine, "The Dangers of Denial: The Need for a Clear-Eyed Understanding of the Power and Accountability Structure Established by the Delaware General Corporation Law," *Wake Forest Law Review,* vol. 50, p. 761, 2015.

[31] C. Marquis, "Public Benefit Corporations Flourish in the Public Markets," *Forbes,* 14 June 2021.

[32] N. G. Mankiw, *Principles of Economics* (2nd edition), Orlando, FL: Harcourt College Publishers, 2000.

[33] "2020 Flash Report S&P500," Governance & Accountability Institute, Inc., New York, 2020.

[34] M. Thompson and N. Valencia, "Corporate ESG/Sustainability Reporting – Does It Matter? Analysis of Fortune 500® Companies' ESG Reporting Trends & Capital Markets Response," Governance & Accountability Institute, Inc., New York, 2011.

[35] D. Hitchcock and M. Willard, *The Business Guide to Sustainability: Practical Strategies and Tools for Organizations*, New York, NY: Routledge, 2015.

[36] L. Fink, "Larry Fink's 2018 Letter to CEOs: A Sense of Purpose," 2018. [Online]. Available: https://www.blackrock.com/corporate/investor-relations/2018-larry-fink-ceo-letter. [Accessed 2 January 2021].

[37] L. Fink, "Larry Fink's 2020 Letter to CEOs: A Fundamental Reshaping of Finance," 2020. [Online]. Available: https://www.blackrock.com/corporate/investor-relations/larry-fink-ceo-letter. [Accessed 2 January 2021].

[38] J. Powell, "Chair Powell to Sen. Schatz 4.18.19," 18 April 2019. [Online]. Available: https://www.schatz.senate.gov/imo/media/doc/Chair%20Powell%20to%20Sen.%20Schatz%204.18.19.pdf. [Accessed 3 January 2021].

[39] J. Rainbow, "Space and the New ESG Business Climate," *SpaceNews,* 5 March 2021.

[40] "JPMorgan Chase Expands Commitment to Low-Carbon Economy and Clean Energy Transition to Advance Sustainable Development Goals," 25 Febuary 2020. [Online]. Available: https://www.jpmorganchase.com/news-stories/jpmorgan-chase-expands-commitment-to-low-carbon-economy-and-clean-energy. [Accessed 3 January 2021].

[41] K. Schwab, "Davos Manifesto 2020: The Universal Purpose of a Company in the Fourth Industrial Revolution," 2 December 2019. [Online]. Available: https://www.weforum.org/agenda/2019/12/davos-manifesto-2020-the-universal-purpose-of-a-company-in-the-fourth-industrial-revolution/. [Accessed 3 January 2021].

[42] P. Hawken, *The Ecology of Commerce, Inc.,* New York, NY: Harper Bussiness, 1992, pp. 93–97.

[43] R. Henderson, *Reimagining Capitalism in a World on Fire*, New York, NY: Public Affairs, 2020.

[44] P. Hawken, A. Lovins and L. H. Lovins, *Natural Capitalism: Creating the Next Industrial Revolution*, New York, NY: Little, Brown and Company, 1999.

[45] J. Elkington, *Cannibals with Forks: The Triple Bottom Line of Sustainable Development*, Oxford, UK: Capstone, 1997.

[46] J. Elkington, "25 Years Ago I Coined the Phrase, "'Triple Bottom Line.' Here's Why It's Time to Rethink It," *Harvard Business Review,* 25 June 2018.

[47] J. Mackey and R. Sisodia, *Conscious Capitalism*, Boston, MA: Harvard Business School Publishing Corporation, 2014.

[48] A. Edmans, *Grow the Pie*, New York, NY: Cambridge University Press, 2020.

[49] G. Friede, T. Busch and A. Bassen, "ESG and Financial Performance: Aggregated Evidence from More Than 2000 Empirical Studies," *Journal of Sustainable Finance & Investment,* vol. 5, no. 4, pp. 210–233, 2015.

[50] R. E. Freeman, *Strategic Management: A Stakeholder Approach*, Boston, MA: Pitman Publishing, 1984.

[51] D. Chandler, *Sustainable Value Creation* (2nd edition), Oxon, UK: Routledge, 2021.

[52] M. Carney, *Values(s): Building a Better World for All*, New York, NY: Public Affairs, 2021.

[53] J. Sacks, "Morals: The One Thing Markets Don't Make," *The Times,* 21 March 2009.

[54] T. A. Kochan and S. A. Rubinstein, "Toward a Stakeholder Theory of the Firm: The Saturn Partnership," *Organization Science,* vol. 11, no. 4, pp. 367–386, 2000.

[55] NASA, *NASA Systems Engineering Handbook,* NASA SP-2016-6105 Rev 2, 2016.

[56] R. E. Freeman, J. S. Harrison and S. Zyglidopoulos, *Stakeholder Theory,* Cambridge, UK: Cambridge University Press, 2018.

[57] R. E. Freeman, "Response: Divergent Stakeholder Theory," *Academy of Management Review,* vol. 24, no. 2, pp. 233–236, 1999.

[58] A. B. Carroll, "The Pyramid of Corporate Social Responsibility: Toward the Moral Management of Organizational Stakeholders," *Business Horizons,* vol. 34, pp. 39–48, 1991.

[59] T. Chow and B. Weeden, "Engaging All Stakeholders in Space Sustainability Governance Initiatives," in *International Astronautical Congress,* Beijing, China, 2013.

[60] P. Utting and K. O'Neill, "Corporate Sustainability Accounting: What Can and Should Corporations Be Doing?—Full Report," United Nations, 2020.

[61] T. A. Sutherland, *Stakeholder Value Network Analysis for Space-Based Earth Observations,* Cambridge, MA: Massachusetts Institute of Technology, 2009.

[62] E. Rebentisch, E. Crawley, G. Loureiro, J. Dickmann and S. Catanzaro, "Using Stakeholder Value Analysis to Build Exploration Sustainability," in *1st Space Exploration Conference: Continuing the Voyage of Discovery,* Orlando, FL, 2005.

[63] B. G. Cameron, E. F. Crawley, G. Loureiroc and E. S.Rebentisch, "Value Flow Mapping: Using Networks to Inform Stakeholder Analysis," *Acta Astronautica,* vol. 62, no. 4–5, pp. 324–333, 2008.

[64] Berger, C., Blauth, R., Boger, D., Bolster, C., Burchill, G., DuMouchel, W., Pouliot, F., Richter, R., Rubinoff, A., Shen, D., Timko, M., Walden, D. "Kano's methods for understanding customer-defined quality," *Center for Quality Management Journal,* vol. 4, pp. 3–36, 1993.

[65] W. McDonough and M. Braungart, *Cradle to Cradle,* New York, NY: North Point Press, 2002.

[66] W. R. Stahel, *The Circular Economy: A User's Guide,* New York, NY: Routledge, 2019.

[67] M. Eckelman, L. Ciacci, G. Kavlak, P. Nuss, B. Reck and T. Graedel, "Life Cycle Carbon Benefits of Aerospace Alloy Recycling," *Journal of Cleaner Production,* vol. 80, pp. 38–45, 2014.

[68] E. Asmatulu, M. Overcash and J. Twomey, "Recycling of Aircraft: State of the Art in 2011," *Journal of Industrial Engineering,* vol. 2013, 8 pages, 2013.

[69] V. Smil, *Making the Modern World: Materials and Dematerialization,* West Sussex, UK: John Wiley & Sons, Ltd., 2014.

[70] M. Eckelman, G. Mudd and T. Norgate, "Metals Production and Energy Use," in *Environmental Risks and Challenges of Anthropogenic Metals Flows and Cycles,* United Nations Environment Program, 2013.

[71] S. K. Das, "Designing Aluminum Alloys for a Recycling Friendly World," *Materials Science Forum,* vols. 619–521, pp. 1239–1244, 2006.

[72] J. M. Allwood, J. M. Cullen, D. R. Cooper, R. L. Milford, A. C. Patel, M. A. Carruth and M. McBrien, *Conserving Our Metal Energy: Avioding Melting Steel and Aluminum Scrap to Save Energy and Carbon*, Cambridge, UK: University of Cambridge, 2010.

[73] G. Gaustad, E. Olivetti and R. Kirchain, "Improving Aluminum Recycling: A Survey of Sorting and Impurity Removal Technologies," *Resources, Conservation and Recycling,* vol. 58, pp. 79–87, 2012.

[74] W. Carberry, "Airplane Recycling Efforts Benefit Boeing Operators," *Aero Quarterly,* vol. 4, pp. 7–14, 2008.

[75] H. Jiang, "Trends in Fleet and Aircraft Retirement," in *ASA Annual Conference*, Las Vegas, NV, 2015.

[76] K. Wong, C. Rudd, S. Pickering and X. Liu, "Composites Recycling Solutions for the Aviation Industry," *Science China Technological Sciences,* vol. 60, pp. 1291–1300, 2017.

[77] M. Sheetz, "Elon Musk Touts Low Cost to Insure SpaceX Rockets as Edge Over Competitors," 16 April 2020. [Online]. Available: https://www.cnbc.com/2020/04/16/elon-musk-spacex-falcon-9-rocket-over-a-million-dollars-less-to-insure.html. [Accessed 10 January 2021].

[78] Space X, "Smallsat Rideshare Program," *Space X*, [Online]. Available: https://www.spacex.com/rideshare/. [Accessed 10 January 2021].

[79] NASA, "NASA Commits to Long-Term Artemis Missions with Orion Production Contract," 23 September 2019. [Online]. Available: https://www.nasa.gov/press-release/nasa-commits-to-long-term-artemis-missions-with-orion-production-contract. [Accessed 10 January 2021].

[80] S. Clark, "NASA Taps Lockheed Martin to Build Six More Orion Crew Capsules," 23 September 2019. [Online]. Available: https://spaceflightnow.com/2019/09/23/nasa-taps-lockheed-martin-to-build-six-more-orion-crew-capsules/. [Accessed 10 January 2021].

[81] V. Cox, "Mission Extension Vehicle: Breathing Life Back into In-Orbit Satellites," 19 April 2020. [Online]. Available: https://news.northropgrumman.com/news/features/mission-extension-vehicle-breathing-life-back-into-in-orbit-satellites. [Accessed 10 January 2021].

[82] Aristotle, *Complete Works of Aristotle*, Princeton, NJ: Princeton University Press, 1984.

[83] F. Quesnay, *Tableau Oeconomique*, 1758. Reprint, New York, NY: Macmillan, 1894.

[84] J. S. Mill, *Principles of Political Economy with Some of Their Applications to Social Philosophy*, London, UK: John W. Parker, 1848.

[85] K. Marx, *Capital*, Volume I, Hamburg, Germany: Verlag von Otto Meisner, 1867.

[86] J. Dupuit, "On the Measurement of the Utility of Public Works," *International Economic Papers,* vol. 2, pp. 83–110, 1844.

[87] H. H. Gossen, *Die Entwicklung der Gesetze des menschlichen Verkehrs und der daraus fließenden Regeln für menschliches Handeln*, Friedrich Vieweg und Sohn, 1854.

[88] B. Mosselmans, *Marginalism*, Newcastle Upon Tyne, UK: Agenda Publishing, 2018.

[89] M. Mazzucato, *The Value of Everything: Making and Taking in the Global Economy*, New York, NY: Public Affairs, 2018.

[90] G.E. Moore. *Principia Ethica*, Cambridge, UK: Cambridge University Press, 1903.

[91] C. Batavia and M. P. Nelson, "Goodness Sake What Is Intrinsic Value and Why Should We Care?," *Biological Conservation*, vol. 209, pp. 366–376, 2017.

[92] E. Westacott, "Some Objections to an Objectivist Conception of Intrinsic Value," *Southwest Philosophy Review*, vol. 10, no. 1, pp. 177–186, 1994.

[93] E. Sober, "Putting the Function Back into Functionalism," in *Mind and Cognition: A Reader*, William Lycan (ed.). Oxford, UK: Blackwell, 1990.

[94] G. Moore, "The Conception of Intrinsic Value," in *Philosophical Studies*, London: Routledge & Kegan Paul Ltd., 1922, pp. 253–275.

[95] S. A. Davison, *On the Intrinsic Value of Everything*, New York, NY: Continuum International Publishing Group, 2012.

[96] T. Scanlon, *What We Owe Each Other*, Cambridge, MA: Harvard University Press, 1998.

[97] M. J. Zimmerman, *The Nature of Intrinsic Value*, Lanham, MD: Rowman & Littlefield Publishers, Inc., 2001.

[98] S. Kagan, "Rethinking Intrinsic Value," *The Journal of Ethics*, vol. 2, no. 4, pp. 227–297, 1998.

[99] C. Korsgaard, "Two Distinctions in Goodness," *Philosophical Review*, vol. 92, no. 2, pp. 169–195, 1983.

[100] I. Kant, *Foundations of the Metaphysics of Morals*, Riga: J.F. Hartknoch, 1785.

[101] J. Callicott, "Rolston on Intrinsic Value: A Deconstruction," *Environmental Ethics*, vol. 14, no. 2, pp. 129–143, 1992.

[102] J. Bentham, *An Introduction to the Principles of Morals and Legislation*, 1789. Reprint, Oxford, UK: Clarendon Press, 1907.

[103] J. S. Mill, *Utilitarianism*, London: Longmans, Green, and Co., 1879.

[104] R. M. Chisolm, Brentano and Intrinsic Value, New York, NY: Cambridge University Press, 1986.

[105] A. Leopold, "The Land Ethic," in *A Sand County Almanac*, Oxford, UK: Oxford University Press, 1949, pp. 237–261.

[106] W. K. Frankena, *Ethics* (2nd edition), Englewood Cliffs, NJ: Prentice Hall, 1973.

[107] R. M. *Adams, Finite and Infinite Goods: A Framework for Ethics*, New York, NY: Oxford University Press, 1999.

[108] P. Singer, *Animal Liberation*, New York, NY: Avon Books, 1977.

[109] T. Regan, "The Case for Animal Rights," in *In Defense of Animals*, Peter Singer (ed.). New York, NY: Basil Blackwell, 1985, pp. 13–26.

[110] K. E. Goodpaster, "On Being Morally Considerable," *Journal of Philosophy*, vol. 75, no. 6, pp. 308–325, 1978.

[111] B. Fisher, K. Turner, M. Zylstra, R. Brouwer, R. D. Groot, S. Farber, P. Ferraro, R. Green, D. Hadley, J. Harlow and P. Jefferiss, "Ecosystem Services and Economic Theory: Integration for Policy-Relevant Research," *Ecological Applications*, vol. 18, no. 8, pp. 2050–2067, 2008.

[112] H. Tallis and J. Lubchenco, "Working Together: A Call for Inclusive Conservation," *Nature*, vol. 515, no. 7525, pp. 27–28, 6 November 2014.

[113] T. Milligan, *Nobody Owns the Moon: The Ethics of Space Exploitation*, Jefferson, NC: McFarland & Company, Inc., Publishers, 2015.

[114] S. Reiman, "Sustainability in Space Exploration – An Ethical Perspective," Mars Society, 2011.

[115] H. Jonas, *The Imperative of Responsibility: In Search of an Ethics for the Technological Age*, Chicago: The University of Chicago Press, 1984.

[116] A. Pompidou, "The Ethics of Space Policy," UNESCO, 2000.

[117] D. M. Livingston, "A Code of Ethics for Conducting Business in Outer Space," *Space Policy*, vol. 19, no. 2, pp. 93–94, 2003.

[118] J. B. Campbell and R. H. *Wynne, Introduction to Remote Sensing* (5th edition), New York, NY: The Guilford Press, 2011.

[119] International Space Station Program Science Forum, *International Space Station Benefits for Humanity* (3rd edition), 2019.

[120] O. Gurtuna, *Fundamentals of Space Business and Economics*, New York, NY: Springer-Verlag, 2013.

[121] P. L. Nelson and W. E. Block, *Space Capitalism: How Humans will Colonize Planets, Moons, and Asteroids*, Cham, Switzerland: Palgrave MacMillan, 2018.

[122] N. A. Anfimov, "The MIR Experience and Commercialisation of the Russian Segment of the ISS," *On Station: The Newsletter of the Directorate of Manned Spaceflight and Microgravity*, vol. 6, pp. 21–23, 2001.

[123] Potomac Institute for Policy Studies, "The International Space Station Commercialization (ISSC) Study, PIPS-97-1," Arlington, VA, 1997.

[124] R. Jakhu and M. Buzdugan, "Development of the Natural Resources of the Moon and Other Celestial Bodies: Economic and Legal Aspects," *International Journal of Space Politics & Policy*, vol. 6, no. 3, pp. 201–250, 2008.

[125] M. Borowitz, Open Space: The Global Effort for Open Access to Environmental Satellite Data, Cambridge, MA: The MIT Press, 2017.

[126] A. C. Clark, "Peacetime Uses for V2," *Wireless World*, p. 58, February 1945.

[127] Douglas Aircraft Company, Inc., Santa Monica Plant Engineering Division, "Preliminary Design of an Experimental World-Circling Spaceship, Report No. SM-11827," Santa Monica, CA, 1946.

[128] World Meterological Organization, "Resolution 40 (Cg-XII), WMO Policy and Practice for the Exchange of Meteorological and Related Data and Products Including Guidelines on Relationships in Commercial Meteorological Activities," 1995.

[129] L. R. Shaffer, "NASA Remote Sensing Data Policy," *International Archives of Photogrammetry and Remote Sensing*, vol. 29, p. 21, 1993.

[130] NASA, "Earth Science Reference Handbook: A Guide to NASA's Earth Science Program and Earth Observing Satellite Missions," Washington, DC, 2006.

[131] Intergovernmental Panel on Climate Change, "Climate Change: IPCC Scientific Assessment," Cambridge University Press, Cambridge, UK, 1990.

[132] M. Borowitz, "International Cooperation in Global Satellite Climate Monitoring," *Astropolitics*, vol. 13, no. 2–3, pp. 162–184, 2015.

[133] Intergovernmental Oceanographic Commission (of UNESCO), "From Observation to Action-Achieving Comprehensive, Coordinated and Sustained Earth Observations for the Benefits of Humankind: Framework for a 10-year Implementation Plan," Paris, France, 2004.

[134] GCOS Data and Information Management Panel, "Data and Information Management Plan: Version 1.0 (WMO/TD- No. 677, GCOS- No. 13)," World Meteorological Organization, 1995.

[135] R. Nixon, "Address Before the 24th Session of the General Assembly of the United Nations," New York, NY, 1969.

[136] United States Congress, "H.R.4836- Land Remote Sensing Commercialization Act of 1984," Washington, DC, 1984.

[137] M. M. Waldrop, "Imaging the Earth (I): The Troubled First Decade of Landsat," *Science,* vol. 215, no. 4540, pp. 1600–1603, 1982.

[138] M. Watanabe, "Failure of Landsat 6 Leaves Many Researchers in Limbo," *The Scientist,* 12 December 1993.

[139] Committee on Earth and Environmental Sciences, "The Value of Landsat to the U.S. Global Change Research Program," 1990.

[140] Group on Earth Observations, "GEOSS Data Sharing Action Plan (Document 7, Rev2, as Accepted at GEO-VII)," 2010.

[141] M. A. Wulder, J. G.Masek, W. B. Cohen, T. R. Loveland and C. E. Woodcock, "Opening the Archive: How Free Data Has Enabled the Science and Monitoring Promise of Landsat," *Remote Sensing of Environment,* vol. 122, pp. 2–10, 2012.

[142] NASA, "EOSDIS Distributed Active Archive Centers (DAACs)," [Online]. Available: https://earthdata.nasa.gov/eosdis/daacs. [Accessed 12 April 2021].

[143] European Space Agency, "Copernicus Open Access Hub," [Online]. Available: https://scihub.copernicus.eu. [Accessed 12 April 2021].

[144] Group on Earth Observations, "GEO Strategic Plan 2016–2025: Implementing GEOSS," 2015.

[145] H. M. Miller, L. Richardson, S. R. Koontz, J. Loomis and L. Koontz, "Users, Uses, and Value of Landsat Satellite Imagery—Results from the 2012 Survey of Users: U.S. Geological Survey Open-File Report 2013–1269," United States Geological Survey, 2012.

[146] B. Joffe, "Ten Ways to Support GIS Without Selling Data," *Urban and Regional Information Systems Association Journal,* vol. 16, no. 2, pp. 27–33, 2005.

[147] G. Sawyer and M. de Vries, "About GMES and Data: Geese and Golden Eggs, A Study on the Econpmic Benefits of a Free and Open Data Policy for Sentinel Satellite Data," Brussels, Belgium, 2012.

[148] NASA, "Commercial Smallsat Data Acquisition (CSDA) Program," 11 January 2022. [Online]. Available: https://earthdata.nasa.gov/esds/csdap. [Accessed 5 February 2022].

[149] J. L. Schenker, "Startup of the Week: Planet Labs," *The Innovator,* 10 December 2017.

[150] J. Arnould, *Ethics Handbook for the Space Odyssey,* Adelaide: ATF Space, 2019.

[151] G. Brundtland, "Our Common Future: Report of the World Commission on Environment and Development, A/42/427," United Nations, Geneva, 1987.

[152] United Nations Committee on the Peaceful Uses of Outer Space, Scientific and Technical Subcommittee, "Guidelines for the Long-Term Sustainability of Outer Space Activities," Vienna, 2019.

[153] Secure World Foundation, "Space Sustainability: A Practical Guide," 2018.

[154] The Natural Step, [Online]. Available: https://thenaturalstep.org/approach/. [Accessed 12 April 2021].

[155] F. Guidice, G. L. Rosa and A. *Risitano, Product Design for the Environment: A Life Cycle Approach,* Boca Raton, FL: CRC Press-Taylor & Francis Group, 2006.

[156] Environmental Management—Life Cycle Assessment—Principles and Framework, ISO 14040, 2006.

[157] Environmental Management—Life Cycle Assessment—Requirements and Guidelines, ISO 14044, 2006.

[158] T. Maury, P. Loubet, S. M. Serrano, A. Gallice and G. Sonnemann, "Application of Environmental Life Cycle Assessment (LCA) Within the Space Sector: A State of the Art," *Acta Astronautica,* vol. 170, pp. 122–135, 2020.

[159] M. De Santis, "LCA Ground Segment," in *Clean Space Industrial Days. ESA-Clean Space, ESTEC,* Noordwijk, 2018.

[160] S. Bianchi, L. Grassi, G. Benedetti, R. Giacone, H. Yamashita, K. Dahlmann, P. Leyland, S. Mischler and J. N. Laboulais, "Atmospheric Re-Entry Assessment," in *Clean Space Industrial Days, ESTEC,* Noordwijk, 2018.

[161] A. R. Wilson and M. Vasile, "Integrating Life Cycle Assessment of Space Systems into the Concurrent Design Process," in *68th International Astronautical Congress,* Adelaide, Australia, 2017.

[162] M. Ross, D. Toohey, M. Peinemann and P. Ross, "Limits on the Space Launch Market Related to Stratospheric Ozone Depletion," *Astropolitics,* vol. 7, no. 1, pp. 50–82, 2009.

[163] N. Leary, "Aviation and the Global Atmosphere: Special Report of IPCC Working Groups I and III," in *IPCC Symposium,* Tokyo, Japan, 1999.

[164] J. Wilkerson, M. Jacobson, A. Malwitz, S. Balasubramanian, R. Wayson, G. Fleming, A. D. Naiman and S. K. Lele, "Analysis of Emission Data from Global Commercial Aviation: 2004 and 2006," *Atmoshpheric Chemistry and Physics,* vol. 10, pp. 6391–6408, 2010.

[165] B. Glover, D. Rutherford and S. Zheng, "CO2 Emissions from Commercial Aviation: 2013, 2018, and 2019," The International Council on Clean Transportation, 2020.

[166] International Space University, "ecoSpace: Initiatives for Environmentally Sustainable Launch Activities, Final Report," 2010.

[167] C. H. Jackman, D. B. Considine and E. L. Fleming, "A Global Modeling Study of Solid Rocket Aluminum Oxide Emission Effects on Stratospheric Ozone," *Geophysical Research Letters,* vol. 25, no. 6, pp. 907–910, 1998.

[168] J. Friedberg, "Bracing for the Impending Rocket Revolution: How to Regulate International Environmental Harm Caused by Commercial Space Flight," *Colorado Journal of International Environmental Law and Policy,* vol. 24, p. 197, 2013.

[169] M. N. Ross and P. M. Sheaffer, "Radiative Forcing Caused by Rocket Engine Emissions," *Earth's Future,* vol. 1, no. 4, pp. 177–196, 1014.

[170] P. D. Lohn, E. P. Wong, J. Tyrrel, W. Smith, J. R. Edwards and D. Pilson, "Rocket Exhaust Impact on Stratospheric Ozone," TRW Space and Eleectronics Group, 1999.

[171] A. E. Jones, S. Bekki and J. A. Pyle, "On the Atmospheric Impact of Launching the Ariane 5 Rocket," *Geophysical Research: Atmospheres,* vol. 100, no. D8, pp. 16651–16660, 1995.

[172] M. Ross and J. A. Vedda, "The Policy and Science of Rocket Emissions," The Aerospace Corporation, The Center for Space Policy and Strategy, 2018.

[173] WMO (World Meteorological Organization), "Scientific Assessment of Ozone Depletion: 2018," *Global Ozone Research and Monitoring Project-Report No. 58,* 588 pp., Geneva, Switzerland, 2018.

[174] S. Durrieu and R. F. Nelson, "Earth Observation from Space – The Issue of Environmental Sustainability," *Space Policy,* vol. 29, no. 4, pp. 238–250, 2013.

[175] O. Zhdanovich, "Creation of a Sustainable Space Development Board, and Other Initiatives for Environmentally Sustainable Launch Activities," in *Space for the 21st Century: Discover, Innovation, Sustainability*, 2016, pp. 229–268.

[176] M. Saint-Armand and J. Ouziel, "Eco-Space Project – Environmental Impact of New Technologies," in *5th CEAS Air & Space Conference*, Delft, Netherlands, 2015.

[177] P. Brinkman, "NASA Pursues Greener, More Efficient Spacecraft Propulsion," *United Press International,* 14 June 2021.

[178] J. B. Pettersen, H. Bergsdal, E. J. Silva and J. Ouziel, "Space Propellants and High-Energetic Chemicals Data Barriers, Solutions, Uncertainty and Confidentiality in an LCI Database," in *LCM Conference*, Luxembourg, 2017.

[179] Y. A. Romaniw, "The Relationship Between Light-Weighting with Carbon Fiber Reinforced Polymers and the Life Cycle Environmental Impacts of Orbital Launch Rockets (PhD Dissertation)," Atlanta, GA: Georgia Institute of Technology, 2013.

[180] A. J. Timmis, A. Hodzic, L. Koh, M. Bonner, C. Soutis, A. W. Schäfer and L. Dray, "Environmental Impact Assessment of Aviation Emission Reduction Through the Implementation of Composite Materials," *The International Journal of Life Cycle Assessment*, vol. 20, pp. 233–243, 2015.

[181] S. S. Neumann, "Environmental Life Cycle Assessment of Commercial Space Transportation Activities in the United States (PhD dissertation)," Arlington, TX: University of Texas at Arlington, 2018.

[182] A. Vercalsteren, K. Boonen, T. Geerken, B. Remy and Q. Legasse, "Greensat: Ecodesign of the PROBA-V Mission," in *Clean Space Industrial Days*, Noordwijk, 2018.

[183] SpaceX, "Draft Programmatic Environmental Assessment for the SpaceX Starship/Super Heavy Launch Vehicle Program at the SpaceX Boca Chica Launch Site in Cameron County, Texas September 2021," Federal Aviation Administration, 2021.

[184] Pumpkin, "CubeSat Kit," [Online]. Available: http://www.cubesatkit.com/index.html. [Accessed 12 April 2021].

[185] T. G. Roberts, "Space Launch to Low Earth Orbit: How Much Does It Cost?," Aerospace Corporation, 2020.

[186] Bryce Space and Technology, "2020 Year in Review (through October 31)," 2020.

[187] NASA, "Space Debris and Human Spacecraft," 26 May 2021. [Online]. Available: https://www.nasa.gov/mission_pages/station/news/orbital_debris.html. [Accessed 11 December 2021].

[188] J. C. Wilhelm, "The Keys to Rule Them All: Sustainable Development of Orbital Resources," in *Post 2030-Agenda and the Role of Space*, Cham, Switzerland: Springer International Publisher-Springer Nature, 2018, pp. 59–70.

[189] J. Delaval, "ESA Clean Space Initiative," in *Space for the 21st Century: Discovery, Innovation, Sustainability*, 2016, pp. 213–228.

[190] T. Hitchens, "Forwarding Multilateral Governance of Outer Space Activities: Next Steps for the International Community," in *Space for the 21st Century: Discovery, Innovation, Sustainability*, 2016, pp. 75–118.

[191] J. Foust, "Russia Destroys Satellite in ASAT Test," *SpaceNews,* 15 November 2021.

[192] D. J. Kessler and B. G. Cour-Palais, "Collision Frequency of Artificial Satellites: The Creation of a Debris Belt," *Journal of Geophysical Research*, vol. 83, no. A6, pp. 2637–2646, 1978.

[193] D. McKnight and D. Kessler, "We've Already Passed the Tipping Point for Orbital Debris," *IEEE Spectrum*, 2012.

[194] L. David, "Space Junk Removal Is Not Going Smoothly," *Scientific American*, 14 April 2021.

[195] H. Klinkrad. (ed.), "ESA Space Debris Mitigation Handbook," European Space Agency, 1999.

[196] T. Cross, "International Space Station Robotic Arm Struck by Space Debris," *Spaceflight Insider*, 31 May 2021.

[197] J. Elkington, *Green Swans: The Coming Boom in Regenerative Capitalism*, New York, NY: Fast Company Press, 2020.

[198] United Nations. *United Nations Office for Outer Space Affairs, Space Debris Mitigation Guidelines of the Committee on the Peaceful Uses of Outer Space*, Vienna: United Nations, 2010.

[199] J. Rainbow, "MEV-2 Servicer Successfully Docks to Live Intelsat Satellite," *Space News*, 12 April 2021.

[200] A. Anzaldua, B. Blair and D. Dunlop, "Are Solar Power Satellites Sitting Ducks for Debris," in *Space for the 21st Century: Discovery, Innovation, Sustainability*, 2016, pp. 343–360.

[201] G. Hardin, "The Tragedy of the Commons," *Science*, vol. 162, no. 3859, pp. 1243–1248, 1968.

[202] E. Ostrom, *Governing the Commons: The Evolution of Institutions for Collective Action*, Cambridge, UK: Cambridge University Press, 1990.

[203] M. K. Macauley, "Close Encounters of the Trash Kind," *Journal of Policy Analysis and Management*, vol. 13, no. 3, pp. 560–564, 1994.

[204] M. K. Macauley, "In Pursuit of a Sustainable Space Environment: Economic Issues in Regulating Space Debris," *Resources*, vol. 112, pp. 12–16, 1993.

[205] World Economic Forum, "Space Sustainability Rating," [Online]. Available: https://www.weforum.org/projects/space-sustainability-rating. [Accessed 15 April 2021].

[206] T. E. Diegelman, "An Alternative Model for Space Commerce Sustainability," in *Space for the 21st Century: Discovery, Innovation, Sustainability*, 2016, pp. 295–312.

[207] W. H. Lambright, "NASA and the Environment: An Evolving Relationship," in *Historical Studies in the Societal Impact of Spaceflight*, Washington, DC: NASA, 2016, pp. 383–426.

[208] B. I. Edelson, "Mission to Planet Earth," *Science*, vol. 227, pp. 367–368, 1985.

[209] United Nations Office for Outer Space Affairs, "European Global Navigation Satellite System and Copernicus: Supporting the Sustainable Development Goals, Building Blocks Towards the 2030 Agenda," Vienna, 2018.

[210] European Space Agency, "ESA Activities Supporting Sustainable Development," 2016.

[211] Maxar, "Satellite Data's Role in Supporting Sustainable Development Goals: Empowering Organizations with Earth Observation, Geospatial Information and Big Data," 2019.

[212] NASA, "Sustainable Development Goals," 26 June 2020. [Online]. Available: https://earthdata.nasa.gov/learn/backgrounders/sdg. [Accessed 12 April 2021].

[213] W. M. Forney, R. Raunikar, S. Mishra and R. Bernknopf, "An Economic Value of Remote Sensing Information: Application to Agricultural Production and Maintaining Ground Water Quality," in *2012 Socio-Economic Benefits Workshop: Defining, Measuring, and Communicating the Socio-Economic Benefits of Geospatial Information*, 2012.

[214] J. D. Sachs, *The Age of Sustainable Development*, New York, NY: Columbia University Press, 2015.

[215] M. Black and J. King, *The Atlas of Water: Mapping the World's Most Critical Resource*, Berkeley, CA: University of California Press, 2009.

[216] National Science Foundation, "Scientists Use Satellites to Measure Vital Underground Water Resources, News Release 18–053," 19 July 2018. [Online]. Available: https://nsf.gov/news/news_summ.jsp?cntn_id=295988. [Accessed 12 April 2021].

[217] G. Matloff, C. Bangs and L. Johnson, *Harvesting Space for a Greener Earth* (2nd edition), New York, NY: Springer, 2014.

[218] H. H. Schmitt, *Return to the Moon: Exploration, Enterprise, and Energy in the Human Settlement of Space*, New York, NY: Copernicus Books-Springer Science+Business Media, 2006.

[219] T. Taylor, "Helium 3: The First True Commercial Space Activity and Recovery of Lunar Resources by Mining and Space Transportation Industries," in *Space for the 21st Century: Discovery, Innovation, Sustainability*, 2016, pp. 313–328.

[220] R. M. L. Parrella, "Space as Engine for Growth," in *Post 2030-Agenda and the Role of Space*, Cham, Switzerland: Springer, 2018, pp. 83–96.

[221] The Nathalie P. Voorhees Center for Neighborhood and Community Improvement, University of Illinois at Chicago, "National Aeronautics and Space Administration & Moon to Mars Program: Economic Impact Study," 2020.

[222] European Space Agency, "Space Economy: Creating Value for Europe," 2019.

[223] J. Bivens, "Updated Employment Multipliers for the U.S. Economy," Economic Policy Institute, 2019.

[224] International Telecommunications Union, "Measuring Digital Deveopment, Facts and Figures 2021," ITU Publications, Geneva, Switzerland, 2021.

[225] F. Cingano, "Trends in Income Inequality and Its Impact on Economic Growth," *OECD Social, Employment and Migration Working Papers*, vol. 163, 2014.

[226] I. Brannon, "Privatizing Disaster Relief," *Regulation*, vol. 44, no. 2, pp. 2–3, 2021.

[227] D. Marcelo, A. Raina and S. Rawat, "Private Sector Participation in Disaster Recovery and Mitigation," Global Facility for Disaster Reduction and Recovery, Washington, DC, 2020.

[228] K. Buchholz, "How Has the World's Urban Population Changed from 1950 to Today?," 4 November 2020. [Online]. Available: https://www.weforum.org/agenda/2020/11/global-continent-urban-population-urbanisation-percent/. [Accessed 5 December 2021].

[229] Eurisy, "Ten Success Stories on the Use of Satellite Applications in Cities," 2019.

[230] Global Climate Observing System, "The Global Observing System for Climate: Implementation Needs, GCOS-200," World Meteorological Organization, 2016.

[231] R. S. Nerem, B. D. Beckley, J. T. Fasullo, B. D. Hamlington, D. Masters and G. T. Mitchum, "Climate-Change–Driven Accelerated Sea-Level Rise Detected in the Altimeter Era," *Proceedings of the National Academy of Sciences of the United States of America*, vol. 115, no. 9, pp. 2022–2025, 2018.

[232] D. Wood and K. J. Stober, "Small Satellites Contribute to the United Nations' Sustainable Development Goals," in *32nd Annual AIAA/USU Conference on Small Satellites*, Logan, UT, 2018.

[233] World Wildlife Fund, "Sustainable Seafood," [Online]. Available: https://www.worldwildlife.org/industries/sustainable-seafood. [Accessed 5 March 2022].

[234] R. McKie, "Biologists Think 50% of Species Will Be Facing Extinction by the End of the Century," *The Gaurdian*, 25 February 2017.

[235] C. Arevalo-Yepes, "Space Systems for Sustainable Development on Earth," in *Space for the 21st Century: Discovery, Innovation, Sustainability*, 2016, pp. 387–402.

[236] A. -S. Martin, "Satellite Data as Evidences Before the Mechanisms of International Courts," in *Post 2030-Agenda and the Role of Space*, 2018, pp. 97–106.

[237] M. Wall, "Stephen Hawking Wants to Ride Virgin Galactic's New Passenger Spaceship," *Space.com*, 20 February 2016.

[238] NASA, "The Artemis Accords: Principles for a Safe, Peaceful, and Prosperous Future," [Online]. Available: https://www.nasa.gov/specials/artemis-accords/index.html. [Accessed 11 November 2021].

[239] W. K. Hartmann, "The Next 25 Years in Space," in *Blueprint to Space: Science Fiction to Science Fact*, Smithsonian, 1992.

[240] P. O. Weiland, *Crossing the Threshold: Advancing into Space to Benefit the Earth*, Huntsville, AL: Threshold 2020 Press, 2010.

[241] D. Duemler, *Bringing Life to the Stars*, Lanham, MD: University Press of America, 1993.

[242] T. Milligan, "Property Rights and the Duty to Extend Human Life," *Space Policy*, vol. 27, no. 4, pp. 190–193, 2011.

[243] C. S. Cockell, *Space on Earth: Saving Our World by Seeking Others*, New York, NY: Macmillan, 2007.

[244] J. Arnould, "Space Exploration: An Alliance Between Public and Private," in *Commercial Space Exploration: Ethics, Policy, and Governance*, Jai Galliott (ed.). Surrey, UK: Ashgate, 2015, pp. 61–70.

[245] R. Zubrin, *Entering Space: Creating a Space Faring Civilization*, New York, NY: Jeremy P. Tarcher/Putnam, 1999.

[246] B. Pittman, D. Rasky and L. Harper, "Infrastructure Based Exploration – An Affordable Path To Sustainable Space Development," in *63rd International Astronautical Congress*, Naples, Italy, 2012.

[247] General Social Services, "Interested in Space Exploration," National Opinion Research Center at University of Chicago, [Online]. Available: https://gssdata-explorer.norc.org/variables/3459/vshow. [Accessed 31 October 2021].

[248] D. Thomas, "Virgin Galactic Space Flight Tickets to Start at $450,000," *BBC News*, 6 August 2021.

[249] T. Hoium, "Virgin Galactic Holdings Could Be a Home Run Stock," *Nasdaq*, 9 February 2020.

[250] J. Foust, "NASA Selects Axiom Space to Build Commercial Space Station Module," *SpaceNews*, 28 January 2020.

[251] The Tauri Group, "Suborbital Reusable Vehicles: A 10 Year Forcast of Market Demand," 2013.

[252] J. S. Lewis, *Mining the Sky: Untold Riches from the Asteroids, Comets, and Planets*, Reading, MA: Basic Books, 1996.

[253] M. Shaer, "The Asteroid Miner's Guide to the Galaxy," *Foreign Policy*, 28 April 2016.

[254] A. Toivonen, *Sustainable Space Tourism: An Introduction*, Bristol, UK: Channel View Publications, 2021.

[255] J. D'Onfro, "Jeff Bezos Thinks That to Save the Planet We'll Need to Move All Heavy Industry to Space," 1 June 2016. [Online]. Available: https://www.businessinsider.com/jeff-bezos-on-blue-origin-and-space-2016-6. [Accessed 21 January 2021].

[256] A. Marshall, "Development and Imperialism in Space," *Space Policy,* vol. 11, no. 1, pp. 41–52, 1995.

[257] R. Zubrin, *The Case for Mars: The Plan to Settle the Red Planet and Why We Must,* New York, NY: Free Press-Simon & Schuster, Inc., 1996.

[258] A. M. Hein, M. Saidani and H. Tollu, "Exploring Potential Environmental Benefits of Asteroid Mining," in *69th International Astronautical Congress,* Bremen, 2018.

[259] J. Foust, "NASA Considering Commercial Mars Data Relay Satellites," *SpaceNews,* 5 December 2020.

[260] H. Hertzfeld, B. Weeden and C. Johnson, "How Simple Terms Mislead Us: The Pitfalls of Thinking about Outer Space as a Commons," in *International Astronautical Congress,* Jerusalem, Israel, 2015.

[261] J. Arnould, *Icarus' Second Chance: The Basis and Perspectives of Space Ethics,* Vienna: Springer, 2011.

[262] M. Elvis and T. Milligan, "How Much of the Solar System Should We Leave as Wilderness?," *Acta Astronautica,* vol. 162, pp. 574–580, 2019.

[263] D. Wood, "Creating Our Sustainable Development Goals for Mars," *Walker Reader (The Gradient),* 2 December 2020.

[264] P. Ehrenfreund, M. Race and D. Labdon, "Responsible Space Exploration and Use: Balancing Stakeholder Interests," *New Space,* vol. 1, no. 2, pp. 60–72, 2013.

[265] C. Cockell, "The Ethical Status of Microbial Life on Earth and Elsewhere: In Defence of Intrinsic Value," in *The Ethics of Space Exploration,* James S.J. Schwartz and Tony Milligan (eds.). Switzerland: Springer, 2016, pp. 167–180.

[266] H. Rolston III, "The Preservation of Natural Value in the Solar System," in *Beyond Spaceship Earth: Environmental Ethics and the Solar System,* Eugene C. Hargrove (ed.). San Francisco, CA: Sierra Club Books, 1986, pp. 140–182.

[267] L. Alter, "What Is the Carbon Footprint of the Space Program?," 11 October 2018. [Online]. Available: https://www.treehugger.com/what-is-the-carbon-footprint-of-the-space-program-4857306. [Accessed 2021 October 31 2021].

[268] M. McElroy, "Move Over, Sustainability Accounting: Here Comes Purpose Accounting," 23 July 2018. [Online]. Available: https://sustainablebrands.com/read/finance-investment/move-over-sustainability-accounting-here-comes-purpose-accounting. [Accessed 10 January 2021].

[269] SpaceX, "Smallsat Rideshare Program," [Online]. Available: https://www.spacex.com/rideshare/. [Accessed 12 April 2021].

[270] P. D. Lohn and E. Y. Wong, "The Impact of Deorbiting Space Debris on Stratospheric Ozone," TRW Space and Electronics Group, 1994.

[271] J. Leggate, "How Much Does It Cost to Leave Earth?," *Fox Business,* 26 May 2020.

Index

Printed in the United States
by Baker & Taylor Publisher Services

Printed in the United States
by Baker & Taylor Publisher Services